Dr Peter O'Connor, no
conducts a private pA
substantial part of him
analysis groups in addition to individual therapy. He
previously worked in the United Kingdom as a consultant to
the National Marriage Guidance Council and was also a
clinical associate in the Institute of Marital Studies at the
Tavistock Centre, London.

BEYOND THE MIST

What Irish Mythology
Can Teach Us About Ourselves

Peter O'Connor

ORION

An Orion paperback

First published in Great Britain in 2000
by Victor Gollancz
This paperback edition published in 2001
by Orion Books Ltd,
Orion House, 5 Upper St Martin's Lane,
London WC2H 9EA

A CIP catalogue record for this book is available
from the British Library.

ISBN 0 75284 383 4

Printed and bound in Great Britain by
The Guernsey Press Co. Ltd, Guernsey, C.I.

Many times man lives and dies
Between his two eternities,
That of race and that of soul,
And ancient Ireland knew it all.

Under Ben Bulben
W. B. Yeats

Permission to quote from 'Under Ben Bulben', W.B. Yeats, *Collected Poems*, London, Macmillan, 1982, granted by A. P. Watt Ltd. on behalf of Michael B. Yeats.

CONTENTS

PREFACE AND ACKNOWLEDGEMENTS

This book springs from several sources. The first is my family of origin, particularly my father, who fostered in me a deep and abiding sense of Irishness. Then my own psychoanalysis revealed, amongst many things, a depth of connection through the father to the symbolic Celtic aspects within me, and served as a springboard for turning my attention to these matters. Third, some fourteen years ago I had a dream in which I was wearing an Aran sweater and in a rush to answer a telephone call from a Jungian colleague I caught the sweater on some sort of sharp object. As I continued to walk towards the telephone, which was some distance away, the sweater gradually unravelled, until a voice said to me, 'Go back and trace the thread.' Whilst dreams always have several layers of meaning, are symbolic rather than literal, at one level this book is a tracing of that thread. Finally my son Patrick, as part of his education at a Rudolph Steiner school, where the world of the imaginal and symbolic is so highly valued, brought home from school one day a copy of Padraic Colum's book *The King of Ireland's Son*. I devoured it and knew instantly that this was the sort of material that I needed to be engaged with.

The writing of this book has presented enormous difficulties, since the world of Irish mythology is complex and devoid of the linearity and order that are found in e.g. Greek mythology. It is like being permanently in a dream, and one has to let the material do its work rather than work on it. What kept me going was the hope that I might be able to introduce readers to the world of Irish mythology, along with some reflections on the contemporary value of the stories.

However I must state at the outset that I have approached the subject strictly as a student and there is no pretence on my part of being an Irish scholar. Indeed I owe an enormous debt to the scholars who have translated the material into English and made this rich world available. Without their scholarship this book itself would not have been possible. Three writers in particular stand out: Proinsias MacCana,

Alwyn and Brinley Rees and Marie-Louise Sjoestedt. Their works, apart from being a goldmine of information, have also been inspirational.

It was Marie-Louise Sjoestedt who advised that 'If a student of Celtic can put into some order the rather confused tradition, it is by staying upon his own ground.' My 'ground' is psychoanalytical psychology: as a psychotherapist I listen to the inner thoughts and dreams of individuals. Here one encounters not only the individual struggles of people's lives but also the universal struggles that beset us all. This is the realm where, as Freud found with his focus on the Oedipus myth, mythology can be of considerable value. Whilst I have viewed the mythology through a psychological lens, I have striven to avoid over-'psychologizing' the material. On the contrary, I believe that psychology needs remythologizing, to refind *psyche*, or soul, and thereby redress the imbalance that has come about through the near-obsessive focus on logic, or the rational aspects of being.

'Psychology' literally means 'the logic of the soul', since the Greek word '*psyche*' translates as 'soul'. It is my hope that the world of Irish mythology will reorientate our thoughts to the imaginal and re-establish a sense of awe, uncertainty and mystery concerning the human psyche. Statistics, rats in mazes and ready-made prescriptions for how to behave, solve all your problems and find the love you have never had are of course more comforting, albeit illusory. Mythology is not aimed at proving anything but rather at modifying something, at subtly shifting the sense of ourselves, or the world, that we hold. Unlike much of contemporary psychology, it does not aim for simplistic clarity but rather for the expression and 'holding' of ambiguity and ambivalence.

Apart from the written works, both past and present, of Irish scholars, I also owe a debt to Gearóid O'Crualaoich of University College, Cork. He responded to my rather vague initial approach with enthusiasm, which resulted in my spending time as honorary visiting fellow at the University of Cork. Gearóid was not only an inspirational colleague and teacher but above all he offered me the warmth of his friendship, which served to encourage me to continue with the work. He is however in no way responsible for it, or for any mistakes or omissions. To Gay O'Crualaoich and Sue Alwyn, I also express my thanks for the friendship and many kindnesses they showed me during my stay in Cork. I would also like to thank Jenny Salt who so willingly and ably typed the early stages of the manuscript.

However it is to Clive Bloomfield that I owe my greatest debt. Clive, in addition to patiently teaching me the Irish language, has also been a mentor and friend and helped nurture and sustain my commitment to the world of Irish mythology when at times it was flagging. Ireland, although it is in the process of great change, is for me a culture that values Eros, the force that connects, above Logos, the force that discriminates. Thus it is a place of feeling and relationships, and one can only hope that the current invasion of economic rationalism and material success does not alter this. The mythology reflects this priority of Eros and restores a respect for the unknown, for nature and relationships, in a world that is increasingly obsessed with technology, rationality, things and facts.

Finally, to my wife Margaret I record my deepest thanks. As always she has endured the problems and demands of a writer husband with warmth and respect, and given encouragement when at times the project seemed impossible.

Peter A. O'Connor
Melbourne, October 1998

I

ANCIENT MYTHOLOGY AND MODERN SOCIETY

A question that I have frequently asked myself in recent years is: why is there such a great interest in mythology, and what loss of meaning is being attended to in this contemporary revival?

The *Oxford English Dictionary* defines myth as 'A purely fictitious narrative usually involving supernatural persons, actions or events and embodying some popular idea concerning natural or historical phenomena; in generalized use, as untrue or popular tale.' Longman's dictionary defines myth as follows: 'Myth is a false story or idea, something or someone invented, not true.' Collins's dictionary goes a little further and defines it as 'An untrue idea or explanation; the word often used to show disapproval.' And finally Cassell's dictionary says of myth: 'A fictitious legend or tradition usually embodying the beliefs of a people on creation, the gods, the universe, etc.' However Cassell's goes on to state that myth-making belongs 'to a stage or culture when myths were developed'. This rather ignorantly suggests that we are not always making myths, and fails to recognize that the very process of myth-making will continue so long as human beings exist. But the modern myth makers – scientists, economists, historians, sociologists, psychologists, theologians etc. – are, of course, inclined to believe that what they are constructing is the truth, not yet another myth. The dictionaries quoted, which stand as the authoritative voice of meaning, are aiding this deception. What stands out in all the definitions is the dismissive tone, which implies a defensiveness against some real or imagined threat that generates anxiety. This is part of our illusion that the observable, phenomenal world is the only reality and any other view of reality, or the very notion of other realities, is merely fictitious. Myth is the account of these other meanings and levels of reality and therefore modern rational human beings are inclined to deride it. But what could economic rationalism be other than a myth, 'an untrue idea or explanation', 'some popular idea concerning natural or historical phenomena'? But a myth believed in becomes a 'truth' and other 'truths' have to be dismissed as mere fictions. Christianity is a recent myth that has exhibited this very pattern of deriding other religious myths as false and fictitious. No matter how real something may appear, the narrative that is constructed to account for it is essentially mythic or imaginal. The imagination is the backdrop to the factual and forms the mainspring from which the rational account is constructed. Sigmund Freud, the father of psychoanalysis, said in a letter to Albert Einstein, 'It may perhaps seem to you as though our theories are a kind of mythology ... But does not every science come in the end to a kind of mythology like this? Cannot the same be said today of your own physics?'[1] Freud here is saying that even in the highest realms of objective scientific thinking mythic activity is still at hand.

It is sometimes valuable and illuminating to trace the origins of a word rather than rely on its current definition. The word 'mythology' is derived from the Greek work '*muthos*'. This means 'speech', and *muthos* itself is derived from the Indo-European word '*mudh*', which one can take to mean a thinking-over or reflection. Partridge, in his etymological dictionary,[2] considers *mudh* to mean 'imagine', and he also suggests that another more obscure root of the word '*muthos*' may be the Lithuanian word '*mausti*', which means 'to yearn for'. (Note also that the root of the word 'fable' is the Latin word '*fabula*', which means 'story' (so *confabulare*, 'to talk together'). So I would define myth as 'a yearning for imaginative speech that facilitates a thinking-over or reflection'.

Muthos refers to speech and therefore to the oral tradition. During the late fifth century BC the Sophists launched an attack on this original meaning, since words were seen as coming directly from the gods and myth was therefore a direct revelation. The Sophists sought to replace *muthos* with the new concept of the word, namely *logos*. This preference has come to triumph, and the written word has become the god and source of revelation. Reason, rationality and logical discourse have triumphed over the yearning to talk together and facilitate reflection.

This shift from *muthos* to *logos* has also meant a shift from influencing and modifying to evidence and proof, from circularity and meandering to linearity, from the art of talking together to the art of reasoning and arguing logically, from being together to faxing each other. Mythology is undoubtedly fictitious, but why should this be seen as a negative quality? It is more useful to see mythology as another way of knowing things, a way that does not rely on logic. One could say that science, that archetypal symbol of Logos, is only dealing with the transitory, observable world, whereas mythology is dealing with the profound and eternal realities that make science itself possible. Myth is in fact the distilled essence of human experience expressed in metaphor.

By its very nature, oral communication is more suited to narrative, to confabulation and imagery, than it is to discourse. The written language since it was mastered by the ancient Greeks in the fourth century BC has had an extremely powerful effect on the development of human society. Writing made possible the emergence of abstract language and reasoning, far removed from the poetic quality of the oral tradition. The spoken word allows for imagery, which communicates feelings.

In this context it is important to note that in Ireland the written language did not arrive until the sixth or seventh century AD, almost a thousand years later than in Greece. The effects of this much later arrival are clearly present in Irish literature, both the ancient and the modern, noted for their rich imagery. This is perhaps one reason why James Joyce's famous novel *Ulysses* is difficult to come to grips with, since one actually needs to hear it.

Because the Irish myths remained in the oral tradition until they were written down by the Christian monks around the sixth century AD, they are very different in quality from the Greek myths. They are less linear, less ordered and more richly imaginative. In this sense they are very much like dreams. What myth and dreams have in common is that they are imaginal, not factual productions. What we know from the work of Carl Jung and more recently that of James Hillman is that image is psyche, so that myths are tales from and about psychological life, the subjective not objective life. This is not to suggest that they are unrelated to the outer life, but the subjective account of that outer life.

Since the Greek word '*psyche*' translates as 'soul', Jung declared that one should stick to image because in sticking with images we find soul. Thus mythology provides us with a story that animates us, ensouls us, turns mere events into experiences. We need mythological stories to restore (re-story) our souls, since the most dominant recent myth that has aimed at our souls is Christianity, and it has by and large become imaginatively moribund. This is mostly because it has been theologized, rendered sterile by *logos* and removed from *muthos*. Yet in its origins what else could Easter, the cornerstone of Christianity, be other than a seasonal myth that depicts the cycle of life, death and renewal?

In our modern society, dominated by Logos and rationality, one of the fundamental roles of myth must surely be to restore and reinstate the imaginative life. We enjoy mythological stories because they provide us with a moment when we are connected to our sense of imagination, uncluttered by the demands of rationality, space and time. The soul is fed by myth, the mind by logic. In an alarmingly factualized world, where we are bombarded by fax and e-mail, infotainment and talk radio, is it any wonder that we yearn for mythology? An anthropologist looking at us might well conclude that the tribe needs stories to re-establish the equilibrium that has been disturbed by excessive information. The tribe needs stories in order to balance rationality with imagination and maintain a state of psychological well-being. Imagination in this sense of the word is a way of seeing through and beyond the obvious, the literal, to the metaphorical and the symbolic.

Another way of thinking about images and the symbolic is to describe them as the language of feelings not facts. Feelings represent themselves to consciousness in the form of images, and thus myths and dreams are narrative accounts of our inner life of feelings. Feelings facilitate a sense of connection to events in our lives, and act as a catalyst for the experience of seeing through or beyond the obvious. For example, if one had no feeling for art then a Picasso painting would not be likely to make any sense, in fact it would probably be perceived as nonsense. It is only through allowing ourselves to *experience* mythological and folk stories that we can appreciate that they are not nonsense. At the feeling level they make sense – we feel connected – although we would probably struggle in most instances to articulate logically what we have understood the story to mean. The relationship that people have to their dreams is identical: some declare absolutely that they are all nonsense, whereas others recognize that in some way they make sense.

What we know about dreams today is essentially derived from the works of Sigmund Freud and Carl Jung. It was Freud who brought dreams back to consciousness at the turn of the last century, with his ground-breaking work *The Interpretation of Dreams*.[3] It was Carl Jung who extended our understanding of the dream to include 'collective unconscious' material that he termed 'archetypal themes'.

Freud held the view that dreams served a wish-fulfilling function for desires that were otherwise unacceptable to our conscious minds. Jung added that dreams are not only wish-fulfilling but also compensatory. That is, they compensate for the consciously held view and therefore provide for balance in the human psyche. So if someone is being unrealistically approving of another person they may well dream of that person in a very negative light. Or if they should hold a particularly low view of themselves then they might dream of themselves achieving something remarkable. Jung's other contribution was his opinion that the dream is both an individual and a collective phenomenon, that is, it can be derived from our personal unconscious life (which in turn results from our personal history) or it can be formed from our history as a species, the collective history of the race, and in these situations we have what are termed 'archetypal dreams'. Archetypes refer to patterns of instinctual knowing with which we come into life, not something we acquire. These patterns of knowing are a bit like the instinctual migratory patterns in birds. They are derived from the repeated, universal experiences that human beings have faced such as birth, death, separation, rivalry, relationships, youth, old age, etc. They form the bedrock of the individual psyche and clearly provide the link between myths and dreams. This is succinctly put by E. R. Dodds when he states that myths are 'the dream-thinking of the people, as the dream is the myth of the individual'.[4] David Leeming reiterates these thoughts when he says that 'myths might be called the dreams of mankind'.[5]

Myths therefore are the social equivalent of archetypal dreams and invariably attend to the universal themes that confront human beings. Mythology, as James Hillman asserts, is the 'psychology of antiquity and psychology and mythology of modernity'.[6] Freud's mythology, termed 'psychoanalysis', is essentially a story of the eternal conflict between the life force he termed Eros and the death force called Thanatos. In the later years of his life he said:

And now I think the meaning of the evolution of civilization is no longer obscure to us. It must present the struggle between Eros and death, between the instinct of life and the instinct of destruction, as it works itself out in the human species. This struggle is what all life essentially consists of.[7]

Here we have a mythology, a story called psychoanalysis, that aims to provide some modification and understanding of the experience of life. Eros's role is to draw people and things together; it is the principle of connectedness. Thanatos, or the death instinct, is the force that accelerates disintegration, separates things and people and finds its ultimate expression in the physical separation of death. Thanatos is the entire realm of non-being and non-connection, not just our physical non-being as manifested in death. It is the interplay between these primal forces that forms the basis of creativity. Eros by itself would be insipid, Cupid-like, and Thanatos by itself would be an intolerable emptiness.

What we know about dreams is that they are composed of material that has been repressed from our conscious minds, whether the individual or the collective mind. However they can also fulfil a teleological function, in that they can point to new meanings, reveal new goals, insights and possibilities. It follows that myths will contain the repressed material of the culture, that which is unacceptable to the prevailing values. Yet at the same time myths must also be capable of creating a breakthrough in meaning, offering a sense of renewal where the old meaning is failing to sustain life. If dreams are, as Freud told us, the *via regia* or royal road to the personal unconscious, then myths are the *via regia* to the collective unconscious.

One aspect of human existence that stands out as not being acceptable is death. Death defies our prevailing materialistic values of accumulation. Thus we can witness in Western society an obsession with Eros in all its forms, from hard-core pornography through to the search for spiritual enlightenment. Regrettably its less evolved forms dominate, so that we are inundated with pornography and a sexuality that leads to people being treated as objects, at the expense of the more significant aspects of Eros, namely the values of compassion, relationships and love. This obsession with Eros is evidence of a massive cultural denial of the existence of death and disconnection. The recent emergence of the so-called New Age, for example, shows a marked tendency to see everything as being connected to everything else. This is Eros without Thanatos; discrimination, disconnection, separation and the void of not-knowing are rarely discussed by the gurus of the New Age. However death cannot be permanently denied and whilst in fairy tales it is usually Eros that triumphs, in myths it is Thanatos that triumphs. Myths are able to hold the ambiguity of life and death and therefore one of the roles of myth may well be a compensatory one of redeeming Thanatos from the abyss of cultural unconsciousness and restoring balance to the collective psyche. (For many people this would not be a dream but a nightmare!)

One outstanding feature of New Age philosophy has been the adoration of the goddess, as opposed to the male god. This in part

represents a reaction against the long-standing domination of patriarchal values. But in this adoration only one side of the goddess figure is
considered, and that is the nurturing, life-sustaining aspect, not the
destructive, life-devouring aspect. Eros is held aloof from Thanatos and
in this one can see a defensive and selective reading of myth taking
place. Oswald Spengler in his *Decline of the West* says:

> Today we simply no longer know what a myth is; for it is no mere
> aesthetically pleasing mode of representing something to oneself, but a
> piece of the most lively actuality that mines every corner of the waking
> consciousness and shakes the innermost structure of being . . . in the old
> days men did not enjoy myth. Behind it stood death.[8]

According to Greek mythology, Thanatos is the child of a union
between Erebus, the god of darkness, and Nyx, the queen of the night,
whose earlier partner was Chaos. Thanatos emerges from the union of
darkness and finds his ancestry in chaos. It is a union that returns us to
nothingness, to non-being, the void. Thanatos, along with his five
brothers and sisters, resides in Tartarus, which lies well below the
surface, even further below than Hades. Thanatos is rarely above the
surface, that is, it remains in the unconscious mind. Hence little is
known at the conscious level about this aspect of our psyche. If a plant
is deprived of sunlight it will not develop, but once brought out into the
light it blooms and grows in accordance with its nature. Thus our
conscious knowledge of death is stunted, and we think of it as referring
only to physical death. In contrast, Eros is strongly in the conscious
psyche and we are more than well aware of it. Thus above the surface
we have life but not death, and thus the obsession with the life force
and not death. We in the West see death as the negation of life not as
an aspect of it.

Freud was perfectly correct in expressing the significance of the
polarity between the life and death instincts, but we need to recognize
also the recurring, *cyclical* nature of birth, life and death. This is not
just a linear progression from our physical birth through to our death,
but a process that occurs throughout our lives. The 'death' aspect
surfaces whenever a change occurs. So for example divorce, redund-
ancy, your children leaving home, the death of a parent are all mini-
deaths that exist as part of the eternal cycle. It is the acceptance and
understanding of this broader notion of death that facilitates an
understanding of the process of change itself. This seems to be the

essence of what myth is about, to return us to an awareness of this eternal cycle. Myth enables us to bring some sunlight to bear on the dark, forbidding territory of Tartarus.

In modern society we have lost sight of death and have idealized life. We tend to move from life to renewal and avoid death, thereby only creating an illusion of change. We keep changing in order to create the illusion that renewal is taking place and that death does not occur; *plus ça change, plus c'est la même chose*. In denying death what we want at the ego level is life and renewal without facing death or endings. Yet we know from story after story, myth after myth, that there cannot be any birth or renewal until death has occurred. So, for example, following the loss of a marriage a 'death' has occurred and a certain period of mourning for this loss of a significant aspect of self must occur. However what one sees more often than not, particularly amongst men, is a refusal to undergo this mourning. Instead what they do is quickly find an illusory renewal, or rebirth, by rushing straight into another relationship. This avoids any acknowlegement of the temporary death since to do so means moving into the darkness, into Tartarus territory, where death and endings have to be faced. Thanatos means not only the concrete fact of our physical death but equally importantly the death of certainty – in short, chaos.

Myth after myth confirms this cycle, and Irish myths state it with great clarity. But modern people have moved away from natural cycles. Living in modern houses, working in air-conditioned buildings, having the benefits of modern medicine, knowing and experiencing the world through a television screen have contributed to the fantasy of triumphing over the inevitability of death. While many, for example, embrace the notion of reincarnation literally, it would seem more valuable to see it symbolically as serving to remind us of the inevitable cycle of birth, life and death. But once again the tendency is to choose only two aspects of the cycle and deny the death. It is like wanting only spring and summer without winter or autumn.

As an aside, I often find in my psychotherapeutic work that it is the autumn, the yellowing, the decaying, that is most strikingly resisted, precisely because it heralds the death of the existing pattern of meaning or view of oneself. Many individuals in their initial seeking of therapy want renewal, or change, without the necessary death of the old way of being and experiencing the inevitable mourning that must accompany this death. Paradoxically this old meaning does not have to be a positive one; indeed it is equally difficult to give up the negative and destructive patterns of being. What we resist losing and mourn for is the familiarity that has kept us in the 'life' aspect of the cycle. Myth can help us to grasp some understanding in these areas and assist us in creating new meaning. In this regard Irish myths, with their emphasis on the birth, life and death cycle, are of particular value.

The Greek myths as we have come to know them today are in many respects Logos-based, masculine-ordered and influenced by the emergent urban culture. Most likely they were different from this in the early stages of existence, but over time the male gods came to dominate and the feminine was relegated, in many instances, to a position of inferiority. Irish mythology on the other hand is earlier, more primitive, rural as opposed to city-based, and as a direct consequence the feminine dominates. The Irish figure of the sovereign queen, a personification of nature, is a pre-eminent figure with whom all aspiring kings must mate before they can legitimately rule. This ritualistic mating ensures the fertility of the land. In contrast to the Greek myths, where it is Zeus who is promiscuous, in the Irish myths we have such feminine figures as Queen Medb of Connacht, whom we are told mated with at least nine mortal kings. Her promiscuity clearly symbolizes the ongoing fertility of the land. The contemporary Greek myths show Hera, the wife of Zeus, as a relatively powerless female who has to endure her husband's many infidelities. No doubt in the early stories she was not such a powerless figure, but over time the male scribes have rendered her submissive. Such a pattern is not present in the Irish myths. Here feminine figures are dominant and nature is to the fore, and thus the eternal cycle and the inevitability of death are always present.

So one role of myth, in particular Irish myths, is the redemption of Thanatos from the collective unconscious, and the restoration of an awareness of the natural cycle of birth, life and death. In redeeming death we will also 'differentiate' this aspect of our psyche. Instead of death being seen simplistically as the negation of life, we will understand that the role of Thanatos is to facilitate endings and disconnections, a sense of separateness and boundaries. This is the essential ingredient of any successful process of change.

Reflecting on myths (or dreams) is never a disinterested, objective, scholarly activity, despite the impression given by the construction of various theoretical edifices and the peddling of such material under the guise of research. To reflect on myths is to reflect on oneself. Jung said, 'I had to know what unconscious or preconscious myth was forming me, from what rhizome I sprang.'[9] If myths can provide us with this opportunity to reflect on ourselves, then we need to explore them in a similar way to dreams, given the obvious link between the two types of thinking. First however we need to know something of the history and everyday social circumstances of the people whose myths we are exploring, just as we would need to know the everyday context in working with an individual dream.

2

WHO WERE THE CELTS?

The Context of the Mythology

Any evidence we have concerning the ancient tribe of the Celts is indirect, since nothing was written until the sixth or seventh century AD, when the Christian monks began the task of transcribing the myths and stories. In reading the stories we must always bear in mind that they were originally passed on in the oral tradition, and subsequently transcribed by Christian monks. This does raise some questions regarding the extent to which they may have been tampered with. However some scholars are inclined to the view that the monks would have originally come from the *fili*, or sacred poet, class and were therefore connected to the ancient stories. Nevertheless it is difficult to imagine that the incoming religion would not have made a few strategic changes in its own interests. We shall see this in connection with the early stories that focus on how Ireland was settled, where we find reference to Moses, an indication of Christian imposition upon the ancient stories. The other two major sources of knowledge about the early Celts are archaeological evidence and the descriptions of them by contemporary Greek and Roman writers.

Like most other Europeans, the Celts were initially Indo-Europeans and are conservatively estimated to have first emerged as an identifiable tribe in an area near the source of the Danube River around 1000 BC. However there is strong archaeological evidence to suggest that they may have existed some two thousand years before this. It seems that celticization was a gradual process which must have been well established by the time the classical writers of Greece and Rome began to mention 'the Celts'; this was not until 500 BC at the earliest.

Overall the evidence seems to point to the Celts having their roots in the later Bronze Age culture of non-Mediterranean Europe. Then, around the mid- to late second millennium BC, a new material culture emerged which is referred to by archaeologists as the Urnfest Tradition. This name comes from the burial sites, which included cremation pots, and reveals a new technological ability of manipulating bronze into flat sheets to make shields and armour. This Urnfest Tradition occurred in areas later identified as having been occupied by Celts in the period around 2000–1500 BC.

By the eighth century BC new cultural elements are recognizable. The horse, for example, was adopted for riding, indicating the existence of equestrian warriors, and long swords were in use. This is known as the Hallstat period, taking its name from the site where much of the archaeological evidence has been discovered.

The Hallstat culture seems to have had strong trade links, particularly in salt, with the Romans, Greeks and Etruscans. At this point they appear to be iron-using farmers and traders. As a society it seems they were fairly sophisticated and hierarchically structured. Burial sites at Hallstat and Hochdorff indicate an élite class of princes who appear to have imported luxury goods from Mediterranean Europe in exchange for salt.

Around the early fifth century BC a new period emerges called the Le Tene, named after the lake settlement in Switzerland. This period is characterized by fine artwork, particularly metal decoration, which consisted of free-flowing designs of curves and spirals, still evident in today's Irish craftwork. The Le Tene is considered to be the period during which Celtic culture was at its peak, and unequivocally establishes the Celts as a real civilization.

It is around this time that we first hear from the classical writers, in particular Herodotus, who described the Celts at this time as tall people with light skin, hair and eyes. He also saw them as boastful, a quality that appears regularly in the stories, particularly in what is termed the Ulster Cycle, whose tales are characteristically heroic. He also described them as vainglorious, demonic in battle and ostentatious. Again these qualities are all confirmed in the myths themselves, stories that were recorded some thousand years after Herodotus was writing. Despite these less than flattering qualities, Herodotus also saw the Celts as very hospitable, and fond of music, poetry, feasting and hunting. It could be said that the Celts embody the three Fs, fighting, feeding and fornicating. Herodotus's observations are confirmed both by the vernacular evidence of the stories and by later writers such as Posidonius in the first century BC.

The period from the fifth to third century BC was a time of tremendous expansion. Migration took place in all directions, partly due to the pressure of land shortage and partly to a new expansionist outlook. From their homeland north of the Alps, the Celts migrated south into northern Italy, west into Gaul and east along the Danube into Hungary, Greece and Turkey. Migration also took place across the sea to northern England and from there into Scotland, Wales and Ireland.

According to the Celtic scholar Proinsias MacCana, the Celtic people were in Ireland as early as the third century BC,[1] although it would seem that a megalithic population occupied Ireland already. Reference is made in the stories to groups of people existing prior to the tribe that came to be known as the Celts. Megalithic tombs such as that at New Grange have provided evidence of a sophisticated settlement as early as 3500 BC.

As part of their rise in power the Celts are known to have sacked Rome in approximately 390 BC, and a section of them entered and plundered Delphi in 279 BC. A year later three of these Celtic tribes, known as the Galatae (an equivalent of the commoner terms 'celtic' and '*keltoi*'), crossed into Asia Minor into the region known as Galatia. They then became the Galatians that St Paul refers to in his epistles. However the largest gathering of Celts was to be found in the area known as Gaul, part of which we know today as France.

In all of this expansion, it is claimed, the Celts never wiped out the inhabitants of the regions they conquered, but they did impose their language and traditions. The result of this behaviour was a collection of tribes who shared a common language and culture, rather than a specific tribe of people who were 'Celts'.

However by the late third century BC a clear decline in the power of the Celts in Mediterranean Europe had commenced. In 225 BC they were heavily defeated by the Romans in Italy. In 191 BC the northern Italian Celts were subdued and the Romans took over Gaul on the Italian side of the Alps. Also, from the second century BC the Celts were under pressure from the Teutonic people, the Germans, who were under Celtic domination, but who had not acquired their language. This, it is argued, allowed the Germans a certain measure of independence which enabled them to revolt and finally break away from Celtic domination.

So by the second century BC only fragments of Celtic tribes remained, mostly within Gaul, where they had preserved their independence. Julius Caesar put an end to this when he attacked and conquered Gaul in the first century BC. Under the succeeding Roman emperors, Augustus and Tiberius, the remainder of Celtic Europe was subdued, with Claudius initiating the conquest of Britain in AD 43, subjugating most of the remaining Celtic world. Only Ireland, perhaps because of its insular nature, remained untouched by the Roman presence and this has proved to be a most significant factor in the preservation of the language and culture of the Celts.

It is said often in the literature that the main reason the Celtic empire collapsed was that it lacked the sense of cohesion that results from a centralized organization, which could have consolidated the scattered tribes. Others suggest that a more significant factor was that the Celts were not unified by patriotism, as the classical societies were, nor by personal fidelity to a single chief, as were the Teutonic people. On the contrary, the Celts were ruled by a priestly class, the druids, and according to T. W. Rolleston: 'Here lay the real weakness of the Celtic polity. There is perhaps no law written more conspicuously in the teachings of history than that nations who are ruled by priests drawing their authority from the supernatural sanctions are . . . incapable of true national progress.'[2] He goes on to say that such a form of achieving order and unity as the druidic is inevitably the enemy of criticism and the growth of secular thought, which are the conditions of national development. (The druids, though Rolleston sees them as the cause of the collapse of the Celtic empire, were the central figures in the conservation of Celtic traditions and culture. As we will see a little further on under the pressure from Christianity it seems they later merged into and became the *filid*, or sacred story-tellers.) The root of the success of nations such as Greece and Rome lay in their conception of a civic community, the republic, as a kind of divine entity. The exalted conception of the state forms a kind of practical religion which men were prepared to serve in order to preserve and exalt the life of the nation. Teutonic cohesion on the other hand was derived from the sentiment of personal fidelity to a chief. The relatively recent rise of Nazism would attest to the validity of this assertion.

Against these efficient and organized forces, with their sense of cohesion, the Celts were powerless, and as we have seen were finally overrun and assimilated, except in Ireland, Scotland and Wales. The Irish Celts are sometimes referred to as the 'insular', as opposed to 'continental', Celts.

Apart from the presumed arrival of the Hallstat Celts in Ireland in the sixth century BC, there were other waves of migration of continental and pre-Roman Celts. It is assumed some fled from the Roman invasion of Gaul, and certain writers suggest that perhaps this is the group to whom the myths refer when speaking of the invasion of ancient Ireland by the Sons of Mil. (Others suggest that the Sons of Mil were actually from Spain.)

Apart from the arrival of Christianity in the fifth century AD, Ireland did not experience another invasion until the Vikings came in the ninth century. This was followed by the Normans in the twelfth century, and then Cromwell in the sixteenth. One scholar, Michael Dames, makes the interesting point that a fourth invasion of Ireland was the arrival of scientific rationalism, with its insistence on objectivity and denial of the imaginal and mythic.[3] While Cromwell had a horrendously destructive effect on Ireland, this latest invasion may well prove to be the most destructive of all, since it may yet destroy the Irish sense of connection and the imaginal life itself. Objectivity has become a twentieth-century obsession, one which leads to the denial of the legitimacy of the subjective world of feeling and imagination.

We know something of the continental Celts from the classical writers, though their only substantial contact with the Celts would have been in Gaul. So what we have is really a description of the Gaulist Celts; however, there is every reason to believe in its accuracy, for in the main the observations are confirmed in the later Irish vernacular stories themselves. Whilst these writers have the advantage of being contemporaneous with the Celts, they have the disadvantage of not *being* Celts. Thus there is a likelihood of bias and distortion in Roman or Greek writings. The main classical writers were Posidonius (first century BC), Julius Caesar (mid-first century BC), Diodorus (mid-first century BC), Strabo (early first century AD) and Lucan (first century AD).[4] Outsiders are considered to have over-sensationalized some aspects of Celtic life in order to establish the common perception of such people as barbarians when compared with the Greeks or Romans. The classical writers also tended to impose their own cultural understandings upon the Celts. This is clearly seen in the writings of Julius Caesar, who gave all the Celtic gods Roman names. While there is no doubt that some overlap exists, as in all mythologies, Caesar's description violates the complexity of the Celtic pantheon. The Romans did exactly the same thing to the Greek gods and in the process diminished them, so that the god Dionysus, associated with the Eleusinian mysteries (religious ceremonies in which worshippers saw visions of the underworld), simply becomes Bacchus and is over-identified with alcohol and debauchery. To see the Irish god Lugh simply as Mercury, as Caesar does, is a similar violence. Again the parallel to our modern society is obvious, with missionary Christians often renaming the gods of indigenous peoples in the interests of conversion and a so-called higher cause. The believers of the new gods seem determined to replace the gods of the people they have conquered or destroyed with their own. Again there seems to have been a most peculiar agreement in Ireland not to do this, at least not to any great extent. Perhaps it is because the monastic scribes were drawn from the line of *filid* or sacred story-tellers, since these people would have constituted the educated élite in Ireland.

In fact it seems that on the relatively rare occasions that the classical writers made reference to the Celtic gods they exhibited little or no understanding of them. Their writings tended to be more about appearances and practices, not about the spiritual life of the Celts. The descriptions were of the observable world, not the intangible, which was described at this time only in the oral tradition.

The classical writers such as Strabo and Caesar described the Gaulist Celts as frank, high-spirited, with a tendency towards childish boastfulness and love for decoration. They were also seen as being very willing to invite strangers to their banquets, and only after the meal was completed would they ask who the visitors were and what they wanted. At dinner they were described as being very ready to engage in wordy disputes and, after a challenge, to fight in single combat with little regard for their own lives.

Both Strabo and Caesar suggest that there was a sharp division between the nobles and priestly class on the one hand and the common people on the other. Caesar also spoke of their great courage as warriors and attributed this to their belief in the transmigration of the soul. Diodorus tends to confirm these accounts, adding the observation of their great love of gold and how their temples were full of unguarded offerings of gold, which no one touched. He also mentions the great reverence shown towards bards and how the latter were fond of expressing themselves in enigmas so that the hearer had to guess at what they were saying, a quality that still characterizes Irish conversation! He also noted that the druids were the intermediary between gods and man and no one could perform a religious act without their assistance.

The classical writers also tell us that walled villas were conspicuous on the hills, whereas hamlets dotted the plains. The houses were built of timber and were well thatched. Roads apparently ran from town to town, and bridges spanned the rivers on which barges loaded with merchandise travelled. The Celts of this immediate pre- and post-

Roman period were very prosperous, deriving their income from farming – archaeological evidence reveals that this included the rearing of pigs, cattle, sheep and horses, and they also grew cereals for domestic consumption and export. (A characteristic of Celtic agriculture was the use of storage silos sunk deep into the ground.) Another source of income was the tolls charged for goods moved along the waterways.

As to manners, there seems to be some contradictory evidence. On the one hand they are described as very hospitable, as we have already seen, yet on the other Plato records that they had a tendency towards brawling and drunkenness. Their thirst for Greek wines was said to be such that a wine merchant could acquire a slave girl with a jugful, or a servant for a single draught!

The basic unit of social structure was the *tuath*, meaning 'people' or 'tribe'. The head of the tribe was a king who was elected from a royal class and was not therefore necessarily the son of a king. It is also claimed that land was held in common and could not be disposed of by any one individual.

In Ireland itself, the preservation of the traditions that the classical writers described was mostly carried out by the *filid*, the inheritors of the druidic tradition. The *filid* were sacred poets who also in time claimed the role of bards. They were teachers, advisers to kings and legal witnesses to contracts. Their training consisted of committing everything to memory and lasted between seven and twenty years. Among the tales or verses learnt by heart were ones that concerned the supernatural world, and it would seem that these tales, passed on through the oral tradition, kept the myths of ancient Ireland alive. (In passing it is worth noting that the three roles of druid, warrior and farmer conform to the three functions that the French anthropologist Georges Dumézil claims characterized all Indo-European civilizations, that is, sovereignty, force and nourishment, enacted socially as druid/ king, warrior and farmer.[5] The Irish myths will confirm again and again the validity of Dumézil's theory.) The stories of the *filid* preserved the ancient myths of Ireland, and they therefore constitute the third source of our information concerning the Celts.

3

THE MYTHOLOGICAL CYCLE

The Archetypal Struggle Between Eros and Thanatos

The early Irish stories, as already mentioned, were first written down during the sixth century AD. Moreover, the tales were recorded within a Christian milieu (St Patrick having arrived in Ireland about a century and a half earlier) and compiled by Christian monks. Whilst some scholars have, as a result, been tempted to dismiss the entire compilation as simply medieval works of fiction, others, like Alwyn and Brinley Rees, point out that the monks, or sacred poets, who transcribed the early stories lived much closer to the pre-Christian world than we do.[1] For Marie-Louise Sjoestedt, 'it is imprudent therefore, without good reason, to repudiate the ideas that these authors had of the mythical world of the Celts, to which they were much closer than we can ever be'.[2] Rees and Rees make a further point that the various written works retain certain features in common with other mythologies. Jean Markdale asserts that what matters is that the significant myths have existed since the birth of man, and so they must be related to characteristics and deeds of the very earliest times. But, more pertinently, 'There is no need to establish whether myth is true or false, real or unreal, since its very existence suggests that there is a reality and the different aspects under which these realities appear can only be evaluated in their own context.'[3]

Thus what matters is that myth has a real existence and therefore the question of truth, falsity or distortion, whether by Christian monks or the passage of time, is not a central issue. The reality of myth is by and large a psychic reality, derived in part from, and stimulated by, external phenomena and changing times. Myth is not a static phenomenon but rather a dynamic one.

It is noticeable, however, that the stories reveal little of ancient Celtic views concerning the origins of the world and their religious practices and beliefs. It does seem reasonable to conclude that this is no accident, nor is it likely that they did not exist in some form, since all mythologies include stories concerning creation. The absence could be attributed to the need of the incoming religion to 'forget' the gods of the previous religion without destroying the tradition. This reminds us of the continental Celts' habit when they conquered a country, not to destroy the existing traditions but simply to impose their own language. Perhaps something similar could have happened in the transcription of the myths from oral to written word.

Of the surviving manuscripts, those most frequently drawn upon include *The Book of Conquests of Ireland*, most commonly known as *The Book of Invasions* or in Irish *Lebor Gabála*. This manuscript, compiled around the twelfth century, purports to be a history of Ireland, but most scholars agree that it is rather a mythical history. The two other manuscripts of significance are *The Book of Dun Cow*, or in Irish *Lebor na hUidre*, and one generally known as *The Book of Leinster*. Both of these are also twelfth-century copies with *The Book of Dun Cow* being named after a famous cow belonging to Ciara of Clonmacnois, the monastery where it was compiled. It is now in the possession of the Royal Irish Academy and consists of a remnant of 138 pages which nevertheless preserve a large number of romances relating to the old gods and heroes of Ireland. *The Book of Leinster* consists of 187 pages and includes many stories. Another manuscript of considerable interest is one entitled *Dinnshenchas*, translated as *The History of Places*. This is a twelfth-century compilation that explains the names of well-known places throughout Ireland, a sort of mythological geography to match the mythological history of *The Book of Invasions*. Whilst all these were written in the twelfth century, it is a unanimously held view amongst Celtic scholars that they were copied from earlier ones now lost, for the language of many of the sagas is as old as the eighth or ninth century.

The stories themselves were divided by the twelfth-century *filid* according to their subject matter. It is speculated that they were arranged in this way in order to assist the story-teller in memorizing them and also in selecting his stories to fit different occasions. Rees and Rees conclude that a wedding night, a house-warming, the eve of battle and the bringing-out of ale were some of the occasions when tales were traditionally told.[4] Story-telling was also a feature of the celebration of seasonal festivals, and tales were told before setting out on a voyage. Generally speaking the tales are classified by their Irish titles, for example, destructions (*Togla*), wooings (*Tochmarca*), battles (*Catha*), voyages (*Imm rama*), deaths (*Aitte*), feasts (*Fessa*), adventures (*Echtrai*), etc. Whilst this seems a valuable way to organize the tales, modern scholars prefer to classify them principally according to their spirit, which has resulted in the contemporary classification of four groups of stories, called the cycles. These are:

1   The Mythological Cycle (c. 1500 BC)
2   The Ulster Cycle (c. first century AD)
3   The Fenian Cycle (c. third century AD)
4   The Historical Cycle, or Cycle of Kings
    (c. third to eighth centuries AD)

All of these cycles overlap, and a figure appearing in any one cycle may well appear in a later one. But Irish mythology, unlike Greek and Roman, is not linear but meandering; one might go so far as to assert that it is dominated by an archetypal feminine ambience. There is a sense of connectedness and interconnectedness, not Logos and separateness. This quality is simply captured by Sjoestedt when she says that the peculiar difficulty with the mythological world of the Celts is that when seeking an approach to it you find that you are already in it.[5] So one has artificially to contrive a beginning in what otherwise feels like a cycle of interconnected themes and characters.

Unlike in Greek and Roman mythology, there is no clear-cut pantheon, no obvious hierarchy, but what is abundantly clear is the presence in these myths of a primal feminine energy which informs and shapes the gods and heroes of the stories. The existence of such an all-powerful force is also present, despite the dominance of Logos, in the Greek myths, where even the almighty Zeus is subjected to a higher power that is variously named *fatum* or *moira*, i.e. fate. The gods in any mythologies are never entirely masters of their own destiny. However in Irish mythology this fate in the form of a feminine figure is more explicitly present and recognized. She has many names, amongst which are Anu, Danu, or sometimes Caillech Bhéarra. She is the permanent and abiding presence of nature and is both the creator of the land and the land itself. In this sense she underlines the central motif in Irish mythology of the cycle of life, death and renewal (birth). She is both hag and beauty, mother and virgin, benevolent and destructive.

Irish mythology can be seen as seasonal rather than societal. Agriculture and many of the arts were in the hands of women, and therefore goddesses of culture and fertility preceded the various male gods in time. Their supremacy is also clearly present in the stories where they win and woo heroes and determine whether a king will rule or not. Their capacity for love, their passions, their eternal youthfulness and beauty are all suggestive of goddesses of fertility. Given that Ireland has been a predominantly rural and agricultural country, it ought not be too surprising that the underlying force or archetypal energy that is encapsulated in the mythology is concerned with natural cycles, nor that the dominant motif is one of death and regeneration, of beginnings and endings.

The powerful presence of the goddess reflects how Ireland has both resisted and been protected from the ravages of over-masculinization that so characterize Greek and Roman mythologies. Again one must not forget that the Irish stories remained much longer in the oral tradition than the other two mythologies. There can be little doubt that writing brings with it linearity and logic, qualities that we might normally associate with the masculine principle which can inhibit the imagination. Logos is concerned with order and conceptualization, not with imagination. As we shall see, Irish mythology portrays a tension between the masculine forces, personified in the hero figure, and the universal feminine, symbolized by the land and nature. It is to the earliest depiction of this tension that we now turn, by focusing on the Mythological Cycle.

I should point out that to call this cycle 'the Mythological' is misleading, since it implies that the other cycles concern tales that are not mythological. All the tales are mythological, but there is evidence to suggest that they do vary in their relative mixture of imaginative and factual content. The earliest cycle contains almost purely mythical material, whilst there is a predominance of factual material in the later Cycle of Kings or Historical Cycle.

From the earliest times down to the present day, Irish story-tellers describe a spirit folk who live alongside human beings but who are normally concealed from us. They are the *aes sídhe* (pronounced 'shee'), the people of the hills, known also as *sluagh sídhe*, *daoine sídhe* or *daoine maithe* and in English as fairies. These folk have been seen from ancient times as dwelling in hills or mounds, on faraway islands or beneath the waters of the sea or lakes. We shall focus on these beings and the otherworld that they inhabit in a later chapter. These mythical beings were originally known as the Tuatha Dé Danann; this name means literally 'people of the Goddess Danu'. The Mythological Cycle consists of stories about these people up until their conquest by the ancestors of the modern-day Celts, known as the Sons of Mil. The

Tuatha Dé Danann are the gods of ancient pagan Ireland who have been demoted in modern times to 'fairies'.

The Mythological Cycle gives us the details of the various activities of the otherworld characters, culminating in a mythical history involving the various mythical invaders and inhabitants of Ireland. It is to these invasions, the account of which is contained in the *Lebor Gabála*, or *Book of Invasions*, that we will now turn. The book places the settlement of Ireland within a quasi-biblical context, since the monastic scribes saw fit to establish some relatives of Noah as the first settlers of Ireland. There were five mythic invasions, which were led by (in chronological order) Cessair, Partholón, Nemed, the Fir Bolg and the Tuatha Dé Danann.

Cessair

These invaders represent a clear attempt on the part of the monastic scribes to link the initial settlement of Ireland with the Bible, since the time of the invasion is set just prior to the Great Flood. Cessair is described as Noah's granddaughter and the first person to settle in Ireland. (In a somewhat ironic twist it is stated that most of the intending settlers were shipwrecked before they could manage to land, which suggests that their boats were certainly not in Noah's class!) Fifty women and three men landed, supposedly on what is known today as the Dingle peninsula. Two of these men subsequently died and the third, Finton, survived, leaving Cessair and her tribe to perish in the Great Flood. Finton was Cessair's husband, and he survived first by taking refuge in a cave and then by a process of miraculous metamorphoses into a series of animals ranging from a salmon to an eagle, a hawk and then finally back to human form. Through these metamorphoses he is said to have lived for 5,500 years, and was therefore able to relate the tale of the first invasion and all subsequent ones to the monastic scribes. Clearly he is a symbolic representation of the oral tradition and the sages themselves. Finton finally died of old age, but not before he received the last sacraments: here the Christian monks are busily at work legitimizing their own rituals, but not at the expense of a good story.

Partholón

Following the demise of Cessair and her tribe it is said that Ireland remained vacant for a period of three hundred years, until the arrival of Partholón and his followers. Partholón himself fled from Greece after killing his parents in a dispute over the kingship with his brother. He brought skilled people with him, and it was Partholón and his followers who first established many crafts and customs in Ireland. Ale, for example, was brewed for the first time and the first guesthouse was established, and laws were passed on the ownership of land. It is said that once there had only been one cleared plain in Ireland, but Partholón cleared an additional four. He, like the next three groups of invaders, also fought the monstrous race called the Fomorians. Finally *The Book of Invasions* tells us that Partholón and all but one of his followers were destroyed by a plague. The one survivor is a replication of the Finton figure and is called Tuan mac Cairill, who survives for thousands of years through a series of metamorphoses and thereby lives to tell tales of the invasions. Like Finton he is a symbol of the oral tradition itself.

Nemed

Tuan mac Cairill tells of the next invaders, the Nemedians, who also supposedly came from Greece. These people continued the tradition of cultivating the land and are said to have cleared another twelve plains. They would appear to represent an attempt to explain the beginnings of agriculture in Ireland. They like Partholón also fought the Fomorians and, following the death of Nemed and many of his tribe due to plague, the Fomorians subjugated the Nemedians to their rule. At Samain, the beginning of winter, they demanded payment of two-thirds of all the Nemedians' corn, milk and children. In an act of desperation the Nemedians rose up in revolt, only to be obliterated by the Fomorians. Two small groups survived, one going to Greece, the other to distant northern lands. It is from the remnants of these Nemedians that the next two groups of invaders come.

The Fir Bolg

The Nemedians that went to Greece multiplied and eventually returned to Ireland and are known as the Fir Bolg, which means 'the bag people'. It is said that they were enslaved by the Greeks following their retreat from the Fomorians and as a result they were made to carry bags of soil on to bare rocks to make the land fertile. Others such as T. F. O'Rahilly have suggested that the term 'Bolg' might find its origins in an early race called Builg, and this links them to the continental Celts, since this term has been connected to Belgae, the old word for

Belgium.[6] Here we see the possible overlapping of factual and mythical history.

The Fir Bolg divided Ireland into five provinces, Ulster, Leinster, Connacht, Munster and Meath (Mide, which literally means 'the middle'). This represents a fivefold conception of the universe which is consistent with traditional Indian and Chinese beliefs. The bag people also introduced kingship and the idea of a link between the righteousness of the ruler and the fertility of the land. This idea, which is very strong in Irish mythology, is called sacral kingship, where rule by the mortal king is only possible if he mates with the goddess, the sovereign queen. This is the acknowledgement that the king had to respect and work in harmony with nature. This union is often depicted in the literature by the transformation of the female divinity, following union with the would-be king, from an old hag to a young girl of great beauty. The Fir Bolg are regarded as the first group of invaders to have an actual foot in history. However the same could not be said of the next invaders, the Tuatha Dé Danann.

Tuatha Dé Danann

The people of the goddess Danu belong firmly to the otherworld, and introduce us to the Irish pantheon. Unlike Cessair, Partholón and the Nemedians, the Tuatha did not arrive in boats, but in obscure clouds or mist, and landed on a mountain in the west. Their landing caused an eclipse of the sun which lasted for three days. You will recall that when the two surviving groups of Nemedians fled from the Fomorians one group went to Greece, the other to distant northern lands; it is this latter group that returns as the Tuatha Dé Danann. However the story of their sojourn in the distant lands is embroidered into a mythical tale that they came from four great cities, and from each of these magical cities they brought an equally magical treasure. So from Falias came a stone called the La Fial, a stone of destiny, which would roar when sat upon by the rightful King of Ireland. It has later links to the famous stone of Scone in Scotland and to Arthurian legend. The second city was Gorias, and from here came the invincible sword associated with the god Nuada, wounds from which were fatal. From Filias came the magic spear of the god Lugh, a spear that guaranteed victory. Finally from Murias came the magical cauldron of the god Dagda, which was never emptied.

With these gifts, under the cover of a mist or magic cloud, the people of Danu landed in Ireland. When the cloud lifted (and presumably the eclipse passed) the current inhabitants, the Fir Bolg, discovered the Tuatha inside a camp that the Fir Bolg had already fortified since their king, Eochaid mac Erc, had been forewarned of the invasion in a dream. The bag people sent one of their warriors, Sreng, to talk to the mysterious newcomers. The Tuatha Dé Danann sent the warrior Bres to represent them. (As they were both descended from the same tribe, the Nemedians, they shared a common language.) Bres proposed that the tribes should divide Ireland between them, to which Sreng agreed. However the chiefs of the bag people rejected this idea, and their refusal led to the first battle of Mag Tuired.

The Tuatha Dé Danann were led into battle by their king, Nuada, and the Fir Bolg by Eochaid mac Erc. Nuada was initially assisted by the triple-goddess figure Badb (crow)/Morrígan (queen of phantoms)/ Macha (horse). The triple goddess did not use weapons, but sorcery to destroy the enemy. Whenever the Morrígan appears in battle it is in some magical and mystical way and not with brute force. The goddess sent magical showers of fiery rain upon the Fir Bolg, causing great damage until the bag people's own sorcerers offered some form of counter-attack. Following this struggle between the sorcerers, Nuada again sent an envoy to the Fir Bolg, making them the same offer, but again they refused. Then the battle (as we normally think of one) began, and is said to have lasted for five days, during which much killing took place. On the fourth day Nuada had his arm severed by the warrior Sreng. Meanwhile the Fir Bolg king Eochaid was slain by Tuatha warriors. On the fifth day Nuada again met with Sreng and they made peace. The terms were that the Tuatha Dé Danann received all of Ireland except the province of Connacht, which the Fir Bolg were allowed to retain. Some people from present-day Connaught lay claim to Fir Bolg ancestry.

Because no blemished man could be King of Ireland, Nuada with his severed arm had to forsake the kingship. This was bestowed upon Bres (a different Bres from the one who had negotiated with the Fir Bolg). This Bres was the son of a Fomorian king named Elatha and a Tuatha Dé Danann woman, Eri. However it was not long before Bres, with the assistance and connivance of his ancestors the Fomorians, began to oppress the Tuatha. This took a similar form to the Fomorians' previous oppression of the Nemedians, that is, heavy taxes and tributes. The gods of the people of Danu were made to do menial work, with the Dagda, the lord of perfect knowledge, being forced to build a fort for Bres and Ogma, the god of literature, having to fetch firewood, etc. Bres himself failed in his first duty as a king, in that he was not generous or hospitable. It is said that no matter how often the chieftains visited Bres their breath did not smell of beer, and worse still, he provided neither poets nor musicians to entertain them. In the end retribution was brought about by a poet who was offered neither bed nor fire and was given only three dry biscuits on a small dish. This poet, Cairbre, delivered what is said to be the first 'satire' in Ireland:

> Without food upon this dish,
> without cow's milk upon which a calf grows,
> without a man's abode under the gloom of night,
> without enough to reward poets, may that be the fate of Bres!

The effect of this satire was so powerful that Bres broke out in red blotches all over his face, and since he was now imperfect he was forced to abdicate the throne.

Now clearly something magical is going on here: this is no ordinary verse. As we have already seen, there existed in Ireland a learned class that possessed profound mystical and arcane knowledge. The druids, and later the *filid*, could put spells upon people, and this is what happened to Bres. This magic spell or curse often took the form of a rhythmic malediction and could, we are told, drive out rats, render a province sterile or even kill a man. The parallel to the Australian Aboriginal practice of pointing the bone is striking. This practice of magical incantations is sometimes referred to in Irish as '*a glam*' and it was feared far more than any weapon that the enemy should carry or wield. We shall see that the sacred poet plays a significant and often decisive role in determining the course of events.

Bres sought both refuge and revenge among his ancestral tribe, the Fomorians, who some say lived on Tory Island off the north-west coast of Donegal. His mother, the Tuatha woman, informed Bres for the first time that his father was Elatha, a king of the Fomorians, and she produced a ring which served to identify Bres as the true son of Elatha. With this established he sought help from his father to reconquer Ireland.

In the mean time the former king Nuada had, with the help of the physician Diancecht and the god of smithwork, Credne, had his severed arm (some say hand) replaced with a silver one. Henceforth he is known as Nuada of the Silver Arm (Nuadha Airgedlámh). Now that he was no longer imperfect he was reinstated as the king of the Tuatha

Dé Danann. To celebrate this, Nuada held a great banquet at Tara (Temuir), a sacred site and the seat of kings. It is situated in Meath, middle of the five provinces that were established by the Fir Bolg. As a sacred site it is also the place where many of the stories of the Mythological Cycle are located. Some scholars such as MacCana see Tara's location as a symbol of unity transcending the political divisions of tribes. This he argues is a persistent quality of Irish myths themselves, where unity is combined with disunity. It is as if the centre emerges from the sum of the five parts, yet is greater than the total of those parts.[7]

I have expanded on Tara a little since it is to this place that one of the major gods of the Irish pantheon, Lugh, first comes. His arrival at the banquet celebrating Nuada's return to the throne clearly represents an important turning point in the conflict with the Fomorians. This conflict forms the second battle of Mag Tuired, which takes place on the feast of Samain, the beginning of winter and also as the beginning of the 'death' part of the life, death and renewal cycle.

Lugh is a very interesting figure; to begin with his conception, we can appreciate the similarity of his birth to that of the heroes of other mythologies. It was prophesied, prior to his birth, that Lugh would kill his grandfather, Balor, a formidable Fomorian king. Here the recurrent mythic pattern of a son killing a father figure is apparent. One immediately thinks of the Oedipus myth that forms such a central role in Freud's story of the human psyche. The prophecy resulted in Balor imprisoning his daughter in a high tower accompanied by twelve matrons whose task it was to prevent her ever seeing a man. A further parallel immediately presents itself, the Greek myth concerning Danae, the daughter of Acrisius, King of Argos. Here it was also prophesied that a son of his daughter would kill him and he, like Balor, locked his daughter up in a tower. But Zeus loved her and visited her in a shower of gold and from this union the hero Perseus was born. In Lugh's case the story has it that Balor stole the magic cow of Cian, the son of the physician Diancecht. Cian, determined to avenge himself on Balor, sought the advice of the druidess Biróg. She assisted Cian by disguising him as a woman and together they magically wafted across the seas to the tower where Balor's daughter Ethniu was imprisoned. Disguised as two noble ladies seeking shelter, they were allowed into the tower. Biróg then cast a spell upon the matrons, putting them to sleep, whereupon Cian made love to Ethniu and Lugh was conceived.

The first that Balor knew of this was when he heard that his daughter had given birth to triplets, and he immediately demanded that they be drowned. The servant charged with this duty accidentally dropped one of the infants on the way to drowning them, and it was rescued by a druidess who returned the infant to Cian. This child was of course Lugh. As in some of the Greek myths, Cian fostered the infant out, to Goibniu the blacksmith, who taught Lugh all manner of crafts. Thus Lugh is the child of a union between a Fomorian and a Tuatha Dé Danann, just like Bres. This pattern raises the interesting idea of these two heroes not being as separate as they first appear, or even that they may be two sides of the same coin, so to speak. This is a significant point that we will return to since it allows one to think about the seemingly opposite qualities of good and evil as being two aspects of the one, not separate as the Christian myth would have us believe.

It is interesting to note that both Perseus and Lugh, threatened with drowning, went on to become great heroes who confronted the dark and demonic forces. Heroic figures are almost always unwanted and perceived as threatening by the ruling power of the day. We know from our own mythology of psychology that the ego-based identity is invariably unwilling to accept change and that resistance is the inevitable companion of change itself. One interesting difference between Perseus and Lugh is the gender of the monsters that they slay. For Perseus it is the monstrous female the Medusa, whereas for Lugh it is his one-eyed giant grandfather Balor. It is perhaps of some significance that one culture depicts the destructive forces as feminine and the other as masculine. For the Greeks, with their identity being strongly aligned with the masculine, the feminine may well represent that which had to be triumphed over. On the other hand for the Irish, with the feminine acknowledged as the source of being, it may be that the masculine had to be reminded that it was not invincible. At root they both probably represent the forces of chaos that are for ever threatening to disrupt the existing order of things but without which change cannot occur. In the Greek cosmology, chaos existed in the beginning and out of this order arose. Modern people are in the main terrified by their own chaos and associate it exclusively with destruction and not positive change.

4

THE GODS

The Masculine Archetypes

The gods of the Tuatha Dé Danann are not dominant or all-powerful figures. Indeed it is the goddesses who emerge as the most powerful divinities in Irish mythology. There seems to be within Irish mythology a permanent supremacy of divine women, and the male divinities must acknowledge this supremacy. It is as if the ego, which is identified with rationality and Logos, must accept and concede that it is not master in its own house and that more exists than that which is known, visible and tangible. There is the permanent presence of what we have come to term the unconscious, which is often symbolized in myths and dreams by natural phenomena such as the sea, forests, the moon, and the earth, and is therefore symbolically linked to the goddess and the feminine. This pervasive otherworld of the unconscious governs much of our waking life and rules our sleeping life. The unconscious, not unlike the goddesses of Ireland, is the source of growth and fertility, the spring of renewal, that gives energy to the conscious life and yet, just like nature, can destroy consciousness itself. The hero or heroine must simultaneously yield to and struggle to emerge from the unconscious. If successful in this struggle he creates some order, in the form of discrimination and consciousness. We need to work at consciously knowing these forces that move invisibly within us and determine much of our everyday behaviour. Although the goddesses are more powerful, we must firstly turn to the major male divinities of Irish mythology.

The Dagda
The Dagda is the chief god of the Celtic pantheon and one might consider him as similar to Zeus, Jupiter or Odin. He is a multi-faceted god with various titles, such as Father of All (Eochaidh Ollathair) and Lord of Perfect Knowledge (Ruad Rofhessa). The knowledge being referred to here is not factual knowledge but rather esoteric or arcane knowledge, druidic knowledge.

Nora Chadwick points out that the Irish gods 'are neither worshipped nor sacrificed to ... they are supernatural beings with magical powers'.[1] The Dagda certainly falls within this category and we also know that he is described as the 'good god', not because he is good in a moral sense but because he is good at everything, which includes his magical knowledge and powers.

In some stories he is seen as the literal father of the goddess Brigit and the god Oenghus, in addition to his role as 'father of all'. He is said to have possessed a magical club, cauldron and harp. The club was so massive that it required eight men to carry it and one end could kill nine men in one stroke, whereas the other could immediately restore them to life. This possession highlights his supernatural powers over life and death. His magical cauldron left no one unfed since its supply was inexhaustible. This symbolizes a somewhat more feminine role of the Dagda, as nurturer of his tribe. It is interesting to note that the cauldron in many mythologies is associated with female deities and with the processes of regeneration and rebirth. In Babylon for example the cauldron was under the control of the fate-goddess, Siris, mother of the stars, whereas in Welsh mythology it is the goddess Branwen who is the possessor of a magical cauldron of regeneration. (In nearly all mythologies there exists some form of miraculous vessel connected with rebirth and transformation. Christian mythology includes the chalice of Christ, which is linked to the holy grail legend. The New Testament tells of Christ feeding the multitudes from what may be a magical vessel, since from two fish and five loaves, five thousand were fed and twelve baskets of leftovers were gathered up.[2] The chalice associated with the Catholic Mass is another example of a magical vessel since it is connected with the magical renewal of the body and blood of Christ.)

The Dagda is also often described as a crude, ugly, pot-bellied, coarse figure who was inclined to uncouth behaviour. However he also had a very refined side that is reflected in his third possession, his magical harp. This he could summon by merely calling it and it would fly to him through the air. He played on it to mark the changing seasons, which links him to nature and symbolizes his additional role as guardian of the earth and its fertility.

The Dagda, like various of the goddesses, incorporates both the masculine and feminine principles. A chieftain god, preoccupied with territorial claims, kingship and aggression, is at the same time a nurturing figure, guardian of fertility and restorer of life. This aspect of the Irish gods and goddesses finds its parallel in Jung's notion of the archetype and in particular his concept of the archetypal *anima* and *animus*, the feminine and masculine energies in the collective psyche. In the first half of life, says Jung, we tend to develop only one of these consciously, often in line with both gender and social expectations, leaving the opposite aspect in an underdeveloped state, often identifiable with adolescence. The mid-life 'crisis', the transition which occurs between thirty-five and forty-five years of age, is related to a need from within to attend to the imbalance and to develop the opposite qualities to those that are already present in one's conscious life. Many people around this age begin to experience a loss of meaning and purpose, culminating in feelings of aimlessness and hopelessness. 'What is the point of it all?' is the question that many a person in the mid-life period has found themselves asking. For men this is often a time for developing and understanding their feelings, and moving away from an exclusive reliance on logic for understanding the world and other people. Women, if they have pursued a formal career in the first half of life, experience much the same feelings as men: a deep and abiding sense of futility along with a growing sense that there must be more to life than power and success in the workplace. Some of these women experience the emergence of the feminine side in the form of pondering whether they will have a child or not. Other women who may have forgone or curtailed their careers in the interest of raising children find themselves occupied with thoughts of returning to the workplace or undertaking further study. For these women it is the masculine principle that needs development.

In this sense the Dagda provides an archetypal model for men, albeit a somewhat primitive one, of the integration of these opposite qualities. He would appear to be an advance on the singularly masculine gods of the ancient Greeks, which have played such a powerful role in shaping the psyche of Western man.

Lugh

This god, as we have already seen, is the son of a Fomorian woman and a Tuatha Dé Danann man. However evidence exists to suggest that he was well in existence prior to his appearance in the Irish pantheon. His name is associated with such places as Lugdunum (modern-day Lyon in France) and Luguvallium (Carlisle). This is the god whom Caesar equated with the Roman Mercurius and described as the most worshipped god of the continental Celts. Sanctuaries with dedications to this figure have been discovered throughout Gaulish territories. Thus Lugh probably represents an older continental god who has been incorporated into the Irish pantheon.

One of the meanings of Lugh is 'shining one', which means that he is sometimes considered a solar god. The Welsh god Lleu is equated with Lugh, and Lleu is taken to mean 'light'. Some scholars, e.g. Daithi O'hOgain, point out that Lugh is cognate with the Latin word '*lux*', which also means 'light'.[3] The story of the Second Battle of Mag Tuired tells how Bres, son of Balor, arose one morning and said, 'I wonder why the sun is rising in the west today and in the east every other day?' 'Would it were so,' said the druid. 'Why, what else but the sun is it?' said Bres. 'It is the radiance of the face of Lugh,' replied the druid. His face was as bright as the sun and no one could look upon it. As he approached from the west he was riding on the sea-god Manannán's horse, which was as swift as the wind and a rider who was on its back could never be killed. He was also wearing Manannán's breastplate, which protected whoever was wearing it from being wounded, and he carried Manannán's sword, a magical sword called 'the Answerer'; anyone wounded by this sword was instantly killed. Thus equipped, he came across the Fomorian tax collectors, and killed all but nine of them. These he spared only so they could return to their kinsmen and warn them that the Tuatha Dé Danann were ready for war.

The word '*lugos*', which it it presumed is related to 'Lugh', means 'raven', and this was the sacred bird of the Greek sun-god Apollo. Indeed it was the raven that warned Apollo of the infidelity of his mortal lover Coronis, the mother of Asklepios, the god of healing. Interestingly Cian, Lugh's father, is in turn the son of the Irish god of healing, Diancecht. The healing here could be taken to mean not only medical healing but also the healing power of the sun, following the blight of winter. Thus Lugh's prophesied slaying of his Fomorian grandfather Balor may well be the triumphing of a solar deity over the darkness of winter. The solar deity also suggests, within the modern psychological framework, the rising of consciousness, the illuminating light of knowledge, acting as a renewal to overcome the dark blight of meaninglessness, that winter season of the soul when life is without meaning and a feeling of depression is present. Lugh's feast is called Lughnasa, a harvest festival held on 1 August, thereby associating him with fecundity. Apollo also fulfilled a fertility role as he was seen to make the fruits of the earth ripen and at Delos and Delphi the first crops were consecrated to him. He also protected the crops by destroying mice and driving off locusts.

Apollo's deadly arrows were equated with the rays of the sun, which killed from afar. One of Lugh's other names is Lamfhada, which means Lugh of the Long Arm, since like Apollo he shot his weapons from a long distance.

Finally, neither of these gods is confined to a single role. Apollo, in addition to being a sun-god, was also god of medicine, music, archery and prophecy. Lugh would appear to be even more complex than Apollo, since one of his titles was Samildánach, master of many skills or arts. Thus he is god of craft, magic and warfare, and a druid who sings incantations prior to battle and then becomes the heroic warrior who slays the fearsome giant.

Whilst in many respects Lugh is the Irish Apollo he is in addition Hermes and Ares. He and the Dagda are both masters of all arts, but the Dagda has all the hallmarks of an earlier, agricultural god, with his rough and crude appearance and his link to the seasons via his harp. Lugh by comparison seems a more refined and later god.

It is Lugh, not Dagda, who appears in the later heroic tales, where he becomes the father of the great Irish mythological hero Cú Chulainn.

His role as father of Cú Chulainn may well symbolize his rebirth, emerging from the otherworld following the darkness of winter. His death comes about at the hands of the triple kings of Ireland (who, some say, took over the kingship after Nuada) in revenge for him having slain their father Cermaid. Although Lugh is the shining one and although he may be a symbol of consciousness, we learn that consciousness is a transitory state and that other, often darker forces such as envy and jealousy also reside in the realm of the invisible world we have come to term 'the unconscious'. These can 'cause' a death, or dismembering of the solar qualities of illumination and meaning, only for them to be renewed as we 're-member' it and re-emerge from the sea of unconsciousness. Freud once described the goal of psychoanalysis as equivalent to the draining of the Zuyder Zee – essentially an act of reclamation of an element of consciousness, a sense of 'I', from the vast sea of unconsciousness. This is tantamount to saying that we do not *have* consciousness, but rather that we experience moments or times when we are conscious. The critical mythic pattern to grasp is the continuing interplay in the deepest recesses of the collective unconscious of those opposite forces of darkness and light, life and death, meaning and chaos. Light and dark are in an eternal dance with each other and sometimes we find ourselves being with one partner a little longer than with the other.

Oenghus (Aonghus)

Oenghus is the god of love, born of the union between the Dagda and the river-goddess Boann, who was at the time the wife of King Elcmar, whose residence was at Bruig na Bóinne. The Dagda enchanted Elcmar and sent him on a journey so that nine months passed as if it were a single day. The spell prevented Elcmar perceiving the darkness of night, nor could he experience hunger or thirst. During this time the Dagda slept with Boann, and she conceived and gave birth to a son whose name was Oenghus.

Like his father he possessed a harp made of gold, and its music was so sweet that anyone hearing it was compelled to follow. In this respect he would appear to be very similar to the Greek figure Orpheus. The latter also played a lyre that made all those that heard it follow (and was the means by which he managed to descend into Hades in his attempt to rescue his beloved Eurydice). Oenghus is sometimes known as the Irish Eros, and is the protector of lovers both in the Mythological Cycle and in the Fenian Cycle, where he protects the archetypal lovers Diarmuid and Gráinne. It is also said of Oenghus that his kisses turned into birds which hovered invisibly over the younger maidens of Ireland. This would appear to be an Irish version of Eros's arrows. He also had his fairy palace at Bruig na Bóinne, which he acquired from King Elcmar by trickery.

Oenghus appears as the major figure in three important stories, 'The Wooing of Étaín', 'Diarmuid and Gráinne' and 'The Dream of Oenghus'. All these stories involve lovers, but in the latter it is the god himself who is smitten by love, not unlike the mythic story of Eros and Psyche. Briefly, the story is that Oenghus falls in love with a girl he sees in his dream and after a long search he finds her in the form of a swan and takes her back to his palace at Bruig na Bóinne.

Oenghus's death comes about through a woman named Caitleann, who threw a stone at Oenghus during a battle and struck him a fatal blow on the head. Being a god of youth, love and renewal does not protect one from submission to the inevitability of death as part of the cycle of birth, death and renewal.

The remaining gods all appear somewhat lesser figures, although of course we have no way of knowing whether this is simply because they were gradually written out of the stories by the Christian monks, or whether the manuscripts relating to them have been lost.

Midir

Midir is usually seen as the Dagda's son, although in some versions he is the Dagda's brother. He is also Oenghus's foster-father and counselled Oenghus on how to acquire the fairy palace at Bruig na Bóinne. Midir himself is lord of the otherworld, dwelling at Brí Léith (near present-day Ardagh) and it is to this *sídhe*, or fairy mound, that he brings his lover Étaín. Some see him as the Irish equivalent of Hades, or Pluto, god of the underworld. However this would appear to be a little simplistic since the only characteristics he has in common with Hades are that he is a lord of the underworld and that he takes a woman to this world as his lover, as Hades did with Persephone. All the Tuatha Dé Danann chiefs were lords of an under- or otherworld realm, not just Midir.

His most prominent role in the mythology is in the story of the wooing of Étaín, whom he takes as his lover, thus incurring the wrath of his wife Fúamnach, who transforms Étaín into a butterfly and with a strong wind blows her to the far ends of the earth.

There is a tale in which Midir possesses three hostile cranes who guard the entrance to his fairy palace. Cranes are well represented in Irish mythology and are particularly associated with shape-changing or metamorphosis in females, usually ill-natured women. Sometimes they are also connected with birds of ill omen and there is some suggestion that there may have existed a taboo against eating crane flesh because to do so would have resulted in some negative fate. The sea-god Manannán had a craneskin bag that contained many treasures. Midir's three cranes provide a link with Hades, since it was the three-headed dog Cerberus that guarded this entrance. Are we to assume from this that it is a trio of ill-natured women transformed into cranes that guard the entrance to the underworld we have come to know in our contemporary mythology as the unconscious world? Certainly within Jungian circles it is a commonly held position that moodiness (ill-naturedness) can be a manifestation of an underdeveloped feeling life or *anima*. Jung saw this figure as the mediator between the conscious and unconscious worlds, the figure that stands at the entrance of the otherworld, or unconscious. Thus the three cranes, like moods, not only guard access to the unconscious feelings in us but also locate the entrance to this world. This interpretation gains some added credence when one considers that it is to his palace that Midir takes the feminine, in the form of Étaín, that is, like Hades he abducts the feminine into the unconscious. Modern men also seem to have an abducted feminine side that can only be found when they reflect upon their various moods and their ill-natured, feminine side. The irony is that whilst moodiness points to the existence of deeper, underworld feelings, it can also inhibit and prevent one from entering that world. This happens particularly when moods are simply projected on to others whom we then blame for our ills, and not reflected upon and owned as part of ourselves. Moodiness invariably points to the presence of some undifferentiated or unclear feelings which we need to struggle to bring into conscious awareness by journeying into the unconscious or otherworld.

Lir

Lir is a god of the sea, one of the Tuatha Dé Danann, best known as the father of the sea deity Manannán mac Lir. Both are clearly the same figures as the Welsh sea-gods Llyr and Manawydan. One view is that Lir is a much earlier god than his son and could be seen as representing the Irish Sea itself. Again, comparison is sometimes made with the Greek pantheon, where he is seen as the equivalent of Poseidon. What we know of Lir is almost entirely derived from the story entitled 'The Fate of the Children of Lir'. This story is one of the 'three great tragedies' of Ireland.

After the Tuatha Dé Danann retreated underground to their respective *sídhe*, they elected a new king, Bodb Derg, and Lir was offended that they did not choose him. As an act of reconciliation Bodb offered Lir one of his daughters in marriage. Her name was Aobh and she bore Lir two sets of twins, but she died in giving birth to the second set. Lir was distraught and Bodb, in a further gesture of good will, gave him his second daughter, Aoife, to marry. However she turned out to be the classic wicked stepmother and became insanely jealous of the children. She put a curse on them that changed them into swans for eternity. The eldest of the children, Fionnuala, pleaded for mercy and whilst recognizing that the curse was too powerful to be undone she asked that the enchantment be modified so that they may not be condemned to live as swans for ever.

Aoife relented, and modified the spell so that the children would have to live as swans for nine hundred years; during this time they could never live on land. Indeed they had to live for three hundred years on Lough Derravaragh, where they were when the spell was cast upon them, followed by three hundred years on the Sea of Moyle and the last three hundred on the Atlantic Ocean. Aoife then declared that when a king from the north married a queen from the south they would hear a bell, and they would know that their exile was over. The curse meant that although they were swans they would be able to speak with their own voices, use their own minds, feel with their own hearts and be able to sing beautifully. When Aoife's father discovered what she had done he was so furious he used his druidic powers and turned her into a demon, in which form she was doomed to wander through the air for ever. Lir, whilst grief-stricken by the events, was able for the first three hundred years to stay in contact with his children and talk to them at Lough Derravaragh, where some say a large settlement grew up to listen to the children's singing and storytelling.

When the children moved on to the Sea of Moyle they experienced great hardships, as they did for their final three hundred years by the Atlantic Ocean. Nine hundred years elapsed, and the old chieftain gods of Ireland had all gone underground and a new religion was in place, Christianity, brought by St Patrick. The children were rescued by a hermit monk, who rang a bell every night until the children heard it, and provided them with food and shelter and linked them together with a silver chain so that they would never be parted. But it was not until a king from the north, King Lairgren, married a queen from the south that the curse could finally be undone. After this marriage took place the queen, who had heard about the beautiful music that the swans sang, insisted that they be brought to her. Lairgren, knowing that this was wrong and also knowing that the saintly hermit would not agree, nevertheless went ahead and took the swans by force, whereby they instantly turned into very old and frail human beings. Lairgren fled in horror at what he had done, and the children of Lir, knowing that their life was coming to an end, were baptized and buried by the hermit monk.

Manannán mac Lir

This son of the sea is far better known than his divine father, and appears in many of the Irish myths. As a divine chieftain he is usually seen as lord of the otherworld which is located under the sea or on some magical island. The sea is clearly of great significance to an island race, and it may be for this reason that he appears so frequently in the stories. If we draw a parallel between the sea and the unconscious, then we can appreciate further why this god, like the unconscious, is so ubiquitous.

The world of spirits and gods was commonly said to lie over the water. There were three well known such lands, Mag Mell (Plain of Delights), Tír Tairngire (Land of Promise) and Tír na nÓg (Land of Perpetual Youth). In the Celtic otherworld there was an inexhaustible supply of food, there was no death or decay, and the inhabitants were invisible when they chose to be. Frequently in the stories one finds the hero summoned by a woman of the otherworld with the promise of perpetual sensual delights. Many a modern man at mid-life will admit to experiencing this 'summons' and pursuing it. Narcissistic and idealized longings for paradise exist in all human beings, and in men often take the form of the fantasy of the perfect woman meeting their every need. At the mid-life period it is not uncommon for a man to leave his wife, children and even job to pursue what he perceives as *the* relationship of his life. He has been summoned by his own *anima* or otherworld woman and has projected these qualities on to some mortal woman with whom he 'falls' in love. The passage of time often reveals to him that the woman he fell in love with and the woman he is in a relationship with are not the same person. At this moment he often looks back at a trail of pain and destruction that he has left behind him. Not having the self-awareness to understand the inner summoning of the otherworld woman, he took it to be literal rather than a symbolic expression of part of himself.

These lands of perpetual sensual delight are a stark contrast to the Christian otherworld. But since the gods of the incoming religion usually make devils of the gods of the preceding religion, Christianity has demonized both body and bodily pleasures, and the Christian otherworld, hell, has become a place of punishment for the very same pleasures that the ancient Irish delighted in.

Manannán was also a master of illusion, a shape changer and the possessor of several magical items. One was his curragh, called *Wave Sweeper* or *Ocean Sweeper*, which obeyed the thoughts of those who commanded it and had no sails or oars. Two other of Manannán's magical possessions are the magic sword and breastplate loaned to Lugh. He also possessed the magic horse called Enbharr (literally 'water foam') who was swifter than wind and could run over both land and water. Sometimes white-crested waves were called the Horses of

Manannán. Like Midir he possessed a bag made of craneskin in which the treasures of the Tuatha Dé Danann were kept. He also wore a great cloak that was capable of taking on every colour, just like the sea itself.

In one story Manannán is visited by the ancient Irish king Cormac mac Art. Manannán is described as being finely clad and carrying on his shoulder a branch bearing three golden apples which when rubbed together made delightful music. This he gave to King Cormac, who treasured it all his life and gave it back to the gods at the point of his death. The giving of gifts seems to be another characteristic of the son of the sea and may well symbolize the fecundity of the sea as a provider of food, much as the goddesses represent the fertility of the land.

In some stories, following the defeat of the Tuatha Dé Danann by the Milesians Manannán is seen as coming across the sea and giving the gods of the Tuatha three gifts. The first of these was a magical cloak with which the gods could make themselves invisible. The second was to provide a magic feast (Feast of Age) which warded off age. The third gift was his pigs, which had the magical quality of being eaten one day and replenishing themselves to full life the next.

Manannán does not only appear in the Mythological Cycle but also in the later Ulster and Fenian Cycles, which points to his enduring qualities as a god and perhaps to the enduring meaning of the sea for the ancient Irish. In the Ulster Cycle, the great mythic hero Cú Chulainn falls in love with Manannán's wife Fand, but after a while she returns to Manannán, who shakes a cloak between his wife and Cú Chulainn so that they are invisible to each other for ever. Diarmuid, in the Fenian Cycle, is said to have been a pupil of Manannán in the otherworld and as we have just seen Cormac mac Art was also a visitor there. Manannán is still present in the Christian era. In one version King Fiachna is fighting the Scots and in great danger of his life when a stranger appears to his wife, who promises to save him if she will abandon herself to him. She reluctantly agrees and from this union the seventh-century King Mongan is said to have been conceived. The stranger is none other than Manannán mac Lir.

Manannán is also involved in another of the prominent stories that we will discuss later, 'The Voyage of Bran'. King Bran was enchanted by a fairy woman and set out on a journey to the otherworld during which he came across Manannán, and this moment is said to be the source of some of the most beautiful lyrical poetry of the Irish mythological tradition. It is also a piece of poetry as Proinsias Mac

Cana points out that expresses 'vividly the inversion of reality which characterizes the otherworld vision of things'. Manannán addresses Bran in these words:

> It seems to Bran a wondrous beauty
> In his curragh on a clear sea;
> While to me in my chariot afar
> It is a flowery plain on which I ride.

> What is a clear sea
> For the prowed craft in which Bran is
> Is a Plain of Delights with a profusion of flowers
> For me in my two-wheeled chariot.

> Bran sees
> A host of waves breaking across the clear sea:
> I myself see in Magh Mon
> Red-tipped flowers without blemish.

> Sea-horses glisten in summer
> As far as Bran's eye can stretch;
> Flowers pour forth a stream of honey
> In the land of Manannán son of Ler . . .[4]

Bodb Derg

Bodb Derg succeeded the Dagda as ruler of the Tuatha Dé Danann. Some sources actually have him as the Dagda's son, whilst others regard him as Boann's brother. Bodb was king of the *sídhe* of Munster called Sídhe ar Femen, the modern Slievenamon in County Tipperary. Like Manannán, he had magical pigs that renewed themselves after having been eaten. The pig is strongly associated with feasting and perhaps this gives it added significance within the mythology since we also know from the accounts of the continental Celts that feasting was of considerable importance to them.

Bodb Derg's main role in the mythological stories is in 'The Dream of Oenghus', where he searches for and finds the woman of Oenghus's dream. Bodb Derg has two daughters who appear in the later Fenian Cycle. One of these, Sadb, metamorphosed into a fawn and then back to a human and became the mother of Oisín, the great poet and leader of the *fíanna*. Bodb Derg remains a relatively lesser god in the pantheon and does not appear to have the status or ubiquity of such figures as Manannán.

Ogma

Ogma is depicted as a Tuatha champion and one of the figures who challenges Lugh before he is admitted to Tara. He is also known as Cermait, meaning 'honey-tongued', since he is the god of eloquence and a champion orator. As patron of literature he is seen as the inventor of Ogham, the ancient Irish writing usually seen on standing stones. It is also sometimes described as a form of occult writing.

Ogma is first described by the Roman poet Lucian (second century AD), who refers to him as Ogmios. Lucian regards him as the Celtic equivalent of the Greek god Hercules, presumably because of his abilities as a champion warrior. There is also a suggestion that, like the Greek Hermes, Ogma may well have been a psychopomp, who leads souls from one world to the other and travels freely between them. However it is quite possible that Lucian is simply projecting his Greek divinities upon this Celtic figure.

In some versions of the second battle of Mag Tuired, Ogma is married to the daughter of the physician Diancecht, and among their offspring was Tuireann, whose sons later murdered Lugh's father. Another son is said to be Cairbre, the poet who satirized the Fomorian king Bres, thereby precipitating the battle itself.

Goibniu, Luchta and Credne

These three 'craft gods' are, respectively, the blacksmith, the carpenter and the metalworker. It is difficult to find any reference to these figures having anything to do with mortals, and their activities seem to be confined to the supernatural realm. They may well be early gods, since their triplicate form links them to the triple-goddess figures; and their alternative title, Tri Dee Danann, the 'three gods of Danu', also points to this possibility.

The one aspect of Goibniu that differentiates him a little from the other two is that he supplies the magic ale that is served at otherworld feasts. The partaking of this ale bestowed invulnerability upon the gods, and here there would appear to be a parallel to the Greek blacksmith god Hephaestos, who also served drinks to the gods. Whilst Goibniu does not appear in later stories, his importance can be seen in the fact that his character survives in folklore where he is referred to as

Goibhleann and is reputed to own a magical cow whose yield is inexhaustible.

Nuada Airgetlám (Nuada of the Silver Arm)

The most significant thing about this god is perhaps the story concerning the loss of his arm and its replacement first with a silver one and finally with his own. He has his *sídhe* in a place called Almu which was later wrested from him by the warrior hero Fionn, a central figure in the later Fenian Cycle.

Diancecht

This is the divine god of healing, the god of medicine, the 'leech'. He is, one might suppose, the Irish Asklepios, although he would appear to derive his healing powers from druidic knowledge, whereas Asklepios derived his from dreams.

Several important points emerge from these descriptions. Marie-Louise Sjoestedt raises the first point, the difference between them and the goddesses. She claims that the gods are national and tribal in character, whereas the goddesses are local. The gods govern social events or arrangements such as political power and territorial matters, whereas the goddesses govern the natural events. So from the mytho-historical accounts we learn more about the gods than we do about the goddesses.[5] The goddess is the personification of nature. The physical land of Ireland is her body. The goddesses are the very forces that the male figures struggle to overcome in order to have nature serve them. However Nature is only temporarily overcome, since she can provide or destroy at will. Likewise the logical, rational mind, that weapon of modern man with which the ego is identified, is powerless against the forces of the unconscious psyche which Jung once described as a natural phenomenon. In either mythology, ancient Irish or modern Jungian, we see the struggle to arrive at a workable arrangement with the forces of nature, so that we neither ruthlessly try to triumph over her nor naïvely succumb to her. The first strategy leads to a sense of inflation and emotional sterility, the second to madness.

The second theme is the link between the gods and what Jung has termed the archetypes. Jung himself warns: 'not for a moment dare we succumb to the illusion that an archetype can be fully explained and disposed of. Even the best attempts at explanation are only more or less successful translations into another metaphorical language.'[6] Myths are one such metaphorical language that speak of what we know and yet do not know. Myths are the plots that move behind and form the substrata upon which our individual lives are built. The divine figures of myths are the characters of these plots. The plots themselves are imaginative accounts of ancient patterns of comprehension that lie within us. The realm of the psyche that contains these inborn patterns of comprehension has been termed the 'collective unconscious' by Jung. As previously mentioned, one could consider archetypal patterns to be the equivalent of migratory patterns in birds or the highly elaborate and ritualistic mating patterns of many animal species. No one teaches these animals such patterns, they are simply built into the species. The difference in our human species is that we can represent these patterns to consciousness via images, and it is these images that Jung has termed archetypal images. Mythology is the story of these images and the forces that they symbolize.

So the image of the great mother or earth mother can symbolize instinctual comprehension of patterns of birth, fertility and nurturance. The figure of the great father can be seen to symbolize such matters as knowledge and wisdom. Modern human figures such as Gandhi or Mother Teresa can come, via projection, to represent these innate patterns. Less mature human beings than those mentioned are vulnerable to such projections and begin to believe that they actually are wise old men, etc., rather than merely carriers of the projection. This sense of ego inflation is dangerous and usually leads to the downfall of the person, sometimes into psychosis, as the weak ego identifies completely with the archetypal force. The art is to know that these patterns are within us, to build a conscious awareness and relationship to them, and to draw on the knowledge and wisdom of these in-built patterns of understanding. Natural elements such as volcanoes and storms can symbolize destructive forces or the dark side of the great mother. The sun on the other hand symbolizes the force of life, renewal and the overcoming of darkness. Myths, which existed long before science, express these archetypal patterns in a manner that provides us with a sense of relief, the relief that comes with the sense of recognition of something that was known but had not been rendered conscious.

This brings us to the theme of the Irish gods' multi-faceted nature, so unlike the 'single-issue' Greek gods. Jung's archetypes are also intertwined and interconnected, and as one of his major proponents Marie-Louise Von Franz says: 'In the unconscious all archetypes are contaminated with one another.'[7] She attributes this quality to the relative timelessness and spacelessness of the unconscious, the qualities that are used to describe the Irish otherworld. The Dagda is one example of an Irish god who depicts this overlapping quality of the archetypes. He symbolizes a masculine fertility pattern of energy and a source of great nourishment with his miraculous cauldron of plenty. Archetypally he could be seen as symbolizing the fruitfulness of knowledge since he is, after all, the 'Lord of Perfect Knowledge'. As an image he could possibly represent a pattern that might emerge from the unconscious mind at those times when our knowledge is too intellectual and in need of earthing. We know the Dagda is also an earthy god who can call in the seasons and bring us back to the natural rhythm of things, thereby reducing the possibility of inflation of the ego.

Lugh is a complex god who clearly personifies the overlapping quality of the archetypal forces. However the essential quality of Lugh is light, that instinctual urge to illuminate the darkness. He symbolizes the archetypal pattern that calls us to rail against darkness and to bring the light of consciousness to bear on some issue or aspect of ourselves that has been outside our conscious perception. So perhaps when we feel dark and despondent, or are simply feeling lost and aimless, the archetypal pattern of the figure of Lugh will emerge to compensate our conscious position. This we could experience in the form of some insight that would 'throw light upon' our darkness. Balor, the Fomorian giant, on the other hand, symbolizes the opposite forces of darkness and destructiveness that plummet us into periods of sterility and meaninglessness. Balor is the archetypal expression of not only the disintegrative tendencies in the human psyche, but also and more importantly of the dark and unacceptable side of our personality. Yet these qualities need to be confronted and illuminated, brought into our conscious awareness and ultimately integrated as parts of ourselves. This process Jung has termed 'individuation' and Lugh as a solar deity could be seen as a symbol of the archetypal urge towards individuation.

Oenghus is best seen as the archetypal symbol of Eros, the instinctual desire to connect, whether physically, mentally or spiritually. It is the likes of Oenghus, for example, that might emerge in our psyches in the form of erotic fantasies characterized by a longing and yearning for union at those times when we are feeling desperately disconnected. Yet, regrettably, individuals are susceptible to taking the fantasies literally and concretizing them by projecting them on to someone else. Thus they are lived 'out', rather than 'in', not reflected upon for the possible meaning that may lie within the fantasies. The latter approach demands stopping and asking questions such as 'What image lies within this fantasy?', 'What need or feeling is being depicted by this image?' or 'What is my desire and what am I seeking in this fantasy?' Archetypal images, like dreams, are more often than not compensatory. Thus they arise at times when the consciously held view is in need of correction or a renewed sense of meaning. The great value of mythological stories is that they remind us of certain patterns of truth that otherwise escape attention in a profoundly materialistic and outwardly orientated culture such as ours.

Diancecht/Asklepios symbolizes an archetypal pattern, or instinctive knowledge, that we have to confront and heal the divisions that lie within our psyche. These divisions often arise from a too-drastic severance between our outer and inner lives. Mythological stories evoke images that bridge this gap, returning us to a sense of balance and connection and providing a broader landscape within which we can locate our immediate personal difficulties.

Goibniu depicts another, yet not of course unrelated, archetypal pattern. This is derived from his role as a blacksmith god, who, like the medieval alchemist, knows how to transmute raw material into its higher form. He symbolizes an aspect of the archetypal realm that knows of the need to render base matter, or base feelings, into a higher, more conscious form which enables us to make choices in our lives rather than simply acting out blindly then declaring that fate is so unkind. He is part of an instinctual comprehension that works with, or overlaps with, Lugh the figure of light.

Together these images symbolize the interconnected energy patterns upon which consciousness itself is formed and desired. When Jung said, 'The archetypes are the great decisive forces, they bring about the real events, and not our personal reasoning and intellect . . . The archetypal images decide the fate of man,'[8] he meant that they are present in us from the beginning, will not go away and indeed cannot go away. Mythology is a vital map for helping us to know of their existence and thereby enhance the possibility of making some connection to these archetypal and universal patterns within us. This connection serves to relativize the ego and provide a sense of meaning. This is a necessary antidote to the feelings of rootlessness that are so symptomatic of our modern society. An awareness of the existence of archetypal patterns also connects us to a realm beyond the ego and draws our attention to something beyond the mundane, material and obvious life.

5

THE SECOND BATTLE OF MAG TUIRED

The Archetypal Struggle Between Light and Dark Forces

It is told in some stories that King Nuada, having lost his arm in the first battle of Mag Tuired, had it temporarily replaced with a silver one by the physician Diancecht. But it was Diancecht's son, Miach, who miraculously replaced the silver one with Nuada's original arm, which had been dug up.

The story goes that during the difficult reign of Bres, Miach and his sister Airmid, both of whom were physicians, came to the castle of the deposed King Nuada. Nuada's porter, himself blemished with a lost eye, asked the strangers who they were. When they said they were physicians, the porter asked whether they could give him a new eye. They placed a cat's eye in the porter's eye socket, and he was so pleased that he told Nuada, who requested that the physicians be brought to him to repair his arm. Nuada told them where his severed arm was buried, and they dug it up and placed it on Nuada's stump, which had by now festered where the silver arm had been attached. At the same time they uttered an incantation over the arm and after three days and three nights the arm was healed. (When Diancecht heard of this healing he was so furious that his son had excelled him that he killed him with a sword, but only after four attempts because on the first three Miach managed to heal himself.)

This brief interlude, apart from its magical quality, serves to illustrate the persistent mythological theme of killings between fathers and sons, symbolizing the emergence of a new order and the desire of the existing order to kill it off. The process of renewal is aborted by Diancecht killing his son and perhaps whenever envy is present in the older figure then death, in some form or other, of the younger one is an inevitable outcome. This death, which need not be taken literally, could for example take the form of killing off the younger person's self-esteem and spontaneity. We can see this operating when fathers respond to their adolescent sons in an authoritarian manner that evokes either rebellion or compliance, but in any case impedes growth.

It also serves to draw our attention to a common pattern in a man's psyche, his desire and fear of outstripping his father. There is in most men a taboo that makes them fearful of being more successful or living longer than their fathers. The unconscious association would appear to be that surpassing one's father will entail punishment, in the form of death. This is often seen when a man approaches the age at which his father died. A common experience at this stage is fearfulness, and a man's dream life often depicts a regular theme of death in various symbolic forms, such as the running-out of a road. It is as if unconsciously he is anticipating punishment for daring to outstrip his father by living longer. Freud aptly conceptualized this fear as castration anxiety. This theme of killing between father and son, or grandfather and grandson, returns us to Lugh and his arrival at the celebration of King Nuada.

As the feast was being held a strange company was seen approaching Tara, headed by a young warrior with a king's trappings. He announced himself to the doorkeeper as Lugh of the Fierce Combat and son of Cian and of Ethniu, daughter of a Fomorian king. The doorkeeper asked him what art he practised, for it was the custom of the time that no one without an art could enter Tara. Sjoestedt believes that the continental Celts gave precedence in their divine world to craftspersons over warriors.[1] Within the Irish mythological tradition it is usual to find both these attributes combined in the one figure, as with Lugh.

'Question me,' said Lugh, 'I am a wright.'

The doorkeeper answered, 'We need thee not, we already have a wright called Luchta.'

Lugh said, 'Question me, doorkeeper, I am a blacksmith.'

The doorkeeper answered, 'We already have a smith, his name is Goibniu.'

'I am a professional warrior,' said Lugh.

'We already have one,' said the doorkeeper, 'his name is Ogma.'

'I am a harpist,' declared Lugh, to which the doorkeeper made his standard reply that they already had one and his name was Abhean, son of Bicelm.

'I am a metalworker,' said Lugh, and again the doorkeeper replied that they already had one named Credne.[2]

The dialogue continues, describing all the arts, until finally Lugh asked the doorkeeper if there was any one person in Tara who possessed *all* the skills mentioned, and if there was then there was no need for Lugh to come to Tara. The doorkeeper went inside and told Nuada of the arrival of this young man whom he named Samildánach, meaning 'master of all arts'. Nuada responded by inviting him in. This is a moment in the story that we could take to symbolize the arrival of a new divinity in the mythology, the arrival of a new order that is not killed off. Lugh was immediately challenged, first to a game of chess; then to a test of strength, by the champion Ogma; and finally by the harpist. All these, being a *samildánach*, he won.

Nuada, perceiving Lugh as someone who could help him overthrow the Fomorians, handed the kingship over to Lugh. How different this response to the existence of new and superior talents is to that of Diancecht. In fact it stands as a model for a transition unencumbered by envy, with the leader's focus being the welfare of the group and not the preservation of his personal power, a quality so rarely seen in politics. Lugh accepted the kingship and immediately set about the task of preparing for war against the Fomorians, which became the second battle of Mag Tuired.

Lugh now summoned all the Tuatha Dé Danann, to inform them of the forthcoming war against the Fomorians and to ask each of them what they could do to help. Diancecht replied that he would heal every man that was wounded, provided his head was not struck off or his brain cut through. He promised to make the warrior whole again, ready for battle the next day. The blacksmith Goibniu declared that he would replace every broken lance and sword with a new one, even if the war lasted for seven years. He also promised to make the lances so well that they would never miss their target, a feat he claimed the Fomorian blacksmith could not perform. Credne the bronze worker said he would furnish all the rivets for the lances, the hilts for the swords and the rims for the shields. Luchta the carpenter promised all the wooden shafts for the lances and shields. Ogma the champion warrior pledged to kill the Fomorian king and to capture two-thirds of his army. Cairbre the poet replied that he would pronounce a curse upon the Fomorians by one of his satires so that they would feel a great sense of shame and not be able to stand against fighting men.

Lugh then asked the great sorcerer Mathgan what he could promise to do, and he declared that through his power he would throw down all the mountains of Ireland upon the Fomorians. Then he asked the cup-bearers, who said that they would magically hide the twelve chief lakes and rivers of Ireland, so that the Fomorians could not quench their thirst, whereas the Tuatha Dé Danann would be given drink for as long as the war lasted. Then the druid Figol said he would send three streams of fire into the faces of the Fomorians, which would take away two-thirds of their valour and strength, but that every breath drawn by the people of Danu would make them strong.

Finally it came to the Dagda's turn to say what he could do. His promise was that he himself would do all that the other gods had promised individually. 'The power which ye boast I shall wield it all myself.' Upon hearing this the assembly said, 'Thou art indeed the excellent god.' As we have already said, he is known as the good god, not because he is good in a moral sense, but because he is good at everything related to craft and sorcery.

At this point in the story there exists a separate, yet not unrelated, story that cannot be ignored since it is sometimes referred to as one of the three great tragedies of Ireland. Its title in English is 'The Fate of the Sons of Tuireann'. According to the Irish scholar Gerard Murphy it is probably a later story, perhaps written as late as the fourteenth century, which has been woven into the account of the second battle.[3]

The Fate of the Sons of Tuireann

While Lugh was making all his preparations for the battle he sent his father Cian, along with his two uncles Cu and Ceithin to separate provinces in order to muster armies. There had been a long-standing enmity between Cian and the three sons of Tuireann, Brian, Iuchair and Iucharba, and on this journey Cian was confronted by them. Despite transforming himself into a pig, Cian was killed by the three brothers. When Lugh discovered this, instead of directly ordering their execution, he imposed a set of tasks upon the brothers (a theme which is repeated in other mythologies, for example the twelve labours that were imposed upon Hercules). In Irish these tasks are referred to as an *éric*, literally meaning a fine. They consisted of having to obtain a pigskin, a particular spear, a specific pair of horses yoked to a chariot, three apples, seven pigs, a young hound and a cooking spit, and finally to give three shouts on the top of a specific hill. On the surface these all appear to be relatively simple tasks, but all the objects had magical qualities and great risks would be involved in acquiring them from magical distant lands. Lugh needed them in addition to the magic of his own people for the forthcoming battle; for example, the magical pigskin had the capacity to heal all wounds and ailments, whereas the two horses yoked to the chariot could outpace the wind, and the seven swine could regenerate themselves after being eaten.

The final task of the three shouts from a particular hilltop also appears straightforward, but this turns out to be the critical one that the sons of Tuireann are unable to complete and which results in their death. For the king who owned the hill had placed a curse on it, in honour of the death of Cian. This king was Michan, and the curse was that death would come to anyone who shouted on the hilltop. When the sons of Tuireann arrived on the hill, having successfully completed all the other tasks, Michan welcomed them with all the usual hospitality, then, having ascertained the visitors' intentions, he forbade them to shout on the hilltop.

Aware now of the curse upon them, the sons of Tuireann engaged in a fierce battle in which they killed Michan and his three sons but were fatally wounded in the process. Tuireann begged Lugh to lend him the magic pigskin that could heal them, but he refused and avenged his father's death by letting the three brothers die. This ending illustrates an enduring theme of Irish myths: the inevitability of death when a curse is placed upon a figure. These curses are termed *geasa* (the singular form is *geis*) and consist of an injunction or taboo against performing a particular act, or an obligation to act in a specific way.

Individuals in psychotherapy often manifest something similar to the *geis*. Most commonly they place it upon themselves, sometimes consciously, sometimes unconsciously, and usually in adolescence, or in some instances in early childhood. More often than not it is in response to some particular trauma, and continues to exert an influence throughout their adult lives. For example, a man in his mid-forties was referred to me after extensive medical tests had failed to reveal the source of considerable upper-body and testicular pain. The man had had a series of dreams involving violent acts, and it emerged that as a twelve-year-old boy he had punched a fellow student at school and this student had collapsed. There had been much ado about this and he had been severely punished. As a consequence, he recalled, at or around that time he made a pact to himself that he would never lose his temper again. The truth of the matter was that he never had! This was his 'curse', or prohibition upon himself, and his rigid repression of his anger had driven it into his body, where it had become the cause of his pain. Others can be found to make similar resolutions or pacts that are engendered by trauma, in particular the loss of a parent. Here the 'curse' is sometimes in the form of a resolution never to let anyone get close again, in order to avoid a repetition of the hurt.

Another reading of this story of the sons of Tuireann would take into account the outer events of the lives of the ancient Irish, much as one might consider the outer events of a person's life in reflecting on the possible meaning of a dream. One could argue that this story in fact depicts a historical tribal war, and the ascendancy of one group over another, that have found their way into myth. It then makes some sort of sense that it is woven into the preparations for the second battle and indeed provides for an even more elaborate listing of the various magical gifts. In this way the underlying unity between sorcerer and warrior is reinforced, a quality that is characteristic of Irish myths, unlike the Greek myths where the female figure is the source of enchantment and the male the warrior.

To return to our story, it is said that Lugh's preparations took seven years and were completed a week before Samain, which occurs at the beginning of November. The word itself is derived from the Irish words 'samh', meaning 'summer', and 'fuin', meaning 'end'. It is a time of sacrifice, appeasing the gods in order to lessen the hardships of winter. It was at this time that the Dagda had intercourse with the goddess Morrígan, who promised him that she would destroy Indech, the son of a Fomorian king, and deprive him of 'the blood of his heart and the kidney of his valour'. So this second battle is in essence a myth of Samain, to do with ensuring the renewal of the fecundity of the earth and its people, for it is also said that Samain was a propitious time for a woman to become pregnant.

There are some inconsistencies concerning the order of events around this time, but for our purposes we will assume that following this union Lugh then sent the Dagda to the Fomorian camp in order to effect a further delay. This results in the Dagda being ridiculed for both his appearance and his appetite. In accordance with the Celtic custom of hospitality the Fomorians made him a huge broth which filled the King's cauldron. It consisted of four-times-twenty gallons of milk, goats, pigs and sheep, and was poured into a huge hole in the ground. As it would have been bad *geis* to refuse hospitality, the Dagda, armed with a ladle that was big enough for a man and a woman to lie in, proceeded to eat the lot. He then promptly went to sleep, with the Fomorians laughing derisively at his distended stomach. After he woke, the Dagda had sex with the daughter of a Fomorian king, who promised the Dagda that she would serve him against her father.

While the many versions of this story have in the main chosen to emphasize the grotesque and obscene images, there are some more important themes to consider. In the Dagda's mating with Morrígan and the daughter of the Fomorian king, there is the significant theme of the masculine principle seeking the support and assistance of the divine feminine, union with the feminine being a means of achieving one's goals rather than a simple triumphing over her.

Once the battle began, the slaughter was great on both sides, the Tuatha were healed by Diancecht and the magic pigskin acquired by the sons of Tuireann. The Tuatha chiefs had decided that Lugh was too valuable to be in the actual battle, but he managed to escape from his minders and resorted to his magical powers to rally the men of his army by moving around amongst them on one foot and with only one eye open, chanting an incantation to give them strength and courage. Here again we see the combination of warrior/magician. Horrific slaughter continued, with Balor the one-eyed giant chief of the Fomorians slaying King Nuada. This establishes the fact that Irish gods could be killed and that they are not the creators of man but rather his ancestors. Similarly, in the fairy kingdom the visible and invisible worlds coexist alongside each other. By contrast, in both the Christian and ancient Greek mythologies these worlds are separate and have a rigid patriarchy that places the divine above in heaven, or on Mount Olympus, superior to mankind, not alongside.

The next critical moment in the story is the prophesied confrontation between Balor and his grandson Lugh. Some say that Balor actually had two eyes but that he had to keep one closed for it was so venomous that it killed anyone on whom its gaze fell. Other stories suggest that he only ever had one eye and was known as Balor of the Baleful Eye. This links him to other one-eyed mythological figures such as the Titan Cyclops. The destructive quality of the eye also links him to the Medusa, whose gaze turned people to stone. One story tells that Balor, walking past the house where his sorcerer father was preparing a magic potion, became curious and looked in the window. Some poisonous smoke drifted into his eye and he was then only allowed to live on the condition that he kept it shut. However in battle the lid of his giant eye was propped open and the gaze withered all those before him.

Lugh, aware of this danger, shouted to his grandfather to attract his attention and before the eye was fully opened he catapulted a stone through the eye and out the back of Balor's head. The poisonous eye now faced Balor's own army, and destroyed a great number of his troops. The parallel to the biblical story of David and Goliath is obvious and is perhaps evidence of the Christian scribes imposing an element of their own story upon this ancient pagan one. Thus the prophecy was fulfilled and Balor was killed by his grandson. Following his death the Fomorians were routed by the Tuatha Dé Danann. With the encouragement of the Morrígan, who gave the Tuatha soldiers added strength, they drove the Fomorians back to the territory below the sea.

Bres, the inhospitable former king of the Tuatha, had been captured, and he sought to save his life by promising that the cows of Ireland would always be in milk and that a harvest of grain would be produced every year. However both these promises were rejected by Lugh, and Bres's life was only finally spared when he revealed the best times to plough, sow and reap crops. Proinsias MacCana places this piece of the myth into the broader context of Indo-European myths and Dumézil's three functions. He suggests that Dumézil's first two functions, the sacred/sovereignty and force, were well developed, as depicted by the Tuatha Dé Danann. However the third function, nurturance and fertility and aspects of agriculture, was missing. This MacCana argues was held by the Fomorians, and the knowledge extracted from Bres made the Tuatha culture complete. This agreement extracted from Bres may also represent an expansion of knowledge concerning ways of managing the barrenness of winter, since the Fomorians are linked to winter and the battle itself to Samain.

Another way of looking at this story would be to link it to the recurring mythological theme of the struggle between good and evil, or the mythical struggle between the gods and demonic powers that threaten the cosmic order. This struggle is repeated in many mythological stories such as that between the Titans and the Olympians or the Devas and the Asuras of Indian mythology. It is a theme that seems very ancient and persistent throughout mythology and warrants further exploration. Marie-Louise Sjoestedt, who was primarily a linguist, connects the root of the word 'Fomorian', 'mor', to the Germanic word 'Mahr', which is the name of a female demon who lies on the breasts of people while they are asleep.[5] This links it to the English word 'nightmare' and also to the goddess Morrígan. She is sometimes known as the queen of the night, and also as the triple goddess associated with death. So the Fomorians might be symbolically linked to the under-world that today we term the unconscious, since it also is a source of demons that visit in the night, in the form of dreams and nightmares. It is also the source of death, in the sense that it threatens the death of meaning with the irruption of unconscious material that can create a state of disorder and chaos.

A further, but admittedly tenuous, link is to the Hindu word 'mara', which is the name of the Buddhist demon who tempted the Buddha when he was seeking enlightenment under the tree of wisdom. Mara represents the forces that are antagonistic to enlightenment, which in the Buddhist tradition could be seen as both the desire for life and the fear of death. The Buddha not only overcame the seductive attempts of Mara's three daughters but also various attacks by devils and monsters that Mara had sent. In desperation Mara hurled one of his terrible discs, which were known to cut mountains in half, and the Buddha survived this. Finally enlightenment came to the Buddha in his realization that all living beings live, die and transmigrate. This realization could be rephrased to mean that the Buddha became aware of the inevitability of the natural cycle of life, death and renewal. This of course is the very theme that is the essence of Irish mythology.

If we see death and chaos, and visitors in the night, as intercon-nected, one an aspect of the other, then we can appreciate that it is only by grasping the necessity and inevitability of the disintegrating forces of chaos that we can truly appreciate the underlying pattern of our life. So the Buddha was able to free himself from the illusory duality of life *or* death and to see the inevitability of the continuity of life, death and renewal as the eternal cycle of nature.

The second battle of Mag Tuired is essentially a Samain myth, telling of the necessity of confronting the Thanatos forces of disintegration, chaos and death that are represented in nature by the season of winter. This is the recurring archetypal struggle between the life force Eros and the death force Thanatos. To repeat the thoughts of Sigmund Freud: 'And now, I think, the meaning of the evolution of civilization is no longer obscure to us. It must present the struggle between Eros and Death, between the instinct of life and the instinct of destruction, as it works itself out in the human species.'[6]

Thus the Fomorians are symbolic of the powers of Thanatos, whereas the Tuatha Dé Danann symbolize the life force, or Eros. At the personal level the Fomorians are the ever-present nightmare threatening to overwhelm the existing order of ego/consciousness, in psychoanalytic terms the fear of the return of the repressed. Yet the figure of Bres shows the importance of the role of darkness in engendering fertility, since he knew when to plough, sow and reap. Psychologically this is akin to capturing a specific image when we are in the darkness of our psyche and using this image as a means of reflection upon the possible meaning of the darkness. The Tuatha Dé Danann rejected Bres's original offers of cows permanently in milk and annual harvests of grain. What is needed in the psychological sense is not a fantasy of permanent nurturance or goodness (usually in the form of some idealized mother), but the secret of cultivating these qualities for ourselves. The yearning for the idealized breast can only compound feelings of despair and rage.

Depression is a form of dark chaos that often serves to disintegrate our sense of order and meaning, a Fomorian experience so to speak. Yet such a period of despair often acts as a prelude to a period of renewal of meaning and purpose. But when we are in the darkness of depression there seems no possibility of renewal, and instead of yielding a little to it and exploring its possible meaning we are made to feel ashamed and weak, or given medication to obliterate it altogether. In so doing we forgo the opportunity to 'capture Bres' and learn from him.

Mid-life is one obvious point in the individual life cycle when this occurs. However if this 'death' is faced and explored then new meaning emerges. If the individual cannot do this and instead seeks refuge in any number of distractions or denials, such as overwork, drugs, alcohol or extramarital liaisons, then an opportunity for growth is often forgone. At other times the feelings of Eros triumph, as in the experience of falling in love or becoming obsessed by some new philosophy. At these times the Fomorians are absent entirely. However they are never gone for ever and before long the idealism that is so characteristic of falling in love breaks down, often deteriorating into powerful and destructive denigration.

The second battle of Mag Tuired is paradigmatic of the continuing and ever-changing relationship between the negative and positive divinities, or alternatively between the opposite archetypal patterns that form the bedrock of our psychic life. The Tuatha Dé Danann symbolize the positive forces of light and Logos struggling to overcome the destructive and dark forces symbolized by the evil eye of Balor. We need to know and acknowledge the interplay of these opposing forces within us if any form of conscious awareness is to occur, otherwise we will be constantly buffeted by them and have very little opportunity to experience choice in our lives. Instead we will feel that our lives are completely determined by forces outside our control. This we often call fate. The existence in the collective unconscious of this divine war is symbolized in the continuing struggle of the second battle of Mag Tuired.

The feast of Samain can be seen as a ritualistic honouring of the necessity of accepting the permanent presence of the dark and chaotic aspects of growth and sustenance. At Samain, the ancient Irish believed, a gap opened up in the earth; this is the gap between the end of one year and the beginning of the next. Now the supernatural beings make their presence felt by coming through the gaps. These are the people from the invisible otherworld that exists alongside us. Nowadays we call this otherworld the unconscious, which is also a gap, a space, which exists outside time and from which other 'beings' of our self emerge. These are the figures that people our dreams and enact the plots of our inner life.

The original meaning of the Greek word for 'gap' was 'chaos', which again serves to underline that Samain could well be seen as symbolizing a period of loss of meaning, as a necessary stage in the reconstruction of it. The Fomorians then would represent the primal chaos, the state of distintegration and disorder. Cessair, Partholón and the Nemedians were destroyed by these forces of disintegration in the form of the Fomorians. You will recall that Cessair arrived in Ireland with only three males and all but one of the tribe were destroyed by the Great Flood. Here the masculine principle of Logos is insufficiently developed to withstand the chaos and to make any sense of it, and the people are drowned by the ocean of undifferentiated feeling, swamped by the collective or archetypal forces of darkness and absorbed into the great chaos. With the Partholóns and the Nemedians we can see some development in so far as the forces of chaos are now identifiable in the figures of the Fomorians. But the powers of chaos and disintegration are still too strong and both tribes are wiped out by plague and pestilence. It is only the Tuatha Dé Danann's superior esoteric and druidic knowledge, which we could take to be symbolic of a higher and more developed form of Logos, that can withstand the forces of chaos. In all of us, the powers of chaos and the threat of absorption into the vast world of the collective unconscious are for ever threatening and we, like the Tuatha, need a higher level of awareness and knowledge to confront these forces and to integrate them in a meaningful way that contributes to our continuing growth. To fall into unconsciousness through absorption, or to sever any contact with the Fomorians within us through an over-identification with logic and rationality, can only lead to stagnation. As the myth shows, it is the confrontation which yields the creativity. Without the confrontation we cannot learn these secrets and thus cannot integrate the dark aspects of self. All growth requires the letting go of the existing order, the temporary immersion in the chaos of not-knowing and the successful gaining of self-cultivating knowledge.

Lugh, the 'shining one', is an archetypal solar hero, a light of consciousness that successfully challenges the forces of darkness in the figure of Balor. The fact that Balor is his grandfather reminds us that these aspects are not separate but interrelated. 'The Second Battle of Mag Tuired' can be seen at the level of the collective unconscious as the archetypal desire for the light of consciousness to challenge the forces of darkness. All too often this is manifested as the pursuit of information and knowledge to defend against the darkness rather than to explore it.

Thus the battle of Mag Tuired continues today. Unfortunately the modern ego seems to want to cope with this struggle by over-identifying with the light and denying the Fomorian forces within itself. This results in a stultification of individual growth and fertility and in turn produces a sort of plastic, happy person who adamantly denies the existence within themselves of any aggressive or destructive feelings whatsoever. The experience of a relationship with such a person is in fact not an experience at all, since one senses a vacuum behind the kind and warm appearance. The alternative outcome is that in denying our darkness we readily find it in others, through the mechanism of projection. From this position we wreak violence upon fellow human beings, in the form of war, racial prejudice, domestic violence or any number of social ills.

The denial and repression of dark and unacceptable feelings can also result in the development of physical illness. The repression of unacceptable feelings – whether they be sadness, anger, dependency, envy, or hatred – can manifest itself in a variety of complaints. So some dermatological conditions may arise when something gets under the person's skin. Neck aches can mean that someone is literally giving us a 'pain in the neck', and stomach aches can mean that we have been 'kicked in the guts'. This is not to suggest that the physical pain does not exist, but the cause is often hard to identify because it is emotional in nature. Orthodox medical treatment will often attend successfully to the immediate, literal symptom, but the symptoms are destined to appear again, perhaps in a different guise, until such time as the unacceptable feelings and thoughts are brought into the light of day, confronted and accepted.

As 'The Second Battle of Mag Tuired' shows, it was the moment of accepting Lugh, the solar light of consciousness, into their midst at Tara that enabled the confrontation with the dark forces to be undertaken. The essential requirement for success was the extensive preparation and attention to detail that took place. So we need to prepare ourselves for the confrontation, by cultivating the art of reflection instead of taking immediate action and asking over-rational questions such as 'What is wrong with me?' and 'How can I get it fixed?'. One might instead ask, 'When did I get ill?', 'What was I doing, or not wanting to do, at the time I became ill?' and 'Where am I ill?'. Reflecting on these questions can often release images and thoughts that bring 'Lugh' to bear on the issue, thus throwing some light on the illness beyond the obvious physical explanation.

6

THE GODDESSES

The Feminine Archetypes

Irish mythology has an essentially feminine quality, and female deities feature in so many stories of the land and the islands that lie off the coast. It has been suggested that a matriarchal culture preceded the patriarchal one; while this may be true, the more likely explanation is that the feminine is a personification of the fertility of the land. This personification is often in the figure of the sovereign queen, with whom the mortal aspirant for kingship must have union if he is to rule. The Celtic notion of sacral kingship would seem to find its equivalent in the medieval alchemical idea of the *hieros gamos*, or the chymical wedding, which led to the creation of the philosopher's stone.

Whilst the gods' heroic attributes give them a certain measure of power and independence, there always seems to be another power which ensures that they are not completely masters of their own destiny. The Greek father-god, Zeus, is seen as obeying some higher power, variously named as *fatum* or *moira*. The word '*fatum*' is the origin of our English word 'fate' (in turn derived from the verb *fare*, to speak) and is translated to mean 'that which has been spoken'. In this sense it is a form of divine decree.

Within the Greek mythological tradition the Fates or Moirai were three old women, the daughters of Nyx, the night. Clotho span the thread of life, Lachesis assigned to each person his or her destiny, and Atropos carried the shears that cut the thread at death. It is said that they arrived shortly after the birth of a child to decide upon the course of the child's life. They were also invoked at marriage, to ensure that the union was a healthy one, and finally when the end of life approached they had to be summoned to cut the thread. Indeed the whole of life was shadowed by the Fates and it takes little thought to perceive the parallel of the Fates to the theme of life, death and renewal that so characterizes Irish mythology. It seems plausible therefore that the 'other power' behind the gods is the inevitability of this cycle to which all are subjected, gods included. Irish goddesses are usually depicted as triple goddesses, emphasizing their link to the three Fates. The triple goddess personifies a state of wholeness. She is the symbol of the eternal state and the goal itself, which is the acceptance and integration of the three processes of birth, life and death.

The figure of the triple goddess of Ireland could be seen as personifying the fourth state that emerges out of her embodiment of the three. Often we become preoccupied with renewal, or beginnings, in a pattern that Jung has termed the *puer* (child) archetype. This pattern can most readily be seen in connection with relationships where some people, more often men, can only ever begin relationships, usually in a highly sexualized manner. Yet within a short period of time the relationship ends, since the addiction is to the excitement of beginnings, not to relating and the possibility of growth. Others may become obsessed by the fear of death and lose all sight of life and beginnings as they plummet into depression. Here the relationship pattern is one of not getting involved because of the belief that it will not last. Yet others hang on to life, refusing to concede that the only permanent thing is change itself, thereby denying themselves the possibility of renewal. Relationships caught in this pattern simply become stagnant and often moribund, since change is perceived as a threat to order and fixity. In these relationships libido is often sacrificed on the altar of security.

The goal of individuation as espoused by Jung may well be wholeness, but this in turn constitutes a willingness to accept the inevitability of the never-ending cycle of life, death and renewal. The task of consciousness then would be to come to grips with the realization that we are permanently in flux. We must be prepared at times to let go of our attachment to certain possessions and views in order to let Thanatos do its work, allowing them to die as a necessary prelude to the renewal process. If the ego and the persona dominate our being then we cannot yield to the inevitable, since we would be preoccupied with control, and the end result is that we get stuck in the illusion that what we see is all there is.

Danu (Dana/Anu)

It is generally accepted that Anu, Danu and Dana are one and the same deity, and that she is the mother of the gods. But just as the Dagda is seen as the father of the tribe, Danu was not literally their mother. Rather, Anu or Dana is a fertility goddess, associated with the plenty and prosperity of the land. She is described as the one who 'nurtures well the gods'. The province of Munster in the south-west of Ireland is said to owe its fertility to Anu and two mountains in Kerry are known as the 'Paps of Anu'. The mythical tribe of the Tuatha Dé Danann are of course the 'people of the goddess Danu'.

An Cailleach Bhéarra (The Hag of Beara)[1]

Another, much less written-about, female figure who is also a mother-goddess but possibly much earlier than Dana is the Cailleach Bhéarra, the old hag of the Beara peninsula in west Cork. She is a complex figure and would appear to be a predecessor to the Celts themselves. She is also a corn-goddess and associated with the protection of fertility. Indeed in one story she put to death a succesion of male reapers who failed to match her prowess with the sickle. The story reflects a frequent mythological theme of a local hero and the female deity opposing each other in a reaping contest in which the female deity, symbolizing fertility, inevitably triumphs.

Her other manifestations include a role as shaper of the land itself. It is said that she dropped cairns on the hills of Meath out of her apron, and that she was responsible for creating many of the rocks and islands around the south-west coast of Ireland. Deep ravines and valleys are the result of her having run her nails across the landscape.

In another role she is seen as symbolizing the wild forces of nature, especially storms at sea. This role is strongly associated with the Cailleach by the people of the Beara peninsula.

She is also a symbol of longevity and is said to have passed through seven periods of youth and old age so that her children, grandchildren and great-grandchildren are the people and tribes of Ireland. Thus she represents three aspects of the feminine: young maiden, mother and old crone. The Cailleach is also the sovereign queen; under the name Bui, she appears as the wife of Lugh, the divine prototype of kingship.

These roles all illustrate the mother-goddess function and the associations with nature and fertility, which may suggest that she is a very early goddess whom perhaps the continental Celts incorporated into their pantheon to symbolize the land of Ireland itself. She is believed to be embodied today in a special stone that stands overlooking the sea near Eyeries in Cork, where she awaits the return of her husband Manannán, lord of the sea.

Brigit (Brighid)

Another composite early figure is Brigit, who later became the Christian St Brigid. Sometimes she is seen as interchangeable with

Danu, and she is also described as the daughter of the Dagda. However, she is mostly seen in her own right as the goddess adored by poets, blacksmiths and physicians. She is also associated with childbirth, fertility and the hearth, and in these capacities she could readily be seen as the Irish equivalent of some composite Hestia/Artemis figure from Greek mythology, the latter being associated with childbirth and the former with the hearth.

Her festival on 1 February is called Imbolg, which is one of the four great Irish seasonal festivals. Imbolg is a pagan spring festival and is associated with the lactation of ewes, linking Brigit to fertility and the abundance of animals. She was appropriated by Christianity and became St Brigid, but has nevertheless preserved much of her original character, since St Brigid is associated with childbirth, and folklore has it that she was the midwife of the Virgin Mary. In her Christian capacity she is also considered to bring abundance to the country hearth that she visits and as an Irish saint she takes second place only to St Patrick. She and the Cailleach indicate the persistent presence of these fertility goddesses right up to the present time. The land of Ireland is still the goddess's, no matter what name she goes by.

Macha

Macha is one of a group of Irish goddesses who are concerned with war, fertility and the prosperity of the land. She is sometimes perceived as one goddess and sometimes as three, but either way she represents the sovereignty and fertility of Ireland and covers an enormous period of time, from the mythological prehistory period through to the beginning of the Christian era. She gave her name to Emain Macha, the seat of the ancient kings of Ulster. Macha is connected to the festival of Lughnasa, the harvest festival of 1 August.

An interesting aspect of these later goddesses is the explicit appearance of warlike capacities. In the earlier figures, warlike or destructive aspects are embedded in the goddess's association with nature, such as the Cailleach's personification as a goddess of the wildness of nature. In the later goddesses it is a clearly developed role, perhaps symbolizing the heroic male's increasing consciousness of the power of nature to control his fate.

The first of the three Machas, the wife of Nemed, takes us back to *The Book of Invasions* and the arrival of the Nemedians, the third group of invaders to settle in Ireland following Cessair and Partholón. She prophesied the destruction that would be wrought when Connacht fought Ulster over the great brown bull of Cuailgne, and the burden of this foresight caused her to die of a broken heart. (The account of this battle is known simply as the Tain; it constitutes the greatest heroic tale of Ireland, with the central role being played by the hero Cú Chulainn.) Macha died on one of the twelve plains cleared by her husband Nemed, and the plain is named after her. This figure of Macha is clearly an agrarian deity associated with the clearing and cultivation of the land and hence predominantly a fertility goddess.

The second Macha, Macha the Red, was the daughter of one of the three ancient kings of Ireland who ruled alternately, each for seven years. Mythic history places them around the sixth to fourth centuries BC. When Macha's father died she was elected to rule, but the other two kings refused to give her the throne because she was a woman. In the war that followed, the victorious Macha banished one of her rivals to Connacht, marrying the other and making him chief of her army. The five sons of the banished king then sought to contest the throne, but she visited them disguised as a leper. She enticed them one by one to lie with her and in turn bound each of them to slavery. Macha the Red is clearly the warrior-goddess dominating.

The third of the Machas, the wife of Crunnchu, conforms to the familiar mythological/fairy-tale theme of the supernatural bride who lives happily with a mortal husband until he violates a taboo, with the result that she dies. One day a beautiful young woman walked into the house of a peasant widower named Crunnchu. Without speaking a word she set about doing the housework, and at night she made the ritualistic right-handed journey around the room (anticlockwise being an omen of bad fortune) and entered Crunnchu's bed. She became pregnant by him, and through this union he prospered greatly. At this point in the story Macha embodies the sovereign queen, as union with the archetypal feminine is a source of fertility.

Crunnchu was required to attend an assembly of all Ulstermen at Tara, and before he set off Macha warned him not to mention her name nor speak of her at the assembly. At the assembly much was made of the ability of the King's horses, with the poets singing their praises and exalting their swiftness. Crunnchu forgot Macha's warning and declared that his wife could run faster than any of the King's horses. The King took up the challenge and ordered Crunnchu to bring his wife to race against his horses.

In vain Macha protested and asked for a delay, as she was close to giving birth, but the King insisted that she race or he would put

Crunnchu to death. Reluctantly she raced, and beat the King's horses but as she finished she cried out in pain and gave birth to twins. (The name Emain Macha literally means 'the twins of Macha'.) The exertion proved fatal for Macha and she died in giving birth, but with her last breath she cursed the men of Ulster. For nine times nine generations, at times of greatest peril, the men of Ulster would suffer the sickness of childbirth and therefore would be too tired and weak to fight in battle.

Some scholars have interpreted this curse, which is called the Novena of the Ulstermen, as a form of the practice amongst primitive peoples called *couvade*, whereby the husband of a woman in childbirth has imposed upon him the same seclusion and precautions as upon the mother. The aim of this appears to be that the husband will take on the pain of the woman, thereby assisting in the birth process.

A second interpretation of this curse is that it serves to underline the power of otherworld women, and the superiority of their power to that of the male warrior. A third explanation is that the curse, being activated at a time of war, is a symbolic mime in honour of the mother-goddess. In this sense it is an act of propitiation aimed at giving the warriors protection in the forthcoming battle.[2]

In this third Macha we can see the dominance of the functions of childbirth, nurturance and fertility. Thus the three Machas present maternal reproductive power, nurturance/fertility, and warlike/sexual attributes. Of the three, one can be seen to fulfil Dumézil's sorcerer function with her prophecy of a future period of destruction. Macha the Red fulfils the function of force with her warrior-like behaviour, and the third Macha represents fertility.

The use of threes is a dominant feature of Irish mythology and may well have symbolized some sense of totality itself. For example in the realm of time it might represent past, present and future, and in relation to space the qualities of ahead, behind and here. It could also be seen as representing the dimensions of sky, earth and sea. Christianity uses triplication in the notion of the holy trinity. In Egyptian mythology it is present in the figures of Osiris, Isis and Horus. Within the alchemical tradition it exists in the three stages of nigredo, albedo and rubedo. Philosophy has its own version of it in Hegel's thesis, antithesis and synthesis. Consistent throughout these various examples is the assumption that three equals one and that the whole is greater than the sum of the parts. Irish mythology then is not unique in its incorporation of threes, but the extent to which they are used is striking.

The Morrígna

There is one group of three female deities that can lay special claim to the title of goddess of war, and that is the group known as the Morrígna. The persons of this trio are not always the same but usually comprise the Badb (the crow), the Morrígan (the queen of phantoms) and either Nemain (Panic) or Macha. These war-goddesses do not normally engage in armed combat, as their weapons belong to the magical world of sorcery and inspire dread and terror. Nemain, for example, creates panic amongst fighting men, and in a battle against Cú Chulainn 'a hundred warriors fell dead' when they heard her cry.

Even when the goddess of war is enticed to take part in battle she will do so by magic, often appearing in animal form. So the Morrígan attacks Cú Chulainn in the shape of an eel which winds itself around his legs. At other times she appears as a wolf and drives a frightened herd of cattle at him. Cú Chulainn had spurned her overtures of love and ungraciously declared that he had no need of a woman's help. Badb appears as a crow, and in this form she lands on Cú Chulainn's shoulder as a portent of his imminent death, signalling that it is safe to approach and behead him. Badb is essentially a prophetess of death and finds her direct equivalent in Atropos, the Fate who cuts the thread of life. Badb also finds her contemporary expression in the banshee, the Irish fairy whose crying is a portent of death. She also appears in the role of washer at the ford, washing the arms and clothes of a warrior who is to die shortly. The Morrígan can play a similar role as the harbinger of death.

Both the Morrígan and Badb also have powerful sexual roles, and Badb has been described as a femme fatale who befriends the hero and then leads him to his death. When the Dagda mates with the Morrígan she symbolizes the sovereign queen ensuring the fertility of the land.

These three figures that constitute the Morrígna are interchangeable, but as a single or triple figure they are personifications of nature in both her life-giving and life-destroying capacities. Man, in the form of a hero, sets out to conquer nature in order to have it serve him. This of course finds its psychological parallel in the heroic role that the ego must play in facilitating a measure of consciousness of the life-giving or Eros qualities and the life-destroying or Thanatos qualities of the unconscious mind. But just as the Morrígna is not a figure than can be easily overcome, neither can the unconscious be conquered in any complete sense. This realm, like the Morrígna, is the source of both being and non-being. We may well need our own version of a sacral marriage with the sovereign queen if our lives are to remain fertile. Dreams, and the paying of attention to them, are of course a simple means of enacting this ritual. Ignoring or rejecting the Morrígna, as Cú Chulainn does, can only bring about our death – psychologically speaking, the death of consciousness. The crow of depression sitting on our shoulders, or the eel of anxiety winding around us, can be signs of this death, which we must struggle to understand if we are not to succumb to meaninglessness, a specific form of death in itself.

Queen Medb (Maeve)

Queen Medb (English name Maeve) of Connacht is described as being sexually promiscuous; it is said of her that 'never was she without one man in the shadow of another'. She mated with at least nine mortal kings and refused to allow any king to rule in Tara who had not first mated with her. This marks her out as a mythological sovereign queen, with her promiscuity symbolizing the fertility of the land itself.

The most important story concerning Queen Medb is 'The Cattle Raid of Cooley', which belongs to the Ulster Cycle. Medb is jealous of her husband, King Ailill, who possesses a magnificent white bull. Medb hears of a fabulous brown bull and sends her army to invade Ulster to acquire it. During the battle that follows she appears as a warrior inciting her army to fight, and several times she pits her wits against the Ulster hero Cú Chulainn. So she is associated with war, death and fertility.

(Some may ask why there is no Irish equivalent of Venus/Aphrodite. MacCana suggests that the mythological personification of sexual love is bound up in the role of the Irish goddess as sovereign queen and a personification of the fertility of the land.[3] As Sjoestedt also points out, 'to wonder that we do not find a goddess presenting this character to the exclusion of all others is to judge Celtic mythology by foreign standards and so to condemn oneself to a misconstruction of its intimate system'.[4])

Étaín (Éadaoin)

Although Étaín is not usually presented as a deity, she can nevertheless be considered to be a goddess since she is thrice born and her lives cover an enormous expanse of time. In addition she plays a role as a sovereign queen. In relating the famous story of 'The Wooing of Étaín' I have relied on three major sources. One is a very comprehensive version of the stories by Jeffrey Gantz,[5] the second is from the Irish

66

scholar Myles Dillon[6] and the third, a recent, imaginative version by Marie Heaney.[7]

The story commences with the birth of Oenghus, who was conceived from the union between the Dagda and Boann and was then fostered out to Midir. Midir, who was also known as Midir the Proud because he wore such magnificent clothes, lived with his wife Fúamnach in truly splendid surroundings in the *sidhe* at Bri Léith. Fúamnach was both knowledgeable and clever and was very well versed in magic and sorcery since she had been reared by the druid Bresel.

Midir was very attached to Oenghus and was missing him since Oenghus had moved into his own *sidhe* at Bruig na Bóinne. Midir decided to visit him, and when he arrived he found Oenghus sitting on a mound watching a group of boys playing. Suddenly a fight broke out between the boys and Midir decided to intervene to break it up. It was not easy to part them and as he struggled to do so a sprig of holly was hurled at him, putting out one of his eyes. He gathered his eye up from the ground and returned to Oenghus, complaining that now that he was blemished he would not be able to see and rule over the land he had come from. Midir blamed Oenghus, cursing that he had ever come to see him, but Oenghus told him that they would go and find the physician Diancecht. The latter was summoned and it was not long before he had returned Midir's eye to its socket and the healing process had begun. However Midir demanded compensation for the injury and Oenghus, ever ready to please his foster-father, agreed to meet his request. As part of his compensation Midir wanted the fairest maiden in Ireland. Others say that following the healing of his eye Midir wanted to leave Bruig na Bóinne but Oenghus pleaded with him to stay. Midir agreed on the condition that Oenghus give him 'a chariot worth seven *cumals* [female slaves] and clothing appropriate to my rank and the fairest woman in Ériu'.

Oenghus agreed to the conditions and set off to acquire the fairest woman in Ireland, whom he knew to be Étaín, the daughter of King Ailill of Ulster. When Oenghus arrived at King Ailill's palace he announced that he had come to seek his daughter. The King agreed provided some conditions were first met. The first of these was that twelve plains be cleared so that cattle could graze on them. Oenghus felt overwhelmed by the size of the task and sought the help of his natural father the Dagda, who met his son's request and in one night cleared the twelve plains. But King Ailill now wanted twelve rivers to be diverted from the land to the sea. Again Oenghus felt overwhelmed by the request and sought the help of his father, who diverted the rivers overnight. Ailill now asked for Étaín's weight in gold, since he claimed the other compensations had been for the benefit of the people, not him personally. Thus he was given Étaín's weight in gold and Oenghus left with Étaín for Bruig na Bóinne.

Étaín stayed with Midir for a whole year at Bruig na Bóinne but then he decided to return to his own *sidhe*. When he arrived back at Brí Léith he was welcomed by his wife Fúamnach, who also made Étaín feel very welcome. But appearances were deceptive and Fúamnach was plotting her rival's demise. On the pretext of showing Étaín to her room Fúamnach struck her with a wand that instantly turned her into a pool of water. She then fled to her foster-father Bresel's house, fearing Midir's anger. A fire near the pool of water heated it up, and out of the water emerged a worm which before very long turned into a beautiful crimson fly with jewelled eyes and enamelled wings. When it moved its wings it created wonderful music and wherever it went it left a beautiful fragrance in the air. Though she now had the shape of a fly Étaín retained the feelings of a woman and she went off in search of Midir. She found him asleep in a room and as she flew around creating the beautiful music and fragrance Midir awoke and realized immediately that it was Étaín. From then on she accompanied Midir everywhere, lulling him to sleep with her music and also warning him of any approaching enemies. Midir knew that so long as Étaín was with him he could never love another woman.

When Fúamnach heard of this enduring love she was overcome by a jealous rage and once again began to plot Étaín's demise. She decided to return to Brí Léith, but when she arrived Midir attacked her angrily for what she had done to Étaín. Unmoved by Midir's anger, she began to chant a spell that suspended his love for Étaín and rendered all his magic powerless. She then called up a great wind that blew all through Brí Léith, taking Étaín helplessly before it and blowing her out to sea. For seven years Étaín was continually buffeted by the wind and could find no resting place other than odd rocks in the ocean and on the waves. At last she was miraculously blown over Bruig na Bóinne. Utterly exhausted and barely able to lift her wings, she fell on to Oenghus's cloak and he immediately recognized her. He welcomed her into his house, tended to her needs and then set about building her a glass room to live in. Étaín felt safe and secure in this space and her spirit was uplifted by the strange fragrant herbs that Oenghus had placed in the bower. A great love grew between Oenghus and Étaín, who brought joy and happiness into Oenghus's life, just as she had for Midir.

However yet again Fúamnach heard of this love and happiness and again plotted to destroy Étaín. She knew that she would not be able to get direct access to Étaín at Bruig na Bóinne so she was forced to conjure up a more devious scheme. Midir and Oenghus had naturally fallen out over Étaín, so Fúamnach offered to arrange a reconciliation meeting on a hill outside Bruig na Bóinne. The men waited for Fúamnach to join them there, but such a long time passed that they became uneasy and decided to return to the palace. Oenghus went to the glass bower and to his horror discovered that Étaín was gone. Immediately he knew that the jealous Fúamnach had been at work. Some say that he was so angry that when he found Fúamnach hiding in the palace he cut off her head.

When Oenghus had initially left to meet with Midir Fúamnach had circled around Bruig na Bóinne from the opposite direction, found Étaín in her glass room and once again conjured up a powerful wind that sent her back out to sea. For another seven years she was constantly blown over the land and seas of Ireland and could find no resting place. At last she was blown inland towards the great hall of a castle and there she alighted on a beam high above the floor where a festival was in progress. This was the castle of Étar, a great Ulster champion, and much drinking and feasting was going on. Finally Étaín, exhausted from her long ordeal, could cling no longer to the beam and fell straight into the golden goblet of Étar's wife just as she was raising it to her mouth. She swallowed the wine and Étaín in one mouthful. Étar's wife was unaware of what had happened but nine months later she gave birth to a beautiful girl whom they called Étaín. Thus ends the first story, or rather the first part of the story.

The second story commences when Étaín is about twenty years of age. However, as is the way with myths, a thousand years had elapsed, and Eochaid Airem was now King of Ireland. In the first year of his reign he called together an assembly of all the chieftains and their people, to be held at Tara at Samain. However word came back that the chieftains would not attend because the King did not have a wife, and no man could attend this festival without his wife. Eochaid immediately dispatched his messengers to travel throughout the land to find the fairest woman to become his queen. He insisted that in addition the woman also be a nobleman's daughter and a virgin, and it was Étaín, daughter of Étar, whom the messengers ascertained as being ideal in all respects. The king himself set out to meet her and acquire her hand in marriage. As he and his retinue approached Étar's house they came across a beautiful young woman washing herself beside a well. Eochaid was mesmerized by the woman and instantly fell in love with her. When he asked her name she replied, 'I am Étaín, daughter of Étar, a chieftain and nobleman of Ulster.' Eochaid was overjoyed to discover that this beautiful woman was to be his bride and they married immediately and returned to Tara.

It was said that 'All are lovely till compared with Étaín, all are fair till compared with Étaín,' and it was this beauty that caused Eochaid's brother Ailill to fall in love with her. He would gaze upon her endlessly and his will not to do so was powerless against his desire for her. But he could not reveal these wishes to anyone since it was a transgression to lust after his brother's wife. As the obsession grew stronger and stronger he became weaker and started to waste away. No one knew what mysterious illness had overtaken the King's brother.

A whole year passed with Ailill continuing to waste away until Eochaid insisted that his own physician Fachtna see his brother. The physician put his hand on Ailill's chest and at that instant Ailill let out a huge sigh. Fachtna turned to Ailill and said, 'You have one of two pangs that no doctor can cure: the pang of love and the pang of jealousy.' Ailill knew this to be true, but he could not reveal his secret and continued to deteriorate and move towards death.

King Eochaid had to travel throughout his kingdom, but before he left he gave Étaín instructions for the care and burial of his dying brother. Étaín undertook all these tasks willingly, but as she tended Ailill she noticed that contrary to all expectations he started to get better. Finally out of frustration and desperation Ailill confessed to Étaín that he was in love with her and the only thing that could cure him was if they could become lovers. Étaín could not bear the thought of Ailill dying because of his unmet love for her, yet nor could she bear the thought of betraying her husband in his own house. After an agonizing period of confusion she arranged to meet Ailill on a hill at daybreak. Ailill lay awake all night, excited by the thought of a possible union with Étaín, but at the appointed hour he fell into a deep sleep and did not awake until the third hour of the next day. Étaín in the mean time went to the hill as arranged, and the man she saw waiting for her looked exactly like Ailill. But as she got closer she realized that it was not him and the figure she saw did not speak but merely moved on and went away.

When Ailill finally woke up he was devastated to realize that he had missed the rendezvous with Étaín, and she, out of concern for him, agreed to meet under the same arrangements the next day. But again a strange sleep overtook Ailill at the precise time of the meeting with Étaín and again the stranger appeared to her in his place. For the third time a meeting was arranged between Étaín and Ailill and the same events occurred. However this time, Étaín asked the stranger who he was. He replied that he had come to meet her, but Étaín protested that she had come to meet Ailill, brother of King Eochaid, not the person who stood before her. The stranger replied, 'It would be more fitting for you to come to me, for when you were Étaín daughter of King Ailill I was your husband.' Étaín was startled by this statement and anxiously asked the stranger who he was, since she had no memory of the past that the stranger spoke of. He replied, 'I am Midir of Brí Léith and it was the evil sorcery of Fúamnach that parted us and it was I who put the love into the heart of Eochaid's brother Ailill so that we might meet.' He turned to Étaín and pleaded with her to come to Brí Léith with him where she belonged. Étaín was utterly bewildered by all of this, but somewhere within her there was a haunting sense of familiarity with this figure who called himself Midir. After a while she hesitatingly agreed that she would go with him, so long as her husband agreed. She felt she was on safe ground here since she did not believe that Eochaid would agree to such a thing. Midir smiled and quickly agreed to the terms that Étaín had set out and with that he magically disappeared.

Shortly after, the King returned from his royal circuit and was delighted to find his brother not only alive but well. He thanked Étaín for her exemplary care of him, but Étaín kept her silence on both the cause and the cure. Midir, who had originally created the desire in Ailill, and who had protected Étaín's honour by putting him to sleep at the critical time, had released Ailill from his illness by quelling his desire. Thus ends the second story.

The third story commences with King Eochaid standing on the terrace of his palace, admiring the beauty of the surrounding landscape. On the distant horizon he observed a figure who, as he got closer, appeared to be a warrior who wore a deep purple cloak, had golden shoulder-length hair and carried a shield in one hand and a spear in the other.

Eochaid was perplexed, for he knew that the gates of the fort had not yet been opened and thus the warrior could not belong to the company that had arrived the previous night. By now the stranger was facing Eochaid, who asked him, 'Who are you? I don't recognize you.' The stranger replied, 'Not a famous one. Midir of Brí Léith is my name.' 'Then what has brought you here?' asked Eochaid, to which Midir replied that he had come to play *fidchell* (chess) with the King. Eochaid was taken aback by all this and tried to stall Midir by saying his chess set was in the Queen's quarters and he could not disturb her. To the King's astonishment Midir promptly produced a chess set, and the game was all ready to commence when Eochaid said he would not play unless there was a stake. Midir obligingly invited Eochaid to name his stake and the King nominated fifty of the finest horses. Midir lost, and next morning the King looked out on the grass surrounding the palace and observed fifty magnificent horses grazing contentedly.

Eochaid was delighted with his prize and enthusiastically challenged Midir to another game. The stake this time involved clearing land and rendering it fertile. Midir agreed on condition that if he lost Eochaid had to guarantee that he would prevent anyone in his kingdom from witnessing the clearing of the land. Midir played the second game and did lose, thus being required to clear the land. Eochaid could not resist the temptation to know what was happening, and sent one of his stewards to secretly observe the work. Midir was furious, and demanded that Eochaid pay retribution for the betrayal. Midir said they must play another game and that whoever won that game would name his prize. Eochaid had no choice but to accept Midir's terms since he had violated a trust. This time Midir won. Eochaid was terrified that Midir would name some enormous stake and perhaps take back what he had already won and more besides. To his astonishment Midir stated that he wanted to take the Queen Étaín in his arms and kiss her. Completely thrown by this request, Eochaid hesitatingly agreed but asked that Midir come back in a month to claim his stake.

Sensing some sort of danger in the mysterious stranger's request, Eochaid spent the entire month assembling the warriors of Ireland to protect his palace and prevent Midir from entering. However at the due moment Midir suddenly appeared in their midst while the King was banqueting. Midir declared, 'What is promised is now due.' He then embraced Étaín and as he did so they rose up into the air and were transformed into two beautiful swans who flew out of the palace through an opening in the roof. From there they flew to Brí Léith, where Étaín rejoined her kinfolk, the Tuatha Dé Danann.

Eochaid, full of grief and anger at the loss of Étaín, was also furious that Midir had tricked him, and made up his mind to retrieve his wife. He traversed all of Ireland, digging up every fairy mound he could find, for he now knew that she had been taken by one of the folk of the otherworld. To his dismay, however, every time he dug up a mound, by the next morning all the dirt had been replaced exactly as it had originally been. Eochaid was undeterred, and some say that he continued to dig up fairy mounds for nine years. Finally in desperation he sought the advice of a druid who revealed that Midir and Étaín were at Brí Léith.

Just as Eochaid was making his assault on Brí Léith Midir called a truce and offered to return Étaín to him the next day. But Midir, using his magical gifts, tricked Eochaid and at the appointed third hour of the following day fifty women, all looking exactly like Étaín, appeared. Imperiously Midir declared that Eochaid could have Étaín back if he could identify the true Étaín. Eochaid remembered how beautifully Étaín had poured wine, so he requested that each of the women perform the task. Each woman in turn poured, until there were only two left and as the second-last woman took the jug and started to pour Eochaid spontaneously declared that she was Étaín, claimed her and returned with her to Tara.

Much later, when Étaín was pregnant, Eochaid discovered, again through the aegis of Midir, that the woman he had chosen was not Étaín but his own daughter, since his wife was pregnant with her when she flew away with Midir. Reeling in horror from this incestuous union he declared to the gods, 'Never will I look upon the daughter of my daughter,' and he arranged that when the child was born two members of his household would take the child and throw it into a pit of wild beasts. The two servants could not bring themselves to throw the tiny infant into the pit, but left her in an isolated herdsman's hut with a bitch and her pups. When the herdsman and his wife returned they were astonished to find the infant, but accepted her unhesitatingly and reared her as if she were their own child. She, in accordance with her divine heritage, prospered and displayed exceptional beauty and skill.

In due course she was dicovered by a prince, of whom it had been prophesied that he would marry a woman of unknown origin and that she would bear him a child. This duly happened, and that child became the legendary King Conaire Mór, the central character in a later Ulster story entitled 'The Destruction of Da Derga's Hostel'.

'The Wooing of Étaín' is a mysterious and haunting tale that captures the essence of the Irish mythological world. It has a sense of timelessness as it moves between two worlds, the natural and the supernatural, the mortal and the divine.

Étaín is undoubtedly a symbol of life, death and renewal. Some scholars, notably MacCulloch and Gantz, have suggested that the ancient Irish held ideas of reincarnation which are symbolized in the mythic theme of rebirth.[8,9] Certainly the archaeological evidence points to the ancient Celts burying their dead with the clear intention of providing for a journey, indicating a firm belief in the otherworld and perhaps rebirth.

Many of the Irish divinities do not appear to die *per se* but live from generation to generation, as seen in the figure of Étaín. The fact that Étaín was transformed into a beautiful crimson fly is also of some significance in a mythological context. For example, the ancient Greeks believed that the soul could travel from one life to another in insect form. The idea of incarnation would presumably have been anathema to the Christian scribes and it is possible that many more direct references to these beliefs have been edited out. Hence we are left with stories that merely point towards these beliefs rather than stating them. However belief in rebirth is entirely consistent with the pattern of life, death and renewal that so pervades Irish mythology. In this context we can also see Étaín as a seasonal goddess symbolizing the death and rebirth of the crops, which links her to Demeter and Persephone of Greek mythology.

Étaín is also of course a sovereign queen figure. When King Eochaid summons his people to Tara and they refuse to come because he is without a wife, he is reminded that in order to be a rightful king of the land he has first to be accepted as the legitimate spouse of the goddess who personifies the land itself. Without this union the land could not prosper and would remain infertile.

Finally, within the Jungian mythological framework Étaín is an archetypal feminine, or more precisely the archetypal *anima*. Her archetypal status is confirmed by the company she keeps, the gods Midir and Oenghus. The gods of mythology are the archetypes of Jung and their territory, so to speak, is what Jung has termed the collective unconscious. The collective psyche is not something we acquire as a result of our personal history but rather as a consequence of the history of the species. In this sense it is permanent and continuous and like the divine figures cannot die, but merely passes from one generation to the next. Eochaid, as a mortal figure, has to compete with a supernatural rival for a relationship with the feminine in the figure of Étaín. This represents the task of building a personal relationship with the *anima* or feminine aspects of our being, the task of developing a conscious awareness of our feelings and an enhanced capacity both to connect to and communicate them.

If the feminine remains at the archetypal level then feelings remain impersonal, stereotyped and invariably projected out rather than seen as part of ourselves. So a man, for example, will project a fantasy image of the ideal woman on to a real woman and she will have the unnerving feeling that the intense relationship she is experiencing is really not much to do with her but with some fantasy about her. The same pattern is manifested by women when they project the archetypal *animus* on to mortal men. The relationship will have a peculiar impersonal quality about it. Being on the receiving end of such projections is often described by the phrase 'He (or she) is full on.' Relationships starting out with this intensity usually finish as quickly as they started and very often have a distinctly obsessional and possessive quality. To be in the grip of archetypal images and energy is to be impersonal and not really present to the self or others. This can take the form of idealization, where there is absolutely no perception of negatives, or intense denigration and rage, where there exist no positives. From this latter position murder and mayhem are easy since the constraint of the awareness of the other, as such, does not exist. This we normally call madness.

The figure of Eochaid is the hero of this story and within contemporary psychological mythology he is associated with the ego. The role of the ego, like that of the hero in the ancient stories, is to journey to unknown lands (the unconscious) and there to confront unknown and frightening figures that symbolize aspects of our own being. These are figures for which Jung would use such terms as the shadow or *anima* and *animus*. If the hero, or heroine, successfully completes the journey then the ego is altered by the experience. This is usually manifested in a maturing of the personality, which in turn is reflected in an increase in tolerance of ambiguity. However the heroic figure is often reluctant to undertake the journey, preferring instead to adhere to fixed views about him- or herself and the world. In Jungian psychology the figure of the King usually represents the ruling principle of the psyche, or those values and attitudes with which the ego is identified and which govern everyday behaviour. Thus we could see King Eochaid's relationship with Étaín as the interaction of the ego with the archetypal feminine, a necessary first step in ensuring the fertility of one's growth and maturation as an individual.

Midir is a complex figure, but perhaps could be seen as the negative *animus*. The 'negative *animus*' is considered to represent archetypal negative masculine qualities such as fixed opinions, and is essentially antagonistic to feminine values such as relationships, receptiveness, ambiguity and feelings. The desire of the negative *animus* is to disconnect. As we have already seen, disconnection is at times a vital factor in enabling the process of change to occur and is an essential part of the cycle of eternal change. However if the negative *animus* is a dominating force within a woman's psyche it can result in a sad history of unfulfilling relationships with men, and finds its parallel in Midir's actions with regard to Étaín. Midir keeps Étaín to himself and prevents her having a relationship with Eochaid. This is another way of saying that the archetypal negative *animus* resists any emergence of the feminine attribute of feeling. The conscious development of this more Eros-based quality would create a sense of connection and this is the very phenomenon that the negative *animus* works against.

Like his Greek equivalent Hades, Midir abducts the feminine into the otherworld, below the surface of consciousness. From the outset we see his disdain of the feminine as he simply demands the most beautiful woman in Ireland and then returns with her to his wife. Whilst Fúamnach may well be a negative *anima* figure, her rage is understandable. Other people's positions or needs seem irrelevant to Midir the Proud. In some women the negative *animus* can lead to a certain immaturity, with anyone holding a different view seen as unequivocally wrong. The extreme wings of the women's movement, with their rigid adherence to ideological purity, reflect the presence of the negative *animus*. In men this presence is seen in a rigid patriarchal position that does not allow feminine attributes any legitimacy. Midir's hope is that Étaín will simply stay in the otherworld of Brí Léith with him for ever and not have a life in the everyday world. Midir the Proud may also symbolize a narcissistic structure within the personality that yearns for possession, not relationship, for power over others rather than a relationship with others. This is a typical masculine pattern and men as part of their maturation have to work against a narcissistic position that regards those who are different as inferior. This applies particularly to their perception of women and feminine values.

Eochaid's behaviour throughout the story depicts the psychological task of forming a personal relationship with the feminine attributes within himself and not leaving them entirely in the original archetypal form. His first contact with Étaín is essentially archetypal in so far as he 'falls in love' and projects on to her his fantasy of the ideal woman. He 'instantly knows' that she is *the* one.

The figure of Ailill, Eochaid's brother, is interesting. In a stereotypical male way he perceives that the solution to his despair and depression lies in being able to have sex with Étaín. Within Jung's theoretical framework the brother figure is sometimes seen as the shadow, a figure that symbolizes attributes that are unacceptable to the conscious view we hold of ourselves or other people. Ailill symbolizes Eochaid's shadowy, obsessive desire for Étaín and further depicts the absence of an actual personal relationship with the feminine. Étaín, seen through the eyes of the shadow, no matter how benevolent and caring Eochaid may appear, is simply an object of sexual desire, not a person. Sex for many men is often a substitute for intimacy, not an expression of it, particularly when there is a poorly developed relationship with his feelings. When the ego figure of Eochaid is absent, busy with the demands of his job, as many modern men find themselves, the shadow really comes to the fore. It is aided and abetted by the archetypal figure of Midir, who uses Ailill to seduce Étaín. Thus in a psychological sense the archetypal masculine power aids the perception of women as sexual objects to be conquered, not people to be connected with in a meaningful relationship.

Eochaid fails to develop a personal relationship with Étaín, and thus the feeling side of his personality is regressed and is symbolized in the shadow of his brother. If a man's conscious view of himself centres around power, as Eochaid's can be seen to do, then the inevitable shadow that this casts is a dark, often obsessive and impersonal sexuality that denigrates women. The outcome for Eochaid is a complete loss of contact with the feminine, not only at the personal but also at the archetypal level. The feminine finally regresses to the otherworld in the arms of the archetypal negative masculine and disappears from consciousness. Whilst this spurs Eochaid into action, what he is driven by is the loss of an idealized fantasy, and when he discovers that he has chosen his own daughter he rejects her vehemently, sending his child/grandchild to her death. This outcome in the story requires further thought.

Jung's position on incestuous figures is informative and valuable. 'Incest symbolizes union with one's own being, it means individuation or becoming self . . . incest is simply the union of like with like and is the next stage in the development of the primitive idea of self-fertilization.'[10] He is of course referring to the symbol of incest in dreams and not the acting-out of this image.

So Eochaid rejects the possibility of a union with his own personal feeling life, symbolized in the figure of his incestuously begotten daughter. Instead he continues to yearn for the idealized other woman. After all his pursuing of Étaín throughout the otherworld and all the digging up of the unconscious, Eochaid remains unchanged. He still rejects the development of personal feeling that he has banished and condemned to death. This reminds me of certain individuals who relentlessly pursue therapy in a variety of forms and settings, but after all the digging up they remain as uninsightful as when they started. The failure to accept aspects of ourselves, whether masculine or feminine, is a pervasive theme in human beings. In relationships this can be experienced as a constant pressure that one partner exerts on the other to be who they want them to be. The desire to change one's partner is very often a refusal to accept them and a violation of their individuality. It is also, not infrequently, a means by which people avoid looking at themselves and asking what aspects of their own being they might need to change.

The final part of this story may represent an alternative strategy to the one of rejection that Eochaid chose. The herdsman and his wife are a pair, and as such symbolize the integration of the masculine and feminine at the human, not the archetypal, level. (The presence of royal figures in myths and dreams symbolizes the archetypal or impersonal level.) It is this integration of opposites that enables the acceptance and maturation of the feminine in the figure of Étaín's daughter.

The couple also represent opposite qualities to the King. For Eochaid, power and status dominate, whereas the herdsman and his wife are characterized by acceptance and humility. From this symbolic position within the psyche the rejected feminine can be nurtured and renewal found. With the birth of a new king in the figure of Conaire Mór, we can see the transformation of the ego, or ruling principle, that occurs as a result of the development of feminine attributes. Humility and acceptance provide the essential conditions for change, since they facilitate the emergence of unconscious images and thoughts without the interference of a defensive and judging ego. When the sense of who we are is derived from an over-identification with the ego or the persona, the image we project to the world, we are often very dismissive of thoughts and images emerging from the unconscious. Such phrases as 'that's stupid' or 'that is illogical' often point to the presence of the 'old king' ruling the psyche and refusing to disconnect or die.

The Irish goddesses tend to conform to what Jungian mythology has termed the great mother or earth mother archetype, because they are so closely connected to nature and natural events. Mythologies offer many variations of this figure, e.g. Demeter, Cybele and Gaia, beloved of the New Age movement. Other symbols of this archetype are a ploughed field, a garden, a forest or the sea, or animal symbols such as the cow, sow and mare. The great mother is a symbol of both the creative forces and the destructive ones. Like all archetypes she has both a positive and a negative side.

Alongside the goddess's nurturing qualities is the feminine wisdom that transcends logic and asserts the inevitability of the eternal cycle of birth, life and death. The Machas and Danu are unequivocal examples of this. The Caillech Bhéarra is a fine example of the archetypal hag, the holder of wisdom and knowledge of spiritual matters. When women are able to establish a conscious awareness of the relationship to these archetypal figures within themselves, they are able to stand back in any situation and 'know' the inevitability of change. This is not passivity or compliance, but rather an action of acceptance taken in the light of knowledge. It is a yielding and not a giving in. To many men such acceptance is misconstrued as weakness. However men of course are so poorly connected to this feminine archetype and so preoccupied with taking action that they cannot discriminate between acceptance and giving in. However, if a woman is disconnected in this way, which is often true of very intellectual women, then they are often prone to inertia and despair when faced with some life situation that demands the acceptance of change. This could be the birth of a child, marital separation or the death of a loved one. Once caught in the grip of such inertia, it is very difficult to have any sense of the dynamic process of change and the emergence of fertility that comes from the acceptance and the waiting. This requires the presence in a woman's conscious life of the Caillech Bhéarra or the wisdom of the crone. In our masculine-dominated, action-orientated, rational world this figure has experienced enormous denigration and derision. Rationality wants to triumph over life, not participate in and acknowledge the inevitability of the cycle of change.

Jung captures the full complexity of this archetypal figure of the great mother when he describes her as 'the loving and the terrible mother'. [11] Hindu goddess Kali is a good example of this, and just as Mother Nature has a destructive side – earthquakes, bush fires, droughts and floods – so also does the great mother. The negative side of the archetype includes such attributes as the desire to dissolve all boundaries, and the view that everything is connected to everything else and that discrimination and separateness are of no value. In this way the negative face of the great mother works against the emergence of consciousness and the development of boundaries. Yet this return to chaos and the obliteration of boundaries is of course often the beginning of a period of creativity. But such a return as we will see in the stories of the heroic quest, requires discrimination of conscious awareness and not a submissive, compliant giving in.

For some women it is easier to identify, and indeed in some situations to over-identify, with the positive nurturing qualities of this figure, to such an extent that the archetype dominates their psyche. The end result is that they become nothing more than a mother, with no sense of their own individual identity. Changes in this fixed role can therefore bring about a major identity crisis. The children of such women can experience their mothers as extremely possessive, sometimes resulting in the child escaping into sickness, madness or even death. The mother whose entire identity revolves around being a mother needs to 'possess' the child as a means of keeping her own identity intact. As the child emerges into young adulthood he is imprisoned in the mother's psyche and the engulfing face of the great mother comes into operation, preventing the forward movement of growth and development.

Other women react so strongly against the nurturing aspects of this archetype that they appear to place a curse upon themselves that they will never be like their own mother. This may mean a determined avoidance of motherhood, and recalls the mythological role of the *geis*. Over-identification with the destructive aspects of the archetype, meanwhile, may mean that nurturance is perceived as a weakness, and such women are not only unable to nurture others, but also unable to nurture themselves. The masochistic martyr is one manifestation of this pattern, as also is its seeming opposite, the driven corporate woman, who is unable to stop and take stock of the direction of her life.

The power and wisdom of the triple goddess lies in the incorporation of all three attributes of fertility, nurturance and aggression. Perhaps it is because the goddesses are so close to nature that these three qualities have not been split or intellectualized into separate and discrete entities. Again and again the myths reveal the existence of this wisdom and the desirability of holding and containing opposites.

7

THE OTHERWORLD I

The Mythology of the Unconscious

Following their conquering of the Fomorians in the second battle of Mag Tuired, the divine race of the goddess Danu, the Tuatha Dé Danann, ruled over Ireland, some say for eighty years, others say for hundreds of years. According to *The Book of Invasions*, the Tuatha were later invaded by a group called the Sons of Mil or the Milesians.

These partly fictitious and partly historical people derive their name from the Latin phrase 'miles Hispaniae', which translates as 'soldiers of Spain'. They are said to be a group of people who journeyed from Egypt via Crete and Sicily to Spain and settled there. It may well be that they represent a later invasion of Ireland than the continental Celts, who in turn were probably preceded by earlier settlers. On traditional, historical and linguistic grounds T. F. O'Rahilly places this invasion around the period 150–50 BC,[1] at the end of the Bronze Age and the beginning of the Iron Age. It is these invaders who are said to be the ancestors of the present inhabitants of Ireland.

According to myth, Mil can be traced back through Hebrew names to Adam, no doubt due to the interfering hand of the monastic scribes of the twelfth century. Mil was the grandson of King Breogan of Spain, who had two sons, Ith and Bile, Mil's father. King Breogan had built himself a huge tower and from this tower, on a clear winter's evening, Ith saw Ireland and decided to explore this distant land. He set off with thrice-fifty warriors, and when they landed they came across the three Kings of Ireland, who were meeting to decide how to divide up the country's treasures. Ith, who it is said spoke the same language as he was of the same seed, offered the three kings counsel on how to divide the treasures. At the same time he admonished them about their quarreling, particularly given the beautiful and fertile land that they had inherited. But his praise of the land proved to be his undoing, since the three kings became suspicious that he might be planning to take it for himself. They temporarily forgot their quarrel and killed Ith before he was able to return to his ship. His kinsmen returned to their homeland, taking Ith's body with them, whereupon the eight sons of Mil vowed to avenge his death. These eight sons, along with their own sons and families and other kinsmen, set out for Ireland. They arrived at the time of Beltaine, 1 May, the time when many of the previous invaders had arrived. Beltaine celebrates the end of the darkness of winter and the beginning of summer. Thus all the invaders, with the exception of the Fir Bolg, represent a spirit of renewal.

It wasn't long before the Milesians came across the three sister goddesses of Ireland, Ériu, Fódla and Banba. The sons of Mil met each of the sisters separately and each in turn prophesied that Ireland would belong to the Milesians so long as they named the island after the goddesses. One of the leaders of the Milesians, Amairgin, who was a druid and poet, thanked the goddesses and agreed to name the island after them. But another brother, Donn, refused and rudely declared that it was the goddesses who should be thanking the Milesians. Ériu objected to this and prophesied that neither Donn nor his children would ever set foot in Ireland. Amairgin, in agreeing that the island should be named after the goddesses, embraced and acknowledged the power of the sovereign queen, here in the image of the triple goddess of Ireland. Donn refused to acknowledge the sovereignty of the land, and in accordance with the prophecy he drowned before he could settle in Ireland. He was buried on an island off the south-west coast which came to be known as the House of Donn (Tech Duinn). It is said that this island is where the descendants of the sons of Mil follow him after death.

The sons of Mil, having made an agreement with the goddess, reached the seat of the kingdom at Tara and there confronted the three Kings of Ireland, Mac Cuill, Mac Cecht and Mac Greine, and demanded combat or sovereignty. The three kings, who were married to the three goddesses, refused the demand. They asked that they hold the country for another three (some say nine) days, and that during this time the Sons of Mil retreat to beyond the ninth wave. The ninth wave was a sort of magical boundary, perhaps that boundary beyond which the divine world held sway over the ordinary world. Amairgin agreed to these conditions and judged them fair. However he declared that they would then take the island unless the Tuatha could prevent them from landing. If the Tuatha *could* prevent them from landing, they would return to their homeland. Thus Amairgin, the poet and druid, not a warrior or a king, is portrayed as the most powerful figure amongst the Milesians. This reminds us of the position of the druid-poet figure in pre-Christian Ireland, a status upon which the later Christian clergy have been able to build their own power.

So Amairgin and his brothers put out to sea beyond the ninth wave; and when they turned to head back to shore they were immediately confronted by a huge wind. The sea boiled up with gigantic waves, the Milesian boats were scattered in all directions, and many were drowned. It was at this time that Ériu's prophecy was fulfilled and Donn and his family were drowned.

Amairgin and his fellow leaders knew that this storm had been called up by the Tuatha Dé Danann druids. Some say you can tell a druidic wind from a natural one because the former blows no higher than the ship's mast. Amairgin sent his brother up the mast to ascertain where they had been blown to, but the brother was flung from the mast by a huge gust of wind and fell to his death on the deck below. Just before he hit the deck he shouted out that there was no wind above the mast. The sailors were by now extremely frightened and agitated and demanded that Amairgin use his powers to calm the sea. Amairgin battled his way to the bow of the boat and from there he raised his voice above the roar of the sea and sang an invocation to the land of Ireland, to the goddesses Ériu, Fódla and Banba.

> I invoke the land of Ireland.
> Much coursed be the fertile sea,
> Fertile be the fruit-strewn mountains,
> Fruit-strewn be the showery wood . . .[2]

Immediately the wind dropped and the sea became calm. (The Christian tradition has of course a similar story, with Christ calming the Sea of Galilee.) Just as he had done in agreeing to name Ireland after the goddess, Amairgin has acknowledged the sovereignty of the goddess. As soon as he put foot on Ireland Amairgin sang another poem:

> I am the wind on the sea
> I am a wave of the ocean
> I am the roar of sea
> I am a powerful ox
> I am a hawk on a cliff
> I am a dewdrop in the sunshine
> I am the fairest of flowers

I am a boar for valour
I am a salmon in a pool
I am a lake in a plain
I am the strength of art
I am a spear sharp in battle
I am a god that puts fire in the brain.[3]

In this poem Amairgin is claiming to subsume all beings and the creative universe within himself, just as Lord Krishna does in the *Bhagavad Gita*. Amairgin is declaring his druidic powers over those of the Tuatha Dé Danann druids. At the same time he is heralding the moment when man claims sovereignty over the earth and the moment when Irish history, as such, begins. It is the ritualistic creation of a new order; as Marie-Louise Sjoestedt says, 'The day on which the race of men triumphed over the race of gods marks the end of the mythical period when the supernatural was the undisputed master of the earth and the beginning of the new period in which men and gods inhabit the earth together.'[4] We might see this as the moment when the spark of consciousness emerges, the moment when the ego begins to emerge from the undifferentiated world of the collective unconscious, and the self and other are dimly perceived as separate but connected. This process continues throughout life, with the perception of separateness continually moving between clarity and confusion as we struggle with regressive wishes to reunite with the great mother in some replay of a uterine paradise. The arrival of the Sons of Mil symbolizes the emergence of a separate identity, one which demands recognition of the source of being if it is to be achieved at all and not simply drowned.

Upon landing, the Milesians nevertheless had to do battle with the Tuatha Dé Danann. The three kings of Ireland and their queens were killed, and as a result the Tuatha Dé Danann conceded victory to the Sons of Mil. This second landing may well symbolize a 'second birth', the psychological birth of the individual identity. The element of water, so important in this story, is universally regarded as a symbol of birth and renewal.

Although defeated by the Milesians, the Tuatha Dé Danann still possessed their magical powers, and they used these to deprive the Milesians of corn and milk until the Sons of Mil were forced to seek a settlement. It was agreed that the country would be divided into two halves. Amairgin made the division, whereby the territory under the earth was given to the Tuatha Dé Danann and that above the surface to the Milesians. Thus the Tuatha Dé Danann retreated underground and each of the chiefs was assigned as *sídhe* or fairy mound of his own. The gods took possession of the hills, the mounds and lakes, and in due course the Tuatha Dé Danann became the fairy folk of Ireland. In this way the Irish landscape came to be the dwelling place of the gods. They live in close proximity to the human population, and render the land sacred. The parallel to the Australian Aboriginal people and their view of the land is striking, since for them the land also contains the spirits of the ancestors. It was once said of the Aboriginal people that they do not live on the land, but *in* it.

These underground fairy kingdoms became the otherworld, the invisible world alongside the visible. There are similar such worlds in Irish mythology, below the sea and lakes, on distant islands, or sometimes appearing as a mysterious land or building that suddenly appears, surrounded by a mist.

The significant point to note is that the otherworld stands for that which is invisible. Indeed the otherworld is the mysterious space that lies beyond the physical world of the senses. For the so-called primitive person the unknown wilderness, peopled by powerful and dangerous forces, lies immediately beyond the gates of their village. For modern people the otherworld is the realm of the unconscious that lies beyond the area illuminated by consciousness, the land from which we dream and which we visit in our dreams. Little wonder then that some tribes have seen dreams as a visitation by the gods. The arrival of the mortal Sons of Mil in the land of the divine marks this division between the known and the unknown, the visible and the invisible, the material and the non-material universes.

The belief that human beings exist in several dimensions of reality is almost universally held. One way of speaking of these other realities is by referring to them as 'the otherworld'. Nearly every culture from the earliest times to the present has held a view about the nature of this otherworld; in most it is associated with death and the life after death. The particular culture in which a person finds themselves will inevitably shape and determine the view they hold of the otherworld.

The Irish people, like their Celtic forebears, have a rich, living view of the otherworld. Indeed, as we have just seen, it is right alongside and around them all the time.

According to many scholars, in particular Proinsias MacCana, the ancient Irish believed in life after death and the transmigration of the soul.[5] Archaeological evidence and the vernacular tradition both confirm this belief in an otherworld to which the soul goes after death and to which certain select souls go during their life. In Wales it was called Annwin, whereas in Ireland there is a series of otherworlds, but the *sídhe* (shee) are the most commonly known. In the pagan culture of ancient Ireland the people experienced nature as a cycle of eternal return which knows no beginning and no end. Death and rebirth then are merely the end of one cycle and the beginning of another. Physical death simply marks the point of transition between one state and the other. Today we tend to see death as the end, not as a transition, because we have a logical, linear view rather than a circular one. Within the Celtic tradition the natural world forms the basis of the belief in rebirth, not some notion of an omnipotent and distant god in the sky. Myth functions as a prototype, or psychological model, for humans to conduct their lives in accordance with this knowledge of the cycle of eternal return.

The otherworld is essentially a timeless place that transcends spatial definition. Usually a short period spent in the otherworld by a human being is equivalent to an exceedingly long period in our known visible world. Thus a mortal returning from the otherworld may suddenly and dramatically age when they make contact with the material world. Oisín, the great poet, fell in love with the otherworld maiden Niamh, one of Manannán mac Lir's daughters, and followed her to the otherworld where he had many adventures. After a period he started to pine for Ireland, and Niamh gave him a magical horse to take him home, but warned him that it had been three hundred years since he left Ireland. If he dismounted from the horse, she said, time would catch up with him. Oisín had an accident and fell off the horse, whereupon he was instantly transformed into a blind, withered old man.

An otherworld may suddenly appear and disappear, surrounded by a mist. Alternatively it may be located under a lake or the sea, in a mound or hill, or perhaps on a distant island. In short it cannot be given a definite spatial dimension, other than it coexists with the temporal and spatial world, in the landscape and inseparably connected to it. It is, as W. B. Yeats says of the Irish peasant, 'all about him'.[6]

A further quality of the otherworld is its beauty. Almost every tale related to the otherworld describes the beauty of its landscape, its trees and inhabitants. An early Irish lyric verse captures this beauty:

There, there is neither 'mine' nor 'thine';
White are teeth there, dark the brows;
A delight of the eye the array of our hosts;
Every cheek there is of the hue of the foxglove.
Purple the surface of every plain,
A marvel of beauty the blackbird's eggs;
Though the Plain of Fál be fair to see,
'Tis desolate once you have known Magh Mar.
Fine though you think the ale of Ireland,
More exhilarating still is the ale of Tír Már;
A wondrous land is the land I tell of,
Youth does not give way to age there.
Sweet warm streams flow through the land,
The choice of mead and of wine;
Splendid people without blemish,
Conception without sin, without lust.[7]

The Irish otherworld is a joyous, sensuous place, rich in fruits and flowers, with men and women being eternally youthful and beautiful. They dwell in palaces sparkling with precious stones and partake of mead and food from inexhaustible vats while being lulled by beautiful music from the many birds. It is an idealized and paradisaical version of this earthly life. When the fairy maiden invites the warrior Connla to Mag Mell (the Plain of Delights) she tells him: 'I have come from the lands of the living where there is neither death, nor sin, nor transgression, in which there is no one save only women and maidens.'[8] Connla does not hesitate to jump into the fairy maiden's crystal boat and sail away to the otherworld.

The fairy's words mention another feature of the island otherworlds, that they can be peopled exclusively by women. Such a world is called Tír na mBan, the Island of Women. Similar islands are known in Greek mythology, with such figures as Circe and Calypso and their respective islands.

The otherworld is also sometimes known as the Land of the Living, Tír na mBeo. This title refers to the eternal youthfulness of its inhabitants. However it is also known that people of the otherworld *can* die and even be killed by mortals. This is less confusing if we remember that the immortality of the otherworld inhabitants is derived from the intemporal character of their world. In one story Fionn Mac Cumhaill slays the otherworld spirit that breathes fire on Tara every year. 'Immortality' means living outide time as we know it, not the avoidance of death. This immortality reminds us of the eternal cycle, which itself is timeless.

Another quality that is common to most otherworlds is that immortality was more or less dependent on the eating of some specific food and the drinking of a particular drink. The sea-god Manannán had a magical pig that was killed one day and came alive the next, and eating this pig conferred immortality upon the Tuatha Dé Danann. Another god connected to these practices was the blacksmith Goibniu, whose ale was drunk at otherworld festivals and is therefore associated with immortality. (In Greek myth, the blacksmith god Hephaestos served wine to the gods.) Humans partaking of such food and drink experienced immortality in the sense of freedom from the constraints of time and therefore remained young until they set foot back into the material world. At other times a mortal, having eaten and drunk from the offerings of the otherworld, found himself bound to that land for ever. This is precisely what happened to Connla when he first encountered the fairy woman: she gave him an apple to eat while he thought over her invitation. Each time Connla ate a piece of the apple, it replenished itself, but he was now destined to stay in the otherworld for ever. Fruit, in particular berries and nuts, is often mentioned, and it may well be that these were used to produce some sort of intoxicating effect. This links the Celtic mythology to the Greek, in particular the divine figures of Demeter and Dionysius and their connection with the Eleusinian mysteries, which were also concerned with knowing about death, rebirth and immortality.

The inexhaustible supply of food is a common theme, most notably in the magic cauldron of the Dagda. The otherworld cauldron possesses three distinguishing features: inexhaustibility, inspiration and regeneration. In a word, fertility. The cauldron is sometimes coveted by mortals, and various stories tell of attempts to steal it from the otherworld.

Finally the partaking of food and drink from the otherworld may best be seen as depicting an initiation ritual into the otherworld. An intoxicating drink could be associated with an altered state of consciousness, in which the possibility of seeing through the material world is enhanced and a transitory union with the otherworld becomes possible.

The inhabitants of the otherworld are not only immortal; they are also invisible at will. Sometimes they make themselves visible to one person and invisible to others. This serves to emphasize the immaterial nature of the otherworld. It also draws our attention to the fact that beyond the horizons of physical sight lies an unseen but nevertheless real world, which sometimes we can see and which at other times we cannot. It is a realm that some people simply do not know exists.

Up until now we have been describing the otherworld as a place of beauty, peace and harmony. However its inhabitants are also described as fighting and warring with each other. Perhaps somewhat unexpectedly, mortals are sometimes sought as allies and mediators in these disputes. For example Laegaire, son of the King of Connacht, agrees to assist Fiachna, a man from the otherworld, to win his wife back from the enemies who have abducted her. Laegaire and fifty warriors visit the plain of Mag Mell and duly overcome Fiachna's enemies. As a reward he and each of his warriors are given a wife from among the women of the beautiful Plain of Two Mists (Mag Dá Chó). He returns briefly to the upper world to inform his father that he and his men have decided to stay in the otherworld.

If it seems odd that this harmonious and beautiful otherworld should also be characterized by conflict and territorial disputes, it is helpful to see the otherworld as a mirror image of this one. Clearly it will reflect conflict as well as harmony. The usual pattern is that if a mortal is invited to the otherworld it takes on an appearance of peace, beauty and contentment, as we saw with Laegaire; if however a mortal enters uninvited, perhaps to plunder it for treasures or to steal a cauldron, then it becomes dark, inhospitable, its rulers becoming formidable enemies and many obstacles and monsters having to be faced. So the approach one makes to the otherworld determines one's experience of it. But unlike the Christian concept of the otherworld, here good and bad are not split and located separately; they are two sides of the whole.

This ambivalent quality of the otherworld is most clearly seen when it is represented as a hostel, a *bruiden*. These are usually set in the countryside, and most commonly appear from nowhere, surrounded by a mist, and then disappear with the same ease. Each of the hostels is equipped with an inexhaustible cauldron and the never-ending pig. They seem to have been spacious festival halls, and there is frequently a competition for what is known as the champion's portion, a chosen piece of meat, sometimes the thigh, that is given to the outstanding warrior amongst those present.

Yet this place of great festivity can also be a dark place of death. This is no more clearly seen than in the tragic story entitled 'The Destruction of Da Derga's Hostel' ('Toghail Bruidhne Da Derga'). It was at this hostel that Conaire Mór, the rightful and just King of Ireland, met his violent death after he had unintentionally violated his *geasa*. On the way to the hostel he encounters an ominous portent in the image of three red horsemen and a monstrous one-eyed, one-legged figure and his wife. All these figures were otherworld portents of death. For Conaire Mór the hostel of Da Derga, which means Red God, was a place of destiny; the hero, no matter how powerful, has to face the inevitability of death. Proinsias MacCana argues that Derga is one and the same as Donn, and those who enter his abode are either dead or foredoomed.[9] You will recall that Donn was the Milesian who refused to acknowledge the authority of the triple goddess of Ireland and was doomed never to land in Ireland. He was drowned and buried off the south-west coast of Ireland on an island that bears his name, Tech Duinn, 'the House of Donn'.

The otherworld, albeit ambivalent, is nevertheless basically an Elysium and finds its direct parallel in the Greek mythological Isle of the Blessed or the Elysian Fields. However the Irish Land of the Dead, although named separately, as indeed are Hades and Tartarus in Greek myth, is considered an aspect of the otherworld. Celtic mythology allows for and contains this ambiguity, and indeed it is probably accurate to state that containing ambiguity is a fundamental role of mythology. The intolerance of ambiguity would seem to be an artefact of logic and a reflection of the ego's insistent demand for clarity.

The house of the dead, whether the House of Donn or Da Derga's hostel, belongs to a male being. Is it possible that the land of the dead symbolizes a refusal to yield to the feminine principle? Donn could be seen as symbolizing the struggle for power over the feminine and the subsequent banishment that results. The heroic ego finds it very difficult to yield to a pattern older and more powerful than itself, and Donn would appear to be an apt symbol of this attitude. Such a yielding demands a giving-up of our fantasies of omnipotence, but the failure to do this may well mean that we travel to Tech Duinn, since the manner in which we approach the otherworld determines our experience of it. Perhaps on Tech Duinn we are 'dead' because we cannot see through the materialistic universe to the existence of that timeless, invisible space. Such knowledge is only possible when we are connected to the feminine perspective of continuity and do not see the world exclusively through the masculine eyes of logic and linearity.

It is interesting that most, if not all, the male voyagers to the otherworld, whether they go by invitation or on their own initiative, are mortal heroes in the prime of their life. When in the otherworld they undergo an initiation, or rebirth, and gain an awareness of the non-material universe. Voyages to Tech Duinn, on the other hand, happen at the end of one's life, and an invitation to the House of Donn is an invitation to die, not to be reborn. The House of Donn could be seen as symbolizing an absence of awareness of the eternal cycle, and perhaps mortals are destined to stay there until such time as they are able to see through the material world. Is it possible that Tech Duinn finds its later equivalent in the Catholic idea of purgatory?

The voyage to the otherworld is only made by heroes and kings, and there has been some speculation that people of lesser status were destined to a less distinguished afterlife, in the Land of the Dead. But perhaps kings and heroes are symbols of an archetypal pattern of the development of consciousness? The king within alchemical symbolism depicts the evolved ruling principle of consciousness, which needs to be united with the feminine symbol of the queen in the chymical wedding or *conjunctio*. These figures would be receptive to the invitation to see through the visible world into the invisible, well before their actual physical death. A modern parallel can be seen in those individuals who have reached a certain level of self-awareness and are able to sustain a self-reflective and insightful mentality towards their own behaviour. And by 'self-awareness' I do not mean some ego-driven psychological-jargon cliché about oneself, I mean a deep-felt sense of the forces that move us, those invisible aspects of psychic life that lie beyond the realm of our ego and immediate consciousness. This is a state of seeing through the objective to the subjective realm.

The final aspect of the otherworld that needs to be discussed is the pagan festival of Samain, so significant within Irish mythology. Samain is strongly associated with major mythological events such as the divine mating of Dagda with Morrígan. It is a time that is set apart and charged with supernatural energy. At Samain the curtain or veil separating the known world and the otherworld is drawn back, and free communication exists between the two. This is a temporary return to the mythic period prior to the arrival of the Sons of Mil, to the golden age when gods and mortals shared the same space. It is a ritualistic recognition of the permanent presence of the non-material-istic universe, both benevolent and malevolent.

Samain marked the end of one year and the beginning of the next.

The eve of Samain, 31 October, was considered to stand independently between the two years, a period outside time during which the normal order of the universe was suspended. It is the gap between, and 'gap' means chaos. The otherworld opened up, came through the gaps in the earth. Sjoestedt puts this eloquently when she says, 'It seems that the whole supernatural force is attracted by the seam thus left at the point where the two years join, and gathers to invade the world of men.'[10]

(Christianity has renamed Samain as All Saints Day, and Samain eve is of course Halloween in the secular realm.)

Samain has an obvious link to the world of dreams. At night we are also in an otherworld, without the constraints of time and space. Dreams could be seen as the confrontation of the ego, that is the visible world, with the invisible or unconscious world. Sometimes this meeting is full of destructive ambience and themes and at other times it is helpful and benevolent. Upon waking we realize that we have temporarily seen through to the invisible realm that we inhabit also. Dreaming is a return to our own mythic world, both collective and individual. Mircea Eliade reminds us that 'Reality is acquired solely through repetition or participation; everything that lacks an exemplary model is "meaningless". i.e. it lacks reality.'[11] The Irish gods and the festival of Samain are an exemplary model to remind us of the permanent existence of an invisible world that shapes our very being.

8

THE OTHERWORLD II

The tales relating to the otherworlds fall into two broad categories, those classified by the ancient Irish story-tellers as adventures (*echtrai*) and those known as voyages (*imrama*). However, in many of the tales an overlap between the categories can be seen. Whilst the tales come from a wide period of Irish mythology they are clearly pre-Christian in origin, although the later tales reveal a Christian influence.

In Lady Gregory's rendition of the story of Étaín, we are given a description of the land below the surface as Midir makes his plea to Étaín to return with him:

> 'Oh beautiful woman, will you come with me to the wonderful country that is mine? It is pleasant to be looking at the people there, beautiful people without blemish ... the young never grow old; the fields and flowers are as pleasant to be looking at as the blackbird's eggs; warm sweet streams of mead and wine flow through that country; there is no care and no sorrow on any person; we see others but we ourselves are not seen ... Oh beautiful woman, if you come to my proud people it is the flesh of pigs newly killed I will give you for food ... it is a crown of gold you will have upon your hair.'[1]

We see in this description the now-familiar qualities of the otherworld: beauty, eternal youth, feasting and the art of invisibility. We also learn later in the story that Midir's *sídhe* was below the ground, since King Eochaid literally digs up Midir's *sídhe*, only to find that it restores itself overnight and his digging is to no avail. This story would also appear to indicate that the otherworld below the surface existed prior to the arrival of the Sons of Mil, who are said to have driven the Tuatha Dé Danann underground where they formed their various *sídhe*. Such is the nature of Irish mythology, that things can exist both before and after their 'beginning', and this is also the nature of the otherworld, that it defies any linear sense of time.

'The Dream of Oenghus' focuses on the relationships between the various *sidhe*. My telling of this story is broadly based on Kenneth Jackson's translation of an eighth-century manuscript.[2]

Oenghus woke suddenly one night. The most beautiful woman he had ever seen was moving towards him. He leant forward, stretching his hand out to her, but at that very moment she vanished. In the morning when he awoke there was no sign that the woman had ever been in his room. However her image disturbed Oenghus deeply and throughout the day he was listless and could not eat. That night he went to bed eager to see the beautiful maiden again. Sure enough, she appeared again; however this time she carried a harp which she played for him till he went back to sleep. He slept through the night but the next morning felt as wretched as he had the previous day, still listless and unable to banish the image of the beautiful woman of his dreams.

A whole year passed for Oenghus in this manner. The beautiful maiden would appear each night, would not speak or be touched, but played beautiful music on her harp until Oenghus fell into a deep sleep. Each day for a whole year her image tormented him and distracted him from any meaningful activity. Gradually his health deteriorated and his mind became increasingly troubled. He would not tell anyone why he was not eating, and many physicians came and went, all unable to say what was wrong with Oenghus.

Finally the King's own physician was summoned to see Oenghus. He was known throughout the land to be able to tell from the smoke which came from a house how many people were ill in it, and he could tell from a man's face what the illness was. When he arrived to see Oenghus he knew immediately that the source of his malaise did not lie within his body but within his mind. He turned directly to Oenghus and said, 'I think it is for the love of a woman that you are wasting away like this.' Oenghus hastily and nervously agreed, and then told the physician the story of how the beautiful woman had visited him every night and played the harp to him and how she vanished without him ever being able to touch her or know her name. 'No matter,' said the doctor, 'it is fated that you are destined to make a match with this woman,' and he immediately sent for Oenghus's mother, Boann. He instructed Boann to tend to her son by searching throughout Ireland for this beautiful and mysterious woman. Boann was deeply concerned about the health of her son and for a whole year she searched all of Ireland for the woman. But the search was without success, so once again the physician was summoned, and this time he ordered that the

Dagda be summoned and told of his son's dangerous condition. The Dagda was less receptive than Boann and asked why he had been called. The physician went through the situation again; 'What is the use of telling me?' said the Dagda. 'I know no more than you.' The physician reminded the Dagda that he was the King of all the fairy kingdom and that in this role he should summon Bodb Derg, the King of the *sídhe* at Munster, since Bodb Derg was regarded as a very knowledgeable king.

The Dagda finally agreed and sent messengers to Bodb Derg's *sídhe*. When they had explained their mission, Bodb Derg replied, 'The search will be made, but I need a year to carry it out.' At the end of the year Bodb Derg sent some of his messengers to the Dagda, to say that they had found a young woman who possessed all the attributes that Oenghus had described, at Loch Bél Dragon in the Galtee Mountains. 'Bodb Derg bids Oenghus to come with us to see whether it is the same woman that appeared to him in his dream.'

Oenghus was taken to Bodb Derg's *sídhe*, and there they feasted for three days and nights until finally Bodb Derg said, 'Come with me now to see that this is the same woman who appeared to you in your dreams.' But he warned Oenghus that even if it did prove to be the same woman he could only see her, as it was not within Bodb Derg's power to give her to him.

They travelled to a distant lake, and before him Oenghus saw three-times-fifty women, each pair linked by a silver chain, but one woman stood out clearly from the others because she was by herself and was head and shoulders taller than the others. This one also wore a beautiful silver and gold necklace. Bodb Derg asked Oenghus, 'Do you recognize that maiden?' 'Indeed I do,' he replied. 'Do you know who she is?' Bodb Derg answered, 'She is Caer, daughter of Ethal Anbual, from a fairy kingdom in the province of Connacht.'

With a heavy heart Oenghus returned to his parents at Bruig na Bóinne. Bodb Derg accompanied him and together they told of how they had found the woman and knew her name, but the god had no power to give her to Oenghus. He advised the Dagda: 'Go and visit King Ailill and Queen Medb of Connacht and seek their help, for the maiden is in their kingdom,' advised Bodb.

So the Dagda and a convoy of sixty chariots set out for Connacht, and when they arrived they were welcomed by the King and Queen with a week-long feast, at the end of which King Ailill asked why the Dagda had come to Connacht. The story was told again, and at the end

Ailill asked, 'Who is she?' 'She is the daughter of Ethal Anbual,' replied the Dagda. But Ailill said that he did not have the power to give her to Oenghus. The Dagda thought for a while then said he thought the best thing would be to ask Ethal Anbual to come and see the King and Queen to discuss the matter.

A messenger was dispatched, but Ethal Anbual was king of a fairy mound; he had the gift of foresight, and knew why he was being asked to visit the palace of King Ailill and Queen Medb. He said to the messenger, 'I will not come and I will not give my daughter to the son of the Dagda.' The messenger returned and conveyed this reply to Ailill. 'No matter,' said Ailill; 'he will come, and the heads of his warriors with him.' At that the King and the Dagda set off to attack the fairy mound of Ethal Anbual. They destroyed the entire fairy fort and captured Ethal along with many of his warriors. Ailill then said to Ethal, 'Give your daughter to the son of the Dagda,' but Ethal replied, 'That I cannot do, because her power is greater than mine.' Ailill, exasperated, demanded to know the nature of his power that was greater than Ethal's own. 'She is enchanted, and takes the form of a swan one year and of a human the other.' Ailill asked which year she was a bird. But Ethal said he could not reveal this as it would mean betraying his daughter. At this refusal Ailill's frustration boiled over and he threatened to behead Ethal. So Ethal finally revealed that at the next Samain Caer would be in her swan form at Lough Bél Dragon and that if Oenghus went at that time he would see her.

The Dagda returned home with this information, and at Samain Oenghus set off for Lough Bél Dragon. He stood at the edge of the lake and called, 'Caer, Caer, come and speak with me.' From the flock of swans came a voice: 'Who calls me?' 'Oenghus calls you.' 'I will come if you swear on your honour that I may come back to the lake again.' Oenghus agreed, Caer came to him, and he cast his arms around her and both fell asleep in the form of two swans. After a time they awoke and flew around the lake three times so that the promise might not be broken, and then they flew to Oenghus's fairy kingdom at Bruig na Bóinne. As they flew the music they created by their singing was so beautiful that the people slept for three days and three nights. Caer stayed with Oenghus for ever after and from that time on a great friendship grew between Oenghus, King Ailill and Queen Medb.

This story includes several themes that recur in Irish mythic literature: love at first sight; the wasting sickness caused by love; the father who is unwilling to give his daughter away; the otherworld woman taking the initiative in the seduction; the swan; and Samain as a significant time for these mystical happenings.

The fairy woman Caer seduces and enchants the masculine figure, rendering him powerless. Where this unconscious plot is enacted in men we see a repetitive, at times compulsive, 'falling' in love, and an accompanying wasting-away of discrimination and maturity. Carl Jung has called this female figure the *anima*; her mysterious anonymity is typical, and compels men to seek to know her. To come to know the feminine or *anima* aspects of being is, according to Jung, an inevitable part of the individuation process. She is a personification of the unconscious world and the process of establishing some knowledge of her is the process of becoming conscious of aspects of ourselves instead of projecting them out on to others. This pattern of the presence of the unknown woman and the desire to know and form a relationship with her is repeated night after night in men's dreams. It is the constant calling to know oneself. As I have discussed elsewhere, a man's behaviour towards this figure in his dream often reveals the nature not only of his relationship to his own inner world, but also the pattern of his relationships with women in the outer world. One man might dream of letting the unknown female figure drown, whereas another might rescue her. One might dream of rape, another of making tender love to the mysterious female; one might dream of stealing from her, whereas another will dream of receiving a gift with gratitude.[3] Jung draws a direct comparison between this unknown *anima* figure and fairies when he asserts:

> The unknown woman, therefore, has an exceedingly contradictory character and cannot be related to any normal woman. She represents some fabulous being, a kind of fairy; and indeed fairies have the most varied characters; they can change themselves into animals, they can become invisible, they are of uncertain age, now young, now old, elfin in nature, with part-souls, alluring, dangerous and possessed of superior knowledge . . . the figure of the unknown woman is a personification of the unconscious, which I have called the 'anima'.[4]

In reading this description of Jung's, written in 1935, one can sense an almost uncanny retelling of the ancient mythological story of 'The Dream of Oenghus'. This serves to further highlight the mythological status of modern psychology. These mythological images reach deep into the human psyche and connect us to our historical foundations, where reason and logic have not penetrated. 'The Dream of Oenghus' speaks to us today just as powerfully as it ever did, since it touches those deepest and oldest recesses of the psyche, the collective unconscious.

Oenghus's dream is often relived in the lives of men at mid-life who, like Oenghus, initially find their feminine soul or *anima* in their dreams. They then pursue her in the outer world in the form of either a string of love affairs or the fantasy of such affairs, as they seek to know her name. When such relationships fail, then the mourning and the wasting sickness sets in. Today we call it depression, a state in which a person often loses their appetite and pines the return of their idealized lover. The wasting sickness is a prelude to change, as long as we can continue to reflect and come to know the figures of our dreams and not stay stuck in mourning for a lost fantasy. Giving the fantasy imaginal form enables it to be known and located, as we see in the story. Imagination and images are solid vehicles to convey us over the ground of our being, whereas fantasy is a flying carpet that sets us adrift from reality and prevents us from developing. Fantasy always keeps needs in the form of 'if only'; images transfer them in such a manner that needs can be deciphered and the task of meeting them in reality becomes a feasible and practical one. Images thereby set up an interaction with the outer reality, whilst fantasy denies it and causes a 'wasting sickness'. The physician is the unconscious wisdom within each of us, or what Jung would term the wise-old-man archetype, which knows the truth and senses the link in a man's psyche between the *anima* and the mother. The mother is our first and hence very powerful experience of the feminine and as such exerts an enormous influence on the nature of our personal *anima*. If a man cannot separate these two figures then his emotional growth is stunted and he often seeks in other women the idealized mother who he fantasizes will meet his every need. Like the classical description of the ancient Celts he is characterized by feeding, fornicating and fighting. The only problem is that he tends to get the feeding and the fornicating confused if he cannot separate the mother from the *anima*, and when not fed he frequently resorts to rageful and violent outbursts. Oenghus's mother cannot find the unknown woman; it is the masculine energy of the father and other male figures that provides for the separation between mother and son. He can discover the name and whereabouts of the unknown woman. This process establishes that she belongs to the otherworld and has her own power, and that to have a relationship with her demands a certain degree of yielding. But in this yielding a man needs to stand firmly on the shore, the solid land of consciousness, otherwise he 'falls in love' and as in Keats's 'La Belle Dame sans Merci' people will ask:

> 'Oh what can ail thee, knight at arms,
> Alone and palely loitering?'

to which the man replies:

> 'I met a lady in the meads
> Full beautiful – a faery's child
> Her hair was long, her foot was light
> And her eyes were wild.'[5]

If men fall in, rather than relate with, it is often because they are still dominated by the archetypal mother image and are seeking paradise and fusion, not union. The fairies have seduced such a man, and consciousness has been the price.

Swans are usually considered to be symbolic of creativity, in that they are linked to three elements, earth, air and water. They also represent a transition between the unconscious realm of water and the conscious world of air. Caer's terms for the union with Oenghus are that she can return to the lake, symbolizing the role of the feminine in a man to return him to the source, the eternal spring of the inner life. So many modern men ignore the water, the realm of the feminine. This absence of feeling makes them dry and boring, and they are apt to self-combust in displays of hot fiery rage or die in parched sterility.

Whilst the *sidhe* are near the human world in the hills, mounds and caves of the land, another form of otherworld is yet closer to us. This is the world that is usually referred to as being coextensive with the visible and physical world, and is usually both seen and then entered through a mist. The principal tale about this otherworld is 'Cormac's Adventure in the Land of Promise' (Tír Tairngire).

Cormac mac Art was the son of Art, King of Ireland, who in turn was the son of Conn, High King of Ireland and more commonly known as Conn of the Hundred Battles. So Conn was Cormac's grandfather and Connla, who was lured to the otherworld by a fairy woman, was Cormac's uncle; Cormac's male relatives had preceded him in making journeys to the otherworld. Connla we have already discussed; here is a brief outline of Conn's journey.

One day Conn of the Hundred Battles was walking with his druid on the ramparts at Tara when he trod on a stone, which emitted a number of screams. The druid told Conn that the number of screams indicated the number of his descendants that would rule over Ireland. At this moment they were enveloped in a mist and lost their bearings. When the mist lifted they found themselves on a beautiful plain; before their eyes was a magnificent palace, beside which was a golden tree. They entered the palace through an exquisitely carved door. Inside they found a beautiful woman with a crown of gold, seated on a crystal chair, and in front of her was a gold cup. She was the sovereign queen, and next to her was the god Lugh. The woman served Conn some meat and a draught of red ale in the golden cup. Lugh then recited the future Kings of Ireland and the druid wrote them down on staves of yew; then the vision disappeared. Conn was left with the golden cup and the staves of yew.

These objects from the otherworld serve as a connection to the gods, and also as a reminder of the reality that lies beyond the visible world. Cormac mac Art has some similar experiences to his grandfather's.[6]

Early one morning in the month of May, Cormac was alone on the rampart of Tara when he was approached by a splendidly dressed, handsome, tall, grey-haired warrior. He was carrying a branch with golden apples on it and whenever this branch was shaken it emitted the most beautiful music, which comforted the sick, the wounded and women in childbirth by lulling them to sleep. Cormac and the unknown warrior acknowledged each other and then Cormac asked where the warrior had come from. 'I come from a country where only truth is spoken, and where nothing or no one ages or decays and where there is no sadness, no jealousy, no hate and no pride.' Cormac replied that this was certainly not how things were in his own world, and warmly welcomed the stranger. As King, Cormac was entitled to seek a gift from a visitor and he asked the warrior for the silver branch with the golden apples. The stranger agreed, on condition that Cormac granted him three wishes. With that the regal stranger disappeared as magically and suddenly as he had come. Cormac turned and walked back into his palace, and the entire household marvelled at the branch. Cormac shook it and immediately they were all lulled to sleep and did not wake again until the same hour the next day.

A year and a day later the mysterious stranger returned to Tara, seeking the granting of the first of his wishes, which was for Cormac's daughter. Cormac had no choice but to hand over his daughter, and when he had done so the stranger left. The women of Tara wailed with grief, but Cormac shook the branch at them and they fell asleep.

A month later the stranger returned. When Cormac asked him what his second wish was, he said that he now wanted Cormac's son. The King agreed, and once more he had to quiet the grief of the women by shaking the magic branch at them. The stranger returned a third time and Cormac nervously asked what he wanted this time. He replied that he now wanted Cormac's wife. Shortly after he had handed her over, Cormac felt such great grief that he summoned his army and pursued the stranger. They chased him on to a wide open plain, in the middle of which Cormac suddenly found himself engulfed in a very thick mist. When it lifted he found he was completely alone; before him he saw a great fortress surrounded by a wall of bronze. Once inside this wall, he came across a house that was made of silver and was half thatched with white bird feathers. There were men thatching the roof but each time they laid the feathers a gust of wind blew them away. A man was tending a fire, but every great log he put on the fire had burnt to ashes by the time he got back with a second log.

Out of the corner of his eye Cormac caught sight of another royal-looking fortress surrounded by a bronze wall; within this were four houses. Once inside the wall, he saw a wonderful palace, and in the forecourt a fountain with five streams flowing from it. He also observed nine ancient hazel trees growing in the courtyard. Some people were drinking from the fountain, and five salmon were eating the hazelnuts that dropped into it. The sound of the five streams that flowed from the fountain was more beautiful than any music Cormac had ever heard.

Cormac entered the palace to find a noble warrior and a beautiful woman waiting for him. He bathed in water heated by magical hot stones, and as he finished a man appeared carrying an axe, a club and a live pig. With his axe he killed the pig, split the club in half and then cut the pig into four parts, tossing each part into a huge cauldron of boiling water. But as he tossed them in he declared that the meat would not be cooked until a truth was uttered for each quarter.

The man himself started by telling a truthful tale; the beautiful woman followed and then the noble warrior. With each telling of a truth the quarters cooked. It was now Cormac's turn to tell a truth. So Cormac told them how his daughter, son and wife had been taken away and how he had followed until he had finished in the place he now found himself. With that the whole pig was cooked and Cormac's share was placed before him.

But Cormac complained that, as a king, he had never eaten with only three other people, and requested a company of fifty. The warrior now began to sing, and his singing put Cormac to sleep.

When he awoke he found standing before him fifty men and his wife, son and daughter. There was much rejoicing, and a great feast was held during which Cormac expressed admiration for the host's magnificent golden cup. 'There is something even more marvellous about it than its beauty,' said the noble warrior. 'Let three lies be told under it and it will break into three, but tell three truths and it will become whole again.' To prove his point the warrior told three deliberate lies and sure enough the golden cup shattered into three pieces. He then turned to Cormac and said that he would make it whole again by telling three truths. 'Your son has not seen a woman, your wife and daughter have not seen a man since they left Tara.' At this the cup magically restored itself and stood before Cormac as beautiful as ever. Cormac was amazed and said to the warrior, 'How could this be?' 'I am Manannán mac Lir, King of the Land of Promise in which you now find yourself; I brought you here so that you could see it for yourself.' He gave the cup to Cormac and in doing so said, 'Take your family and the cup, so that with it you may discern truth from falsehood, and keep the branch to delight your people with music. On the day that you die, both will be taken from you.'

Then Manannán explained to Cormac the riddles of the palace. The thatchers represented poets who tried to hoard wealth; this is a futile thing to do as the world blows the wealth of poets away. Poets, he went on to say, must not accumulate perishable wealth; theirs is another form of wealth. The man tending the fire represented a thriftless young chief who spent more than he could afford. The fountain in the courtyard was the fountain of all knowledge and the streams flowing from it were the five senses through which knowledge is obtained. It was, he said, necessary to drink out of both the fountain and the streams and in this way the accomplishment of excellence in the arts was achieved.

The next morning Cormac arose and found himself on the green of Tara with his family, the branch and the cup of discrimination, which from then on was known as Cormac's cup.[6]

This tale reiterates many of the themes of the otherworld – beautiful people, palaces and magical objects – but also elements that are familiar from other mythologies. The branch is the most obvious, the same object with which Aeneas, in the classical epic *The Aeneid*, descended into Hades. There is also the theme of initiation into the mysteries of the otherworld. Manannán admits that he brought Cormac to the otherworld so that he could see it for himself. This constitutes the initiation into the mystery.

The importance of truth in this tale is striking. Cormac is initiated into the truth that all knowledge lies in the world beyond the visible one, in particular in the knowledge of the eternal cycle of life, death and renewal. The cup symbolizes the gaining of this knowledge, and the branch symbolizes the peace that comes with it. To drink from the fountain of eternal youth confers understanding that death is not final.

It is interesting to note that it is only the experience of grief, when he loses his wife, that motivates Cormac to undertake the journey. Up until that point he has been willing to tranquillize the grief of others by shaking the magic branch. But in facing grief we accept and allow for the separating work of Thanatos to occur, facilitating a renewed sense of being.

In today's society the undergoing of a prolonged and thorough psychoanalysis holds similar possibilities for shedding some of our self-deceptions and previously unacknowledged losses and grief. The contact with the unconscious that should occur in psychoanalysis is in itself transformative, as was Cormac's journey to the otherworld. From this contact the ego begins to realize that it is not master in its own house. Just as for Cormac, psychoanalysis demands that we respond to the inner call to explore the unknown, and give up some of our habitual views of ourselves. All initiatory journeys, including psycho-analysis, demand separation, followed by the initiation itself and then the return. The story of Cormac mac Art tells of this process and of the reward of an enhanced capacity to discriminate between falsehood and truth that results.

In addition to the subterranean and coextensive otherworlds there also existed an otherworld that lay beneath water, in the form of a lake, a well or the sea. This otherworld was known as Tír fo Thuinn, the Land Under the Waves.

Passing mention has been made of the story of the Sons of Tuireann, the three brothers who killed Lugh's father Cian and had several fines imposed upon them as punishment. One of these was to acquire a cooking spit from the island of Fiancara (Inis Fionnchuire) which was protected by warrior women. For three months the brothers searched for the island, which was said to lie somewhere between the east coast of Ireland and Scotland. Finally they met an old man who told them that in his youth he had heard of the island of Fiancara, but it lay deep below the sea. At this the eldest brother Brian put on his 'water dress', with a helmet of crystal on his head, and leapt into the sea. He swam for a whole fortnight, until he came across the magical island beneath the sea. He saw a great palace and upon entering its doors he observed only women, all beautiful, engaged in needlework and embroidery. When he saw the spit he quickly walked towards it, seized it and walked purposefully towards the door. At this point all the women burst into laughter and ridiculed Brian for the boldness of his deed. They reminded him that they could have prevented him from taking the spit even if he had had his brothers with him. But they also admired his boldness and let him take the spit.

This brief synopsis establishes the dominant role of women in the Irish otherworld and the latent power that they possess. Brian's diving garment may well relate to a firm belief amongst Irish seafarers that a child born with the caul, i.e. the embryonic sac, intact over its head would never drown. Brian clearly needed the magical garment and helmet to descend to the land below the waves.

Some have suggested that this land below the waves, although having many features in common with the other otherworlds, also had about it an air of danger and evil. Perhaps this belief came from the very nature of the sea and its capricious moods that could be fatal. It is sometimes seen as being characterized less by the life-giving qualities of the goddess and more by her dark, negative aspect.

In the story of Ruad, who set out with three boats to converse with the King of Lochlann, we clearly see this other side of the women below the sea. Half-way across the sea Ruad's three boats were magically becalmed, as if anchored. Ruad dived under the sea to investigate, and to his astonishment he saw nine beautiful women, three under each boat, holding them still. They carried Ruad off and each night he lay with one of them, 'without gloom, without tearful lament, under the sea free from waves on nine beds of bronze'.[7] One of the women became pregnant by him and Ruad, needing to continue his present journey, promised to return. The women agreed to let him go, and Ruad stayed away for seven long years, then on his return trip to Ireland he failed to visit the women. They were furious, and pursued

Ruad but could not overtake him. Finally the mother of Ruad's son grabbed the child, threw him head first against the shores of Ireland, and killed him.

Irish literature, as we have seen, abounds with the figures three and nine. As a multiple of three, nine has many meanings, one of which is wholeness. Nine months of pregnancy would be associated with fertility. In spite of this, the nine women in the story of Ruad represent the dark, destructive side of the otherworld women.

Another story of the Land Under the Waves is that of Laegaire, who intervened in a conflict between the chiefs of two fairy kingdoms. Laegaire and his fifty warriors had to dive into a lough to enter the otherworld. As reward for their success, Laegaire and his men were each given a wife. He returns briefly to see his father, and is given a horse by the King of the otherworld, Fiachna, for the purpose. He is told not to dismount from the horse, since to do so would result in instant ageing and an incapacity to return to the otherworld. Laegaire's reply to his father's plea for him to stay is very revealing of the land below the waves.

> A marvel this, O Crimthann Cass,
> Beer comes down with every shower!
> The driving of a batallion of a hundred thousand,
> They go from kingdom to kingdom.
>
> The noble wistful music of the *sídhe*
> Going from kingdom to kingdom,
> Drinking from crystal cups,
> Holding converse with the loved one.
>
> My wife, my own unto me,
> Is daughter of the sun, Fiachna's daughter.
> Besides I shall tell thee,
> There is a wife for each man of my fifty.
>
> We have brought from the fort of Mag Mell
> Thirty cauldrons, thirty drinking horns.
> We have brought the plaint that the sea chants,
> The daughter of Eochaid the Dumb.
>
> A marvel this, O Crimthann Cass,
> I was master of a blue sword.
> One night of the nights of the *sídhe*
> I would not give for thy kingdom.[8]

Once again there are the bounty, the women, the inexhaustible cauldron, the music and even the 'beer that comes down with every shower'. Although this otherworld is below the waves it does not seem to be characterized by the dark side of the feminine. However the seductive power of otherworld is clearly seen in the decision by Laegaire and his warriors to abandon life above the surface despite the treasures offered to him by his father. This abandonment of the world above the surface finds its modern equivalent in psychotic states where the lure of retreat into the unconscious realm results in a complete withdrawal from the observable world. Another, less severe form of this is the embracing of a cult religion, a similar pattern of being seduced by the world below the surface and turning against the gifts of Logos or the father. The art surely is to be able to stay connected to both realms and not to choose one at the expense of the other.

The fourth otherworld location is that of the distant islands across the sea. The island Elysium is found in several tales right up to the Christian era (in the celebrated voyage of St Brendan). After the *sidhe*, the island realm is the most frequently mentioned otherworld in Irish mythology. The sea is both bountiful, a supplier of food, and destructive, in its drowning of sailors. Traversing it as an ordeal to be undertaken in order to reach the otherworld makes sense within this context.

The most famous of the voyage stories is 'The Voyage of Bran' ('Imram Brain'). Bran was King of Ireland, and he had gathered his chiefs together to celebrate the summer festival of Beltaine on 1 May. After a while Bran felt the need to withdraw and seek some peace in the silence outside the walls of his fort.

Suddenly the silence was broken by the most beautiful and plaintive music he had ever heard. He looked around to see who was playing, but nobody was to be seen. He had no sooner turned his back than the music started again. This time he waited a while and then turned round swiftly, hoping to catch the player by surprise, but again there was nobody to be seen.

He then realized that the music was from the *sidhe*, made by the Tuatha Dé Danann. As if consoled by this knowledge, he allowed himself to listen and refrained from trying to see who was playing. Before long the music induced a drowsiness which Bran could not resist, so he lay down and slept. When he woke there was no music, and everything was as it had been before. Suddenly out of the corner of his eye he noticed something glistening in the grass. He picked it up and saw that it was the branch of an apple tree with white blossom on it. But it was not an ordinary branch: it was made of silver, and the blossom shone like crystal.

Bran returned to the gathering in the great hall and an immediate hush overcame the gathering as they caught sight of the branch. Bran was just about to tell them how he had heard the music and come across the branch when a woman appeared from nowhere in the centre of the hall. Her beauty, her dress and her magical entrance left no one in any doubt that she was from the otherworld. Turning towards Bran, she began to sing, extolling the delights of the otherworld. Marie Heaney gives a rich and lyrical version of this ancient verse:

'This silver apple branch comes from a distant isle, the playground of the horses of Manannán Mac Lir.

In the south of the island is a glorious plain raised high by four shining columns.

Huge crowds hold their games on this silver-white plain, boats race against chariots and blossoms fall from the trees.

From one ancient tree, a chorus of birds sings out the hours.

All is harmony and peace in this fertile, well-tilled land.

Music sweetens the ear and colour delights the eye.

Brightness falls from the air and the sea washes against the cliffs like a crystal veil.

In this fair island there is nothing rough or harsh.

No weeping or sobbing is heard there and treachery is unknown.

There are no cries of lamentation or grief, no weakness or illness.

No death.'

She finishes the song with an invitation to Bran to visit the island:

'Though all can hear me, Bran, my song is for you;
Don't let tiredness delay you.
Don't wait to drink the wine.
Begin the voyage across the clear sea to the beautiful land I have promised.'

At the moment she finished the song the branch flew from Bran's hand to hers and she departed as magically as she had appeared.

The next day Bran gathered together three-times-nine men, who were willing to set sail for the island described by the woman. They rowed for two days without seeing anyone, then suddenly on the horizon, on the white crest of a wave, they saw a chariot coming towards them. As it got closer they saw that it was Manannán mac Lir himself who was driving the chariot. He stopped and spoke to Bran in verse, telling him that whilst all Bran could see from his boat were waves, to Manannán it was a plain profuse with flowers.

> 'Steadily then let Bran row.
> It is not far to the land of women . . .
> You will reach before the setting of the sun.'

Manannán then disappeared. Bran and his men, inspired by the appearance of the god of the sea, rowed on, and before long they came to an island. Bran cautiously ordered his men to circumnavigate the island before they put ashore. He noticed a large crowd gathered on the shore, laughing uncontrollably and pointing at Bran and his men. Bran shouted that he was Bran, King of Ireland, son of Febal, and they were looking for the Island of Women. This only served to send the people into even more uproarious laughter. At this Bran chose to send one of his crew ashore, but when he reached it he simply turned around, pointed at Bran and broke into laughter. Bran called his name again and again, but the sailor just kept on laughing. Finally Bran set sail for the Island of Women, leaving the crewman behind on what is known as the Island of Joy.

As the sun started to set they saw a jetty and on it a woman, waving at them. Whilst Bran thought that this was probably the Island of Women, since Manannán had prophesied that they would reach it before sunset, he was nevertheless cautious. Suddenly the woman on the jetty threw a ball of thread at Bran's head, and instinctively he put up his hand to protect himself, but the ball struck his hand and stayed stuck to it. No matter what Brand did he could not dislodge it, and slowly the woman began to pull the thread, and Bran and his men found themselves being drawn to shore. The woman led them to a large house full of women in which was laid out a magnificent feast. The men ate with relish, but no matter how much they ate the plates remained full of food. When they had eaten their fill, each man was provided with a bed and a female companion. This pattern continued day in and day out, until Bran and his men forgot about Ireland and lived a life of pleasure on the Island of Women.

Finally one of the men, Nechtan, became homesick, and pleaded with Bran to return to Ireland. But the others refused to take him seriously and continued to revel in the life. Nechtan persisted and finally forced Bran into agreeing to return. The night before they were due to depart, one of the women visited Bran and told him that he would deeply regret his decision. So Bran went to Nechtan and told him that he was not prepared to go. But Nechtan was not easily persuaded and he reminded his fellow crew members of their former lives and of families they had left behind. This disturbed the men and made them restless, so Bran decided finally that he had no choice but to return to Ireland.

Before he set off the leader of the women came to Bran and gave him two instructions: one, that he must pick up his companion on the Island of Joy, and two, that on no account must he set foot in Ireland. Bran set sail, picking up his companion, who this time did not hesitate to rejoin his friends. After three days they reached the coast of Ireland, where a large assembly of people had gathered. Bran, remembering the instruction from the woman on the island, spoke to the crowd from his boat. One of the crowd asked who he was and he replied, 'I am Bran, son of Febal, and I left Ireland a year ago.'

There was a murmur of bewilderment, then someone from the crowd said, 'We have heard of Bran. He set out hundreds of years ago in search of the magic Island of Women, but he has never been heard of since. We only know of him through an old tale.' At this point Nechtan leapt ashore, but at the very moment his feet touched the ground he disintegrated into dust. Bran let out a loud cry of anguish as he realized that he had been away from Ireland for three hundred years, not one year. He also knew at that moment that he was destined never to set foot on Irish soil again. Bran and his men bade farewell to the assembled crowd and set sail. They were never heard of again.

One other story that deserves brief mention, since it throws further light on the island otherworld, is 'The Voyage of Mael Dúin'. This is considered to be one of the oldest voyage stories and is thought to be the inspiration for the later Christian story of the voyage of Brendan. It also serves as the inspiration for Tennyson's epic poem of the same title.

Mael Dúin was the son of Ailill, an invader who had pillaged a church and raped a nun (the latter sin no doubt being a Christian addition). Ailill was slain not long after this looting and the nun gave birth to a boy who was called Mael Dúin. The nun died in childbirth and Mael Dúin was fostered out to her sister, who was queen of the territory. Mael Dúin grew to manhood but like so many mythic heroes, such as Cú Chulainn and Oedipus, he was taunted about his parentage and sought the truth from his foster-mother. When he learnt the truth he decided to avenge his father's death. He sought the advice of a druid, who told him to build a boat from three skins and set out on a specific day with seventeen men. After Mael Dúin had set sail his three foster-brothers swam after him, pleading to join him on the expedition. Despite the druid's advice Mael Dúin took them on board, a transgression that was to cause later misadventures.

The voyagers first came to two islands with two forts on them and two men quarrelling. One shouted to the other that he was the better man since he had slain Ailill, and no kinsman had ever avenged his death. Mael Dúin was about to land and battle with the arrogant man when a great wind rose up and blew their boat out to sea. Mael Dúin realized that this was a consequence of transgressing the druid's directions and that he had no choice but to yield to the divine forces, so they laid aside their oars and drifted.

This drifting led them to thirty-three islands in all. They include the islands of beautiful birds, of equine monsters and of fiery creatures, a palace with a curious cat, wondrous beasts and trees, and an island with a brass wall with black sheep on one side and white sheep on the other. After these they came to an island with giant cattle and swine that was separated by a river that burnt like fire. Then their journey brought them to the island of the giant miller, followed by the island of black mourners, where everyone was weeping and wailing. (It was on this island that one of Mael Dúin's foster-brothers alighted.) The adventure continued, taking Mael Dúin and his men to the island of the giant blacksmiths, and one on which there was a great fortress that could only be approached by a glass bridge. Many more islands were encountered, including the Island of Women. Just like Bran and his men, Mael Dúin and his company were welcomed and fed by the women. But when they attempted to leave again the queen of the island threw a ball of thread to Mael Dúin; he instinctively caught it and it stuck to his hand. She slowly hauled the boat back towards the shore. This happened three times, and on the fourth attempt Mael Dúin enticed one of his crew to catch the ball. As on the three previous occasions, it stuck to the crewman's hand; however this time the man's hand was cut off and the men were free to leave.

The epic journey continued and they visited many other islands including the Island of Laughter (here another of Mael Dúin's foster-brothers disembarked). They then came to the island of the monk of Torach, who persuaded Mael Dúin to forgive his father's slayers. This he did, and when he returned to the original island he disembarked and made peace with his father's enemies. From here he returned to Ireland.

Both Bran and Mael Dúin journey beyond the ninth wave, the mythic boundary between the visible and invisible worlds, where the pleasures of life are to be had without the loss of either youth or life. They also both voyage to the Island of Women, which is the quintessence of the feminine.

In 'The Voyage of Mael Dúin' each of the islands is characterized by one essential quality, from animals to human attitudes. In Jungian terms one could label these primitive elements 'archetypes'. Jung described these archetypal forces as forming the structural dominants of the psyche: 'They may be compared to the invisible presence of the crystal lattice in a saturated solution.'[10] He further describes archetypes as being in themselves unrepresentable, but making visualization possible by creating archetypal ideas and images. They are forces behind or within the psyche. 'The archetypes are the great decisive forces, they bring about the real events and not our personal reasoning and practical intellect ... the archetypal images decide the fate of man.'[11]

The islands symbolize specific energies that are detached from their usual vehicles in the manifest world, archetypal energies that constitute the subjective life that lies beyond the ninth wave of conscious awareness. Bran and Mael Dúin's voyages symbolize an exploration of and initiation into this vast unknown subjective realm, the collective unconscious. The *Tibetan Book of the Dead* portrays states through which the spirit passes after death in which thoughts and attitudes become solid things, or in Jung's terms archetypal images. Indeed Rees and Rees go so far as to suggest that the voyage stories may well represent the tattered remains of a Celtic equivalent to the *Tibetan Book of the Dead*, and that their function is to teach the 'craft of dying and to pilot the departing spirit on a sea of perils and wonders'.[12]

However I think it is equally valid to see the tales as applying to everyday life as well as to death. They function as models for making the necessary transition in life, from youth to maturity, and finally into old age and death. The mastering of the many tasks that the islands impose may be seen as an initiation into an expanded sense of consciousness, a task that continues throughout one's life, the task that Jung has called individuation.

As in the manifest life, we see that the impetus for the voyages varies from journey to journey. Bran is called by the unknown female, as many males are at or around mid-life, and Mael Dúin is called by the desire for revenge. Whatever the impetus, any renewal requires a symbolic death, or letting go of the familiar, if rebirth is to occur.

The behaviour of the women on the islands, nurturing the mortals and meeting their every need, personifies the life in the womb, and the voyage can be seen as an enactment of the eternal human desire to return to the paradisaical bliss of intra-uterine life. It is likely that these imaginings arise from the biological fact of having lived in another world, and for this reason the womb haunts our psychic life. But we can also think of this desire at a symbolic level as representing the need for a second, psychological birth, to re-enter the cosmic night of the universal mother and embrace a renewed existence. Rebirth demands death, and death begets rebirth. We need to undertake the voyage as part of our individuation and, having experienced some of the forces of the otherworld, or unconscious life, we then need to harness this awareness in the interest of living an increasingly conscious life.

Psychoanalysis is the modern equivalent of voyage tales. It should leave the analysand with a profound sense of awe and mystery about the psyche; yet many people experience the temptation to stay in therapy. This is a shadow side of psychoanalysis, in which a collusion takes place between analyst and patient, and negates the commitment that psychoanalysis has to the pursuit of truth. Others emerge from analysis with a wealth of intellectual insights, words, words and more words that point to the voyage being talked about rather than undertaken.

A voyage undertaken consciously leads to the realization that life and death are not absolute or separate states, but complementary aspects of the eternity of existence itself. This can free us, at least to some extent, of our fantasies of omnipotence and immortality, and facilitate a greater capacity to actually 'be' in the ordinary world.

To enter the otherworld before the appointed hour of death one needs a passport, whether it be acute loss, as in Cormac's case, the invitation of a fairy woman, or simply an intense feeling or traumatic event as in the situation of Mael Dúin. For many people a major disturbance in the *status quo* is the most common passport for the voyage. A marriage break-up, a death, job loss or a major illness can all serve as the beckoning call to voyage beyond the tangible and certain world. Regardless of the initial stimulus, the outcome of a voyage, if undertaken consciously, is the realization of the existence of an otherworld in addition to the manifest one. This other world can tolerate, and indeed thrives on, the existence of opposites, and defies the clarity so passionately sought by the rational mind. Myths act as a sort of trickster who confuses our logical minds in order to give us a glimpse of what lies beyond the material world. Irish mythology is particularly adept at creating this confusion, and evoking the deepest images that lie within us, beyond the edge of conscious thought.

Today's Western world is currently in the grip of a new mythology, 'economic rationalism'. It is clearly a mythology since it is used both to justify and explain a wide variety of phenomena from business, healthcare and welfare through to the environment and warfare. It is a mythology that has the peculiar and perhaps unique quality of not having an otherworld, unless one regards pensions or superannuation as an otherworld! The high priests of money and greed would of course tell us that retirement on a large pension is indeed an otherworld and that we need to strive single-mindedly towards it. Such a world is profane and banally secular, without a sense of mystery and the sacred.

The resurgence of interest in ancient mythology points to a need to address this imbalance. Irish mythology is particularly important at this time since it is so richly imaginative and therefore provides an excellent antidote to the new secular mythology of economic rationalism. Without imagination life is one-dimensional and in due course empty, an emptiness that the economic myth can only attend to by directing us to accumulate more possessions and more wealth. Mythology without an otherworld cannot see beyond the mist, beyond the ninth wave, and is thus blind to the reality in which we actually exist.

9

HEROIC EPICS

The Emergence of Consciousness

Up to now we have concentrated on the Mythological Cycle, the world of gods and goddesses, enchantments, transformations, magic and wizardry. But when we move on to the Ulster Cycle we enter a different world, in which the central characters are aristocratic warriors whose desire is for glory from their heroic deeds, both in this life and after death. For the divine figures of the Mythological Cycle victory in battles, as we have seen, was achieved through magic, whereas for the hero it is achieved through physical prowess and will-power.

The arrival of the Sons of Mil resulted in the banishment of the people of Danu to the world below the surface. This is the point at which the supernatural and the divine are no longer the undisputed masters of the earth, and a new period begins in which mortals and gods cohabit in the earthly realm. Humans have won some of the domain for themselves and with that set up a relationship of rival powers that alternate between hostile and benevolent. This moment symbolizes the birth of the hero, a mortal who embodies the ideal qualities of the race. Whilst there are some similarities between gods and heroes, the hero is clearly in the camp of mortals. The hero is also the protector, a task he carries out sometimes in opposition to the gods and sometimes with their assistance. His function is to mediate between the two worlds, that of mortals and that of gods. As a sort of conduit between the two worlds, he is superhuman but not divine.

Indeed a fundamental concern of Irish mythology is the relationship between men and gods, and the hero is a specific image through which this relationship can be explored. The hero symbolizes the third position that lies between gods and men and he is both mortal and yet sometimes the child of a god. Jesus Christ and Virgil's Aeneas are obvious parallels.

In the secular world we impose a polarity between opposites such as light and dark, day and night, but in nature the world is a continuum. The hero breaks down the notion of opposites. He is a figure that perhaps can be seen as symbolizing an attitude that sees matter and psyche as continuous, not separate. The many journeys that he is depicted as making invariably take him from the known to the unknown and back again. The traveller who is fortunate enough to survive the journey and its perils returns knowing what is enduring in life and what sustains it in an otherwise ego- and time-bound material world. In fact the hero returns with a glimpse, as we saw with 'The Voyage of Mael Dúin', of immortality. 'The glimpse' may well be the point of any heoric journey, whether by a mythic or a human hero. To glimpse immortality, or to momentarily know the truth of the eternal cycle, provides a broad perspective within which one can place the specific events of life. The glimpse of immortality has the effect of reconnecting us to the knowledge of the source and meaning of our being. The self in this sense is a perspective and not a fixed entity. The hero figure personifies the process of acquiring this glimpse and reacquiring it at different stages in life. The fate of the hero is essentially the fate of consciousness itself, and his journeys are the process of seeking, losing, acquiring and reacquiring it. The heroic attitude is the ongoing work of consciousness to be aware that we exist in two worlds simultaneously, the visible and the invisible.

One of the functions of Irish mythology is to provide paradigms that show how we might approach difficult situations in life and bring consciousness to bear upon them. Such archetypal situations as birth, marriage and death are projected on to the mythical level where a model is provided, in story form, for mastering the critical period or transition.

The heroic stories are the symbolic expression of the ego's struggle to separate itself from the vast abyss of the unconscious and the archetypal realm that symbolically we might know as the great mother. One of the tasks of the hero archetypal pattern is to develop the individual consciousness, and in so doing equip oneself to deal with various contingencies that confront us. These confrontations occur throughout life, but we tend to categorize them into patterns that we have come to term 'life stages'. The heroic biography is structured around these identifiable life stages.

The basic heroic story is about how to manage the three major phases of being, that is, birth, life and death, and the various sub-categories that form within this cycle of eternal return. At each stage of our development we experience chaos or disorder as things start to change and fall apart. The function of myth is to provide a model for handling the change and generating the rebirth of meaning and purpose out of chaos or death of change. 'Chaos' is, perhaps, another word for death. At each stage of our development we experience mini-deaths, the moment in time when something has to die, or disintegrate, in order for something to begin. These are the times when we feel chaotic and in a state of profound uncertainty. For example, we experience a death of intra-uterine life when we commence our ordinary life; adolescence and the chaos that it brings is the death of childhood; separation is the death of a particular attachment; and physical death itself of course is the loss of the material life that we have known. Heroic myths depict the process of separation, initiation and return. The hero is initiated at each critical stage as he moves from the chaos and loss into a renewed sense of order and meaning. The figure of the hero shows us how to face both life and death and demonstrates a model for the individuation process itself.

Rees and Rees (in relation to the mythological stories) make the point that 'it is one of the great paradoxes of human life that it derives its deepest meaning from a mythological realm the inhabitants of which conduct themselves in a way that is antithetical to what is normal in everyday behaviour and experience'.[1] The answer to this paradox lies in the similar quality that dreams display. The violations of time and space and the fantastic solutions and adventures that we can have in dreams are familiar to us all. Both myths and dreams are expressed in a symbolic, not literal language. The violation of everyday experiences such as space and time is a necessary narrative device for drawing us away from the concrete and the factual into the feeling, imaginative world of the soul.

In considering the lives of heroes one is immediately struck by the universality of the biographies, the repetition of motifs and themes across many cultures. The Ulster Cycle clearly belongs to the well-established mythological genre of the heroic cycle. There are many overlaps between the heroic figures of the Ulster Cycle and those of other cultures: the odd dragon or monster fight and the liberation of the maiden; an extraordinary birth and childhood; an equally extraordinary death; frequent intervention of the gods, whether malevolent or benevolent. This pattern applies equally well to fairy tales, and several scholars have identified patterns that can be said to characterize the hero. This pattern has been called the International Heroic Biography, and it provides a framework for the elucidation and understanding of the heroic myth from birth through to death.

First J. G. Von Hahn collected stories from the Greek tradition and drew up his 'A Complex of Motifs' in 1876.[2] On the basis of the biographies of fourteen heroes, he identified a pattern he termed the 'Aryan Expulsion and Return Formula'. American scholar Joseph Campbell's more recent work reformulates Von Hahn's original conception with a basic paradigm of separation-initiation and return. It is said that Von Hahn's work was ignored by his contemporaries, with the exception of Alfred Nutt, who in 1881 applied Von Hahn's model to the folk and hero tales of the Celts.[3] In 1909 a disciple of Sigmund Freud, the psychoanalyst Otto Rank, produced a work based on fifteen biographies which included Moses and Christ and which he entitled the 'Myth of the Birth of Hero'. Otto Rank's use of biographies outside the Indo-European area showed that the pattern was not exclusively Aryan, as Von Hahn had implied. Rank tells us:

> The hero is the child of most distinguished parents, usually the son of a king. His origins are preceded by difficulties, such as continence, or prolonged barrenness or secret intercourse of the parents due to external prohibition or obstacle. During or before the pregnancy, there is a prophecy, in the form of an oracle or dream, cautioning against his birth, and usually threatening danger to the father (or his representative). As a rule, he is surrendered to the water, in a box. He is then saved by animals, or by lowly people (shepherds) and is suckled by a female animal or by a humble woman. After he is grown up, he finds his distinguished parents, in a highly versatile fashion. He takes his revenge on his father, on the one hand, and is acknowledged, on the other. Finally he achieves rank and honour.[4]

Here we see the underlying psychoanalytic theme and perhaps even the tailoring of his heroic biography to fit Freud's Oedipal theory.

In 1936 the English scholar Lord Raglan developed a further heroic pattern. He initially studied the Oedipus myth and was struck by the similarity of many of the incidents in that story to the stories of the Greek hero Theseus and the Roman Romulus. To the pattern of twelve traditional Greek heroes he added the biographies of other heroes, including three from the Old Testament – Joseph, Moses and Elijah – and various other figures from Java, Egypt, northern Europe and the Celtic world. The end result was a rather extensive and cumbersome biographical scheme.[5]

Raglan's view is closely tied to ritual, and he asserts that the twenty-two incidents in the hero's life that he established fall neatly into three groups: those concerned with birth, those concerned with accession to the throne and those concerned with death. These correspond to the three principal rites of passage that we have frequently made reference to, birth, life and death.

The next substantial contribution to the heroic biography came from Joseph Campbell in *The Hero With a Thousand Faces* (1949). Campbell's scheme begins virtually where Otto Rank's ends, in that it essentially concerns itself with the second half of life whereas Otto Rank's is concerned with the first half. Campbell's model commences with the hero as a young adult, responding to the call initiating a separation from the known and external world. 'A hero ventures forth from the world of common day into a region of supernatural wonder; fabulous forces are there encountered and a decisive victory is won; the hero comes back from this mysterious adventure with the power to bestow boon on his fellow man.'[6] Thus the formula for Campbell is to do with the rite of passage around separation-initiation-return. He also analyses various sub-themes, such as the refusal to respond to the call in the separation phase, the meeting with the goddess and the father in the initiation stage, and various issues in the return, such as initial refusal and the crossing of the threshold. However despite these details it is a very generalized model and lacks some of the necessary detail that is contained in such models as Raglan's. Death is not part of Campbell's model, and when his hero returns to the ordinary world it is with a changed perspective. Perhaps this changed perspective is the metaphorical death of the ego-based perception of the world. He says of the hero's return that the everyday world the hero left and the 'new world' he now knows as a result of his journey are really one:

> The two worlds, the divine (i.e. new) and the human (i.e. everyday) can be pictured only as distinct from each other – different as life and death, as day and night; nevertheless the two kingdoms are actually one. The values and distinctions that in normal life seem important disappear with the terrifying assimilation of (what is now) the self into what formerly was (to the ego) only otherness.[7]

In short Campbell's hero has had a 'glimpse' and, as for the Irish heroes who travel to the otherworld and manage to return, the visible and invisible are now seen as a continuum, and separateness between the worlds as merely an artefact of the ego. Here in Campbell's model we can already see much that resonates with Irish mythology. The final major contribution is by Jan de Vries, who based his notions on the exploration of fairy-tale heroes but once again found remarkable parallels to myths and heroic legends. De Vries produced his findings in 1959 in his book *Heroic Song and Heroic Legend*. De Vries uses as his basic structure the paradigm of the eternal cycle of life, death and renewal, and sees within the heroic pattern a re-enactment of the primordial acts of the gods as they move from chaos and disorder to life and meaning in a continuing circle.

De Vries identified ten points in the typical hero's life:

1. The begetting of the hero.
2. The birth of the hero.
3. The youth of the hero is threatened.
4. The way in which the hero is brought up.
5. The hero often acquires invulnerability.
6. The fight with a dragon or other monster.
7. The hero wins a maiden, usually after overcoming great dangers.
8. The hero makes an expedition to the underworld.
9. When the hero is banished in his youth he returns later and is victorious over his enemies. In some cases he has to leave the realm again that he has won with such difficulty.
10. The death of the hero.[8]

Whilst De Vries's model has the distinct advantage of parsimony and also allows for flexibility, it is primarily based on warrior heroes and unlike Raglan's model does not include the king figure. Within the Irish tradition the hero can be a seer, a warrior, a king or a saint. But De Vries does specifically include journeys to the underworld, a central theme in Irish heroic myth. Within his broad framework De Vries does give various sub-categories; for example in '1. The begetting of the hero' he includes:

(i) Mother is a virgin who in some cases is overpowered by a god or who has extramarital relations with the hero's father.
(ii) The father is a god.
(iii) The father is an animal, often a disguised figure of a god.
(iv) The child is conceived in incestuous relationships.

Within category 3 he includes various sub-categories for how the life of the child is threatened and sustained.

(i) Exposure: the child is placed in a dangerous situation.
(ii) The exposed child is fed by animals.
(iii) The child is reared by shepherds.
(iv) The child is reared by mythical figures.[9]

The various heroic biographical models have many aspects in common and confirm that whilst the hero is not a god he is clearly a superhuman being who from his very beginning belongs to both worlds, the divine and the human. Insufficient emphasis, I believe, is placed in the International Heroic Biography on the symbolic process of dying itself, and the preparation for death, of which a journey to the otherworld symbolizes the beginning. Much emphasis is placed on the literal death as a static and final stage. This approach diminishes the importance of this dynamic third phase of the eternal cycle. I have compiled a simplified version of these models, drawing most heavily upon De Vries but finding inspiration in Campbell's psychological model.

1. Conception and birth.
2. Youth and education.
3. Transition from boyhood to manhood.
4. Wooing of a maiden.
5. Voyage to the otherworld.
6. Return from the otherworld.
7. Death.

This model is not intended to provide some comprehensive methodology, nor is it meant to be some form of Procrustean bed into which one fits the data, but should be used to aid our reflection and analysis of Irish myths, give us a lens through which we can see some of the material without sacrificing its complexity and ambiguity.

You will recall that, whereas dreams are the myth of the individual, myths are the dreams of the people, derived from our collective history as a race. And just as the outer context is a vital factor in elucidating the meaning of any individual's dream, so is the societal context of myths important in elucidating the meaning of the myths. Myths and heroic biographies do not evolve in isolation; there can be no doubt that heroic epics bear some relation to actual historical events. Such events have made a significant impact, and it is as if they have been lifted out of the course of history and given a lasting glory in the heroic epic. This is not to suggest that the heroic myths are mere history, but rather to indicate that the myths emerge within a context.

We know only too well how a dream mutates and distorts outer events, using them as building blocks, so that the dream involves some sort of personal invention that takes the actual events of life and alters them to construct a dream narrative in accordance with our inner needs and feelings. Presumably the historical events that surround myths experience the same process, and the story we finish up with is one in which the themes attend to feelings and psychological issues built in part on actual historical events.

So what do we know of the society to which the Ulster Cycle is connected? The Ulster Cycle is assigned by learned tradition to the period of history around the birth of Christ, and the stories primarily concern the Ulaid, the dominant people in Ulster. The social and political conditions depicted in the Ulster Cycle confirm again and again the accounts of the Celts given by the classical writers of Rome and Greece. Pre-Christian Ireland was a society based on monarchy, and the King (Rí) reigned over his people (*tuath*) as a judge and a leader in war, but he was not a law giver. Laws were adopted by the people in assembly, with only free men having franchise. The hierarchy was based partly on nobility, partly on learning and partly on wealth.

Celtic society is often represented as consisting of nobles (*flaith*) and churls (*aithech*), although a more general classification divides societies into *soer* (free people) and *doer* (unfree), the latter class including people who rented cattle from members of the wealthy class (free men). The unfree also included slaves (*mug* or *cumal*) and household servants (*gilla* or *inailt*). As a predominantly pastoral society, the chief source of wealth was cattle and swine. Some suggest that the basic unit of value was one cow. Female slaves (*cumal*), as we saw in the story of Étaín, were valued in terms of cows. It is therefore not surprising that the most significant story of the Ulster Cycle, the 'Táin Bó Cuailgne', has as its central theme a cattle raid.

Ireland was divided into five provinces: Ulster in the north-east, named after the Ulaid, Leinster (south-east), Connacht (west), Munster (south-west) and Mide (the middle one). In the ancient tales Ulster (Ulaid) has a proud and antagonistic attitude to the rest of Ireland, though her special enemy is Connacht. The Ulster capital was located at Emain Macha, which is near present-day Armagh and which has been identified as Navan Fort by archaeological research. Here the powerful King Conchobhar ruled, surrounded by a band of chosen warriors known as the Red Branch. Connacht was ruled by the legendary Queen Medb and her husband King Ailill. The ancient capital of Connacht was Rath Cruachan.

The kings and greater nobles dwelt in fortified enclosures (*dun* or *raith*) of earthworks within which there were a number of timber dwellings. The typical establishment of a chieftain consisted of a barn-like structure; in some instances it appears to have been circular, with a fire at the centre and a hole in the roof for the smoke to escape. Perhaps Midir flew out of this hole with Étaín. The hall and adjacent structures were surrounded by moats and earth mounds. The warriors were armed with shields, swords, spears and sometimes javelins, with the greater heroes or warriors travelling in chariots. Victory in battle was completed by bringing home the heads of slain enemies and the challenge of single combat was a prominent feature. Absolutely central to the heroic life as a warrior was the pursuit of fame and the avoidance of blame and shame. The hero/warrior did not pursue this fame for personal reasons but because he was the protector of his tribe and he fought, not for personal honour but for the honour of his tribe. If he failed his entire tribe were dragged into dishonour. The pursuit of fame was a duty towards both ancestors and descendants. Many a modern-day hero is narcissistically based, and hence usually short-lived, whereas the Ulster hero was immortalized in poetry and song. Poets conferred honour and dishonour in their satirical verses, and hence they had a powerful place in the king's court. We have already seen the power of such song in relation to the Fomorian King Bres, who had to forsake his kingdom because he was made imperfect by a poet's satire.

Another powerful influence on conduct was the *geis*, the curse or prohibition. The more eminent a person was, the more *geasa* he had. For example an individual may be forbidden to allow warriors to trespass on their territory without barring their way before morning. The king therefore had many *geasa*, both to limit and govern his behaviour. The great Ulster hero Cú Chulainn has a whole series of *geasa*, the transgression of which eventually brings about his death.

The qualities we will see revealed in the Ulster Cycle are violent assertiveness, invincible energy and great powers of resistance, with the issues of honour and loyalty being central. Again and again the hero is confronted with a choice between evil and duty, with duty being the governing principle and death being valued if it brought fame. All the tales possess the Irish richness of imagination and are in prose form except for expressions of strong emotion, which are in verse. The conflict of loyalty so dear to epic literature is for ever present and forms the basis of many tales.

THE ULSTER CYCLE

The Hero, the Ego and the Shadow

King Conchobhar and his royal court at Emain Macha were the focal point of a society of heroes, of whom the most famous was Cú Chulainn, the Irish Achilles. Other prominent members of this heroic company were the druid Cathbad, who sometimes even took precedence over the King, and Bricriu the Poisoned Tongue, who was an inveterate mischief-maker. The tribal warfare that is such a persistent theme in the Ulster Cycle is, as already mentioned, between the Ulstermen and the Connachtmen under their legendary Queen Medb.

'The Cattle Raid of Cooley' is the central epic, in which the object of Queen Medb's drive against Ulster is to seize possession of the great bull of Cooley, which no doubt is far more than a literal bull and is most likely originally of divine origin, having undergone many metamorphoses prior to its central role in the Táin. However 'The Cattle Raid of Cooley', generally known as the Táin, is only one amongst numerous tales of the Ulster Cycle. A number of these are known as foretales (*remscelá*), and in one sense or another are prefatory to the central saga of the Táin. In the main these foretales cover the birth, youth and adventures of Cú Chulainn. Other tales are less directly connected to the central epic, but 'The Feast of Bricriu', for example, provides us with a rich description of the hero's social life and the communal gatherings at which feasting and various competitions took place. Two tales of particular interest are 'The Destruction of Da Derga's Hostel' ('Toghail Bruidhne Da Derga') and 'The Exile of the Sons of Úisnech' ('Longes Mac nUusnig') or as it is more commonly known the story of Derdriu.

The Destruction of Da Derga's Hostel

In mythology, because the stories are told and retold over such a long period of time, there are often several versions of a figure's life. This is certainly true of King Conaire Mór, a descendant of Étaín who is the main figure in this story. One version appears to have the daughter of Étaín, who is also named Étaín, married to Cormac, King of Ulster, to whom she bears only one daughter and no son. The embittered king banishes Étaín and orders that her infant daughter be thrown into a pit. As in 'The Wooing of Étaín', the servants are unable to carry out their task and instead carry her to a herdsman of King Eterscél. Thereafter she bears the name Mes Buachalla, which means 'the herdsman's fosterling'. In another version, after Étaín's mortal husband dies she marries King Cormac of Ulster, who abandons her because she is barren, apart from one daughter she had previously given birth to through magical means. (This came about after her mother, the original goddess Étaín, made a special porridge for her to eat. She had said to her mother, 'A wrong you have done me, for it is a daughter I will bear.' 'No matter that,' her mother replied, 'for a king will seek the girl.')[1] King Cormac decided to take Étaín back on condition that the daughter be killed as he did not want the mother to rear her. Again the servants are unable to throw the infant into the pit and take it to the cattleshed of a herdsman of Eterscél.

The herdsman fostered the child in secrecy, for fear of discovery, and made her a house that had no door, only a window and a roof opening. The girl blossomed into a beautiful young woman and a very gifted embroiderer. It was said that there was not in Erin (Ireland) a king's daughter fairer than her. However some of King Eterscél's people became suspicious of this strange cottage and noticed the herdsman taking food into it. Finally one man looked through the skylight and saw a most beautiful young woman inside. This news was conveyed to the King, who recalled the druidic prophecy that a woman of unknown race would bear him a son, and he ordered that the woman be brought to him. But that night Mes Buachalla was startled by the appearance of a bird in the opening of her roof. The bird descended into the cottage and then magically laid aside his birdskin to reveal himself as a handsome youth who made love with her and said, 'The King's people are coming to destroy this house and take you by force to him. But you will be with child by me and will bear a son: his name will be Conaire and he is not to kill birds.'

Then Mes Buachalla was brought to the King, who married her. She duly bore a son, whom she named Conaire in accordance with the directions of the bird/god who had impregnated her. So Conaire was brought up the son of King Eterscél. Consistent with traditions of the time he was fostered out, and as a king's son he was sent to three households, along with three foster-brothers, all sons of the warrior champion Donn Désa. Conaire possessed three special gifts, hearing, foresight and judgement, and he taught one of each of these gifts to each of his three foster-brothers. A close bond existed between the four boys.

Then King Eterscél died. It was not automatic that the eldest or only son succeed the king to the throne. In order to ascertain who the successor should be a solemn divination ritual was held, which in English was called the 'bull feast' (*tarbfheis*). A bull would be killed and one man would be designated to eat his fill and drink the broth made from the blood. He would then fall alseep and an incantation was chanted over him. In his sleep he would see the person who would become king; were the sleeper to tell a lie about what he had seen and be found out in his lie, he would be immediately killed. The 'bull feaster' on this occasion had seen a naked man coming along the road to Tara at daybreak, carrying a stone in his sling.

On his way to the bull feast, Conaire saw three huge white speckled birds. He pursued them in his chariot, but could never quite reach them, the birds always allowing him to get within a spear's length then flying off again. Finally the chase ended at the seashore, and Conaire alighted from his chariot and took out his catapult to cast a stone at the birds. At this instant the birds were transformed into armed warriors who threatened to attack Conaire. However one bird/man stepped forward and offered Conaire protection, saying to him, 'I am Nemglan, King of your father's birds, and for this reason you are forbidden to cast stones at birds, for by reason of birth every bird here is natural to you.' Nemglan told Conaire that rather than threaten to kill his kin it would be more fitting if he went to Tara that night, for there was a bull feast on and through it he would be made King. He instructed Conaire to approach Tara naked and with a sling, conforming to the *tarbfheis* vision.

Conaire followed Nemglan's instructions, and as he approached Tara three kings were waiting for him; they clothed him, placed him in a chariot and took him to Tara. However his proclamation as King was resisted by the people of Tara, who declared that the incantation of true spirit had been betrayed because what had arrived was a beardless youth not old enough to be King. Conaire replied, 'No matter that, a young generous king is no blemish and I am not corrupt.' The people then conferred kingship upon him and he declared, 'I will enquire of wise men that I myself may be wise.' These things he had been advised to say by the bird man, who had foretold that his reign would be honoured but that there would be *geasa* to act as restraints upon his rulership.

The *geasa* placed upon Conaire were:

1. Thou shalt not go right-hand-wise round Tara and left-hand-wise round Brega (Brega was a great plain lying to the east of Tara between the Boyne and the Liffey Rivers).
2. The crooked beasts of Cerna must not be hunted by thee.
3. Thou shalt not be away from Tara for nine nights in succession.
4. Thou shalt not stay a night in a house from which firelight can be seen after sunset and into which one can see from the outside.
5. Three Reds shall not go before thee to the House of Red.
6. No plunder shall be taken in thy reign.
7. After sunset a company of one woman or one man shall not enter the house in which thou art.
8. Thou shalt not settle the quarrel of two of thy serfs.[2]

All remained well for Conaire and his subjects, except that his foster-brothers, who had now lost certain prerogatives, had resorted instead to robbery, plunder and murder. Every year they stole a pig, a calf and a cow from the same farmer to see what punishment their foster-brother would mete out. Each year the farmer went to the King to complain, but each year King Conaire refused to intervene and merely told the farmer that he should speak to the brothers directly. Conaire thus violated one of his *geasa*, that is, 'No plunder shall be taken in thy reign.' Finally the foster-brothers' greed and destructiveness went too far and the people brought them and their marauding companions before the King, insisting that he punish them. Conaire was torn between duty and loyalty. This is the dilemma that the hero figure, whether king or warrior, has to face over and over again. Conaire reneged on his duty and ordered that the three foster-brothers be spared but their companions be executed by their own fathers. But no sooner had he made this judgement than he revoked it, declaring, 'No lengthening of my life [have I gained by] the judgement I have given,' thereby recognizing that he had violated one of his *geasa* by allowing the plundering to continue in the first place and another by not punishing his foster-brothers. Instead he decreed that they and their companions be banished to both Scotland and Britain, where they could continue to carry out their plundering. In due course the marauders returned to Ireland to kill Conaire. By breaking the taboo, Conaire destroyed the respect the otherworld personages had for him in their delegation of sovereignty to him. In failing to punish his foster-brothers and in delivering a false judgement he violated the cosmic order with which he had been entrusted. Consequently the otherworld changed dramatically from a benevolent force to a malevolent one and as a result Conaire was drawn into violating all of his *geasa*.

In Jungian mythology, turning one's back on the self leads to a self-destructive life. To recognize and respond in accordance with the self is to find direction from the true centre of our being, not the periphery. In the centre we experience the vital heroic mediation between gods and our personal self, and the cosmic order is not violated. The pursuit of personal power for its own sake is one modern example of a violation of a *geis* aimed at protecting the well-being of the community. It is a *geis* upon us all as members of a civilized society to concern ourselves with the well-being of each other, regardless of race, creed or circumstances, and not to be solely preoccupied with our own well-being.

The reign of Conaire was for a long time characterized by prosperity and peace. But shortly after the foolish judgement on his foster-brothers Conaire was called to intervene in a quarrel between two of his serfs in Munster, lured by the machinations of the Tuatha Dé Danann to break another of his *geasa*. Conaire made peace between the serfs, and in so doing he violated yet another of his *geasa*, for he had stayed five nights with each man, violating the taboo against spending more than nine successive nights away from Tara. One can now sense the inevitable movement towards tragedy and death that is instigated by the breaking of the first *geis*, aimed at protecting the community from plundering. It is as if the *geasa* serve to assert the primacy of the otherworld, or unconscious life over the ego-driven demands for power.

On his return to Tara Conaire's way was blocked by an outbreak of fire and tribal warfare. In order to avoid the conflict he had to turn north-east, and thereby broke another *geis* by going clockwise around Tara and anticlockwise around Brega. At the same time he also engaged in a hunt, only to discover that the animals being hunted were the wild beasts of Cerna. The malevolent intervention of the gods was now apparent, since the fire around Tara was an illusion made by the folk of the otherworld who were now bringing Conaire to his doom.

By this time Conaire was exhausted, and he remembered that he had a friend in the Leinster area, Lord Da Derga. Mac Cécht, his champion warrior, offered to go ahead and arrange the hospitality and light a fire for his king. Conaire agreed and continued his journey alone, and after some time he saw ahead of him three strange horsemen dressed in red tunics and carrying red shields and spears. Even their horses were red. Conaire, for once, but inevitably too late, remembered his *geis* concerning not letting 'three Reds go before him to the House of Red'. Da Derga means Red House, since '*derg*' is a version of the Irish word for 'red'. Anxious to prevent them from arriving before him, Conaire sent his son to intervene, but no matter now fast and hard the son rode the three warriors could not be reached and stayed 'a spear-cast ahead'. The son returned to Conaire with the news that he could not overtake them, and Conaire ordered him to try again and to offer great rewards if they would fall behind the King's company. This happened three times, until finally the men shouted at Conaire's son:

Lo my son, great news. Weary are the steeds we ride, the steeds from Donn Desscorach from the Síd. Though we are alive we are dead. Great will be the cutting off of lives. Sating of ravens. Feeding of crows. Strife of slaughter. Whetting of sword-edge. Shields with broken bosses in the hours after sundown.[3]

They then rode on and alighted at Da Derga's hostel ahead of King Conaire, thereby violating yet another of his *geasa*. Conaire, despairing now yet showing a rare moment of insight, declares, 'All my geasa have overtaken me tonight, and that because of the banishment of my foster-brothers.' In fact not all his *geasa* had overtaken him but they were soon to do so. As the King's party arrived at Da Derga's hostel a solitary woman came to the door after sunset and sought admission. 'As long as a weaver's beam and as black, her two shins. She wore a very fleecy striped mantle. Her beard [some say pubic hair] reached her knees and her mouth was on one side of her head.'[4] Leaning against the doorpost, she cast an evil eye over the King and his retinue, and made the prophecy that neither his skin nor his flesh would escape from the hostel that night other than that which the birds carry away in their claws. 'Who are you and what is your name?' enquired Conaire, to which the woman replied, 'Cailb,' but went on to list her many other names. Essentially she was the death and destruction aspect of the Morrígan, the goddess of war, fertility and death. 'What do you want then?' further enquired Conaire, to which Cailb answered, 'Whatever pleases you.' Conaire told her there was a *geis* against admitting a single woman after sunset, but she replied, '*Geis* or not, I will not go until I have had hospitality from this house tonight.' Again Conaire tried to dissuade her from staying by offering her gifts. But she reproached the King for his lack of hospitality, which we know was of utmost importance. Again torn between the opposing demands of his kingly obligations and his personal *geis*, Conaire agreed to let her in and with that a great fear and sense of foreboding fell upon the gathering. The goddess of death had entered the hostel.

Meanwhile Conaire's three exiled foster-brothers, the sons of Donn Désa, along with Ingcél, a British plunderer and marauder, had returned to raid Ireland. As their boats struck land the hostel shook and there was a loud noise. Conaire, asked to explain the noise, said that it might be the sons of Donn Désa landing. At the same time one of Conaire's foster-brothers said, of Conaire: 'His rule was good. Hence, good will and prosperity marked his reign. May God not bring that man here tonight . . . it is grievous that his life be short.'

The raiding party crossed the marshlands and Ingcél went ahead to the hostel to ascertain who was actually at the gathering. The hostel was so constructed that the River Dodder flowed through it, and there were seven doorways but only one door, which was placed at whichever doorway the wind was blowing towards. Ingcél could see a great fire, and the fact that he had observed a fire from the outside violated yet another of Conaire's *geasa*. When Ingcél related all the details, the sons of Donn Désa identified each figure and, perhaps in an endeavour to dissuade him from attacking the hostel, they related the various heroic details and triumphs of each figure he described. Each of these figures occupied a separate room; in one room was Mac Cécht, Conaire's champion; in another Conaire himself; in another were three giants who were said to have killed three hundred warriors each at the first encounter; in other rooms Ingcél observed three champions from the fairy mounds; and finally he saw the room of Da Derga himself. In this room there was a magical cauldron that was never taken from the fire and which was never empty of food. These descriptions serve to establish that this was no ordinary hostel, but rather an otherworld abode. At each description given by the foster-brothers Lomna the jester exclaimed, 'Alas for him who wreaks the slaughter. If my advice might prevail, the slaughter would not be attempted.' But on each occasion, no matter how terrifying the description of any one inhabitant's prowess, Ingcél merely asserted, 'You do not prevail.' Finally he called upon his raiders to rise up and attack the hostel.

Three times the hostel was set on fire by the raiders, and three times it was extinguished. It is said that six hundred fell before Conaire could even reach for his weapons, such was the prowess of his warrior companions. Once Conaire had acquired his weapons he slaughtered another six hundred, and as a result the raiders were routed. In desperation they turned to their druid, who brought an exhausting thirst upon Conaire. But all the water and drinkable liquids had been used in fighting the fire, and his cupbearers could find no water for him, even in the River Dodder. He pleaded with Mac Cécht to get him a drink, but Mac Cécht declined, stating that his role was to guard Conaire at all times. Finally upon the third request Mac Cécht conceded and he left the hostel with Conaire's gilt cup under his arm, a cup large enough for an ox to boil in.

Mac Cécht searched the rivers and lakes of Ireland, but there was a spell upon them so that they could hide their water. Finally at a lough in Roscommon, which he was able to reach before it could hide itself from him, he managed to fill Conaire's cup.

It was the next morning before he returned to the hostel, and in the mean time the marauders had returned and routed Conaire's retinue. As Mac Cécht approached the hostel he saw two men beheading Conaire. He immediately attacked and killed one of them, and the other ran off with the head of Conaire under his arm. But Mac Cécht hurled a huge stone pillar after him, killing him instantly. He then poured the water into the severed head of Conaire, which said, 'Mac Cécht is a good man. Mac Cécht is a brave man, he gives a drink to the King, he does the work of a warrior.'

Mac Cécht then went in vigorous pursuit of the enemy, and it is said that only nine men fell with Conaire, whereas only five raiders out of five thousand escaped. Mac Cécht buried his king at Tara, and thus this heroic and tragic doom-laden story comes to an end.

Several aspects of this story seem worthy of further comment. First we see that King Conaire Mór's conception conforms to the heroic biographical pattern, since his father is of the otherworld, and his maternal line also links him back to the otherworld. Indeed the presence of the otherworld is a consistent theme throughout the story, and its influence is central to the function of kingship. This reiterates the role of the hero as a mediator between the worlds; the well-being of the kingdom is dependent upon the relationship that the mortal king/

hero maintains with the otherworld. Within this context one can see that a function of a *geis* is to remind the hero of the permanent presence of the otherworld and the need for him to honour it.

This is no more clearly seen than in Conaire's violation of his various *geasa*, which brings about his untimely death, since he was still a young king. His fate was brought about, not by his successive and sometimes unwitting violations of his *geasa* but really by the substantial act of injustice in condemning to death the marauding companions of his foster-brothers and then the sparing of them. He has betrayed truth, wisdom and judicious rule, all of which constitute the cosmic notion of truth located in him as King and protector of the tribe. From this moment on his fate is inevitable, as the otherworld personages intervene at critical moments in his life. Such interventions are characteristic of heroic biography.

Not only do the persons of the otherworld intervene, so also is the place, Da Derga's hostel, a location of the otherworld.

The word '*bruiden*' ('hostel') means 'a spacious hall, especially a banquet hall; and as the otherworld was conceived as a place of perpetual feasting, *bruiden* was applied in particular to the festive hall in the *síd* over which the god of the otherworld presided'.[5] So the hostel is a kind of magic place, and often associated with death, as is clearly so in Conaire Mór's situation. To enter such a place is to face one's death, as prophesied by the loathsome hag, or goddess of death, who challenged Conaire to break his prohibition. The personages that are seen there include several otherworld figures in addition to Da Derga, and the inexhaustible cauldron in his room suggests the presence of Goibniu, the god of the otherworld feast. However this *bruiden* depicts far more the dark kingdom of the dead than the everlasting kingdom of perpetual feasting; it is a place of destiny from which there is no escape.

The threefold nature of Conaire Mór's death also relates to the heroic biography, in so far as it is an extraordinary threefold death: death by fire (since the hostel is burnt three times), death by water (since it is argued that the pouring of water by Mac Cécht down the throat and torso of Conaire is a form of drowning) and finally death by wounding (he is beheaded). Several scholars have noted that Irish stories often portray death as a threefold process, death by iron, fire and water. This threefold death is also predicted in this story by the appearance of the three red horsemen.

One might consider triplication as referring to a triplication of a single person. So we could consider Conaire Mór's three foster-brothers as simply three aspects of himself, especially since he gives each of them one of his three special gifts. Indeed, in the more detailed text of the story the three foster-brothers and Conaire Mór are often described as wearing identical clothing and having identical weapons and horses. Within the mythology of Jungian psychology we could consider the three foster-brothers as shadow aspects of Conaire himself. These aspects bring about his death, since he cannot face dealing with them and instead banishes them. Jungian psychology says that the shadow aspects of our psyche need to be confronted and accepted, and banishing them from conscious awareness simply means that we will act them out unconsciously, just as we see King Conaire did. Repressing the shadow merely relocates it in the unconscious mind, the otherworld of our psyche, which then becomes destructive. If we do not accept the darker aspects of our being then some form of disintegration is inevitable. We will be fatefully driven to break our own taboos, dooming ourselves to some pattern of destructiveness.

The story of Conaire Mór is the story of an unsuccessful hero, an outcome that is not uncommon in Irish mythology. But the unsuccessful outcome allows us to see that the heroic pattern of striving for consciousness is frustrated by our inability or unwillingness to confront our destructive, marauding feelings. No matter how benevolent we may be, no matter how good and noble we are in our outer life, the negative, shadow aspects of ourselves must be acknowledged and accepted if fertile relations are to be maintained with the otherworld that we nowadays call the unconscious. Death is one way of thinking of the loss of consciousness, of the failure of a hero to maintain mediation between the worlds. Consciousness requires vigilance if it is to be maintained. This vigilance demands a respectful relationship with the gods within, otherwise we face disconnection between head and heart, or thought and feeling. This disconnection is symbolized in the beheading of Conaire Mór.

The Exile of the Sons of Uisnech

Two stories that were discussed earlier, 'The Children of Lir' and 'The Sons of Tuireann', are known as two of the three great tragedies of Irish story-telling.

The third great tragedy is 'The Exile of the Sons of Uisnech', ('Longes mac nUsnig'), better known by the name of its central figure, Derdriu

(Deirdre in English), since in a way the longer title does not really capture the main theme of the story.

The story of Derdriu is remarkable, not only because it is a tragic love story, but also because it forms the basis of later romantic stories found in Arthurian legends. It is essentially a story of treachery, honour and romance and the love-triangle jealousy of a beautiful young woman, an ageing king and vigorous, handsome young lover. The mythic subtext of this tale, as for many Irish stories, is seasonal, to do with death and renewal, but it also incorporates a societal plot of power and territory.

The language of the story, as recorded in the twelfth-century *Book of Leinster*, points to its origin in the Ulster period, around the time of the birth of Christ. This is one of the few stories that has been preserved by folk culture right down to our modern time. The earliest written version was composed around the eighth or ninth century, based on the earliest oral tradition, but there are also versions as recent as the beginning of the last century, when it informs several Anglo-Irish dramas, notably J. M. Synge's play *Deirdre of the Sorrows* (1910). There is also a play by the Irish mystic A. E. (the pseudonym of George Russell), and one by W. B. Yeats entitled *Deirdre*, which he completed in 1907. Lady Gregory, Yeats's friend and patron, produced her own version of the story in 1902 which is contained in her collection of Irish tales.[6] Finally the poet and novelist James Stephens created his version of Deirdre in 1923. Thus in its written form the story has been created and recreated for over twelve centuries.

Derdriu finds her parallel in a combination of the Greek figures of Cassandra and Helen of Troy. She is fated from birth to bring great misfortune upon others, and her prophecies are never believed. Though not as well known as her Greek counterparts, Derdriu ranks as one of the great tragic heroines of literature. Jeffrey Gantz, upon whose translation I will mainly draw, describes the story as 'the most stunning tale ever written in Irish'.[7] His translation is of the earliest surviving manuscript, *The Book of Leinster*, and I shall also draw on another translation of the same manuscript by Thomas Kinsella, whose translation of the epic story the Táin is regarded as being most distinguished.[8] The story of Derdriu appears in the Táin because it constitutes a 'foretale' to the main story of 'The Cattle Raid of Cooley'.

As one of the central characters in the story is the King of Ulster, Conchobhar Mac Nessa, it may be helpful to spend a little time focusing on his biography, since it demonstrates how this story is part of the orthodox heroic biography. Conchobhar himself is a composite figure of a heroic king/warrior. There are three separate stories of Conchobhar's conception, reflecting the effect of time and social change on the myth itself. His name however is constant; interestingly it is derived from his mother's name: he is the son (Mac) of his mother, Ness, not his father. Whilst the name of his father changes in the three stories of his birth, the mother, symbolizing his relationship to the sovereign queen, remains constant. It underlines yet again that the power behind the throne, so to speak, was a woman, the goddess, with whom union had to occur if rulership was to be confirmed and the land was to remain fertile.

One story simply has the High King of Ireland, Fachtna Fáthach, as the father of Conchobhar, legitimizing his ascension to the throne through biological means, and the druid Cathbad was Conchobhar's foster-father. In the second version, Ness's twelve foster-fathers were all slain by Cathbad as they drank together one night. The identity of the killer was not known at the time and Ness, utterly outraged, traversed the country in blind fury, seeking vengeance and plundering as she went. One day Ness was bathing in a lake when she was seized by Cathbad, who made her swear to become his wife. This account says that Conchobhar was the offspring of this union.

It is the third version, which continues from the second and elaborates it, which gives an indication of Conchobhar as a true mythic hero. This story picks up from the point of Cathbad seizing Ness and her agreement to become his wife. They decided to return to Ulster and the house of King Eochu; during the night a great thirst overcame both of them, and Cathbad fetched some water from the river, straining it through Ness's veil. In the mean time a light had been lit and its rays shone on the cup, revealing in it two worms. Cathbad compelled his wife to drink from the cup, whereby she became pregnant.

As the time for the birth arrived, Ness experienced great birth pangs but Cathbad told her that if she could just delay the birth until nightfall the child would become a great king, the most renowned in Ireland, because a glorious child, Jesus, would be born the same night in the east of the world. Here we see the hand of the Christian scribes, but also perhaps the linking of the birth of a king, the motif of renewal, to the winter solstice, the point when the sun begins to rise up in the sky from its lowest ebb. Ness did hold out, and the child was born by a river, with a worm in each of its fists. At the moment of birth the infant fell into the river and was rescued by Cathbad, who named him Conchobhar, after the river itself.

This third story accords with the heroic biography, since the conception and birth have a mysterious, magical quality. The worm is often associated with death, yet also with fertility and life, and is usually found in the earth, the womb of the mother goddess, though in this story it is in the water, the water of life. The great thirst that overcomes Cathbad and Ness is like a personal version of the drought and pestilence that often occur as an old king is dying and a new one about to emerge. It may also be seen as the absence of feelings, as water is a typical symbol of the feeling realm.

The three stories of the birth further suggest a triple birth, which is not uncharacteristic of the birth of mythical heroes (Cú Chulainn has three births). There is also the prediction of an auspicious time and the delivery happening in a remote place, in Conchobhar's case the bank of a river, in Christ's case a manger in a stable. The three births establish that the hero is both of this world, son of the High King of Ireland, and of the otherworld, conceived by means of the worms.

We know very little about Conchobhar's early childhood and his biography really only comes alive when he acquired the kingship of Ulster. The reigning King at the time, Fergus Mac Róich, wanted Ness as his wife; she agreed on condition that her son held the kingship for one year. Fergus agreed to this condition, but during the year in which Conchobhar was the King the province prospered enormously, and Ness advised her son to seek the support of the nobles so that he could stay on as King. The strategy worked well, and at the end of the year the nobles decided to retain Conchobhar as their King. The new king ordered Fergus to be banished, resulting in a civil war. Peace was eventually restored, on the understanding that Conchobhar should remain King and that Fergus Mac Róich should become a high official of the province, responsible for feasts and official functions and at times in a semi-judicial role. Conchobhar was a good and able administrator and the crops grew luxuriously, the cattle fattened readily and the rivers and lakes gave plentiful supplies of fish. His role was sanctioned by the sovereign queen, who in this situation we take to be Ness, his mother. He is also said to have been the first consort of Queen Medb, before she reigned as Queen of Connacht, which further points to the involvement of the sovereign queen in Conchobhar's successful reign.

The story of Derdriu commences with King Conchobhar attending a feast in the house of his harpist and story-teller Fedlimid mac Daill. Fedlimid's wife oversaw the festivities, moving amongst the guests throughout the night until finally they were all full of drink and food and began to fall asleep. Fedlimid's wife was relieved that her hostess duties were coming to an end, because she was heavily pregnant. As she walked to her chambers, the baby in the womb suddenly let out an ear-piercing shriek so loud that everyone was woken, and the warriors all grabbed their weapons and rushed to the main hall. Nobody could ascertain the source of the scream, until Fedlimid found his wife, who told him the source of the shriek. The assembled group demanded that Fedlimid bring his wife before them, although she had no idea why the unborn infant had screamed. Anxiously she turned to her druid and seer, Cathbad, and asked him to explain this strange happening.

> 'Fair-faced Cathbad, hear me,
> Prince, pure, precious crown,
> Grown huge in druid spells.
> I can't find the fair words
> That should shed the light of knowledge
> For my husband Fedlimid,
> Even though it was the hollow
> Of my own womb that howled.
> No woman knows what her womb bears.'[9]

Cathbad replied:

> 'There howled in your troubled womb
> A tall, lovely, long-haired woman.
> Heroes will contend for her,
> High kings beseech on her account;
> Then, west of Conchobhar's kingdom
> A heavy harvest of fighting men.
> High queens will ache with envy
> To see those lips of Parthian-red
> Opening on her pearly teeth,
> And see her pure perfect body.'[10]

Then Cathbad placed his hand on Fedlimid's wife's stomach and declared, 'Indeed it is a girl and her name will be Derdriu and there will be trouble on her account.'

Shortly after, Fedlimid's wife gave birth to a baby girl and Cathbad took the infant in his arms:

> 'Though you may have fame and beauty,
> Deirdre, you will destroy much;
> Ulaid will suffer on your account,
> Fair daughter of Fedlimid.
>
> And after that there will still be more deaths
> Because of you, woman like a flame.
> In your lifetime – hear this –
> The three sons of Uisliu will be exiled.
>
> In your lifetime a violent deed
> Will be done at Emhain;
> Repented thereafter will be the treachery
> That violated the guarantee of mighty Ferghus.
>
> Because of you, woman of fate,
> Ferghus will be exiled from Ulaid
> And a deed that will cause much weeping,
> Conchobhar's son Fiachna will be slain.
>
> Because of you, woman of fate,
> Gerrce son of Illadán will be slain,
> And – a crime no less awful –
> Eogan son of Durthacht will be destroyed.
>
> You will do a frightful fierce deed
> Out of anger at Ulaid's high king;
> Your grave will be everywhere –
> Yours will be a famous tale, Derdriu.'[11]

Hearing this prophecy of doom, the Ulster warriors rose up as one and demanded that the infant girl be immediately put to death. But King Conchobhar overruled his warriors and declared that he would take the infant into his keeping, foster her out to a trustworthy foster-parent who would rear her in isolation to prevent any possibility of the prophecy becoming true, and then, when she was of a suitable age, he would take her as his wife.

So Derdriu was reared in isolation and only had contact with her foster-parents and a woman named Lebarcham, Conchobhar's satirist and poetess. She was a very powerful woman, and she became Derdriu's constant companion and confidante. Under her guidance Derdriu grew into a most beautiful young woman, skilled in many things, especially the arts of divination and prophecy. One winter's day when her foster-father was skinning a calf, Derdriu watched as the blood flowed on to the snow and a raven swooped down and sipped the blood. She turned to Lebarcham and said, 'I could desire a man who had those three colours, black hair like the raven, red cheeks like blood and a white body like snow.' Lebarcham replied, 'The luck and good fortune are with you, for such a man is not far away; he is Naoise, one of the three sons of Uisnech.'[12] Lebarcham told Derdriu how the three sons of Uisnech were all known for their outstanding courage as warriors and for their fine singing, which was said to be so melodious that women and men were lulled by it and cows would increase their milk by two-thirds if they heard it. Ardán and Ainnle were the other two sons, but Lebarcham assured Derdriu that it was Naoise who was the strongest and fairest of the three. 'If that is so,' said Derdriu, 'then I will be ill, not have a single day of health, until I see him.'

One day not long after this incident, Naoise was standing on the ramparts at Emain Macha, singing away in his beautiful voice. Derdriu, hearing the singing, slipped away from her guardians and made her way to the rampart, walking past Naoise and pretending not to know who he was, and neither did he realize who she was. 'That's a fine heifer going by,' he said. 'The heifers are bound to be fine where there are no bulls,' replied Derdriu. At this point Naoise recognized Derdriu by her outstanding beauty and quickly replied, 'You have the bull of the province, the King of Ulster.' Derdriu said, 'And if I had a choice between the two of you I would choose you.' 'Not I, not so,' said Naoise; 'because of Cathbad's prophecy you are promised to King Conchobhar.' 'Are you rejecting me?' said Derdriu. 'I am indeed,' replied Naoise. With that an impassioned and furious Derdriu rushed at Naoise, grabbed him by his two ears and shouted at him, 'May mockery and shame fall upon these ears if you do not take me with you.'

Naoise, conscious of the curse upon Derdriu and terrified of the wrath of his king, struggled to free himself from Derdriu and begged her to leave him alone. Derdriu asserted, 'You will do it,' and with that she placed a *geis* on him to take her or lose his honour. At this Naoise began a loud chant that heralded danger to his fellow warriors, and his two brothers ran to him to find out what was the matter. He told them how Derdriu had put a *geis* upon him, and they immediately panicked, remembering Cathbad's prophecy. Naoise was caught between his honour as a man and his warrior bond of loyalty to his king. Finally one of his brothers said that he could not be disgraced so long as they were alive, and suggested that all three of them, along with Derdriu, leave the province of King Conchobhar. 'There is not a king of Ireland who will not make us welcome,' they declared.

So they left that night with a retinue of 150 warriors, their women, hounds and servants, and for a long time travelled safely around Ireland, in spite of Conchobhar's attempts to capture them. Finally however the Ulstermen drove them out of Ireland to Alba (Scotland), where they settled in the wilderness, living off the game they caught and stealing cattle from nearby properties. When the people of Alba got fed up with these thieves and formed a mob to attack them, the sons of Uisnech fled to the King of Alba's palace, seeking protection, and offered to fight for him in exchange for food and sanctuary. The King was glad to have the services of such outstanding warriors and gladly accepted them.

They set up their camp on the green surrounding the King's fort, building their huts in a circle with a secret one for Derdriu in the centre where no one could see her. Nevertheless early one morning one of the King's stewards came past the houses and saw Naoise and Derdriu sleeping together. He immediately returned to the King and woke him, saying, 'I never found a woman fit for you until today. There is a woman with Naoise who is so beautiful that she is fit for a king.' The King asked the steward to go secretly every day to Derdriu and woo her on his behalf. The steward followed his king's order, but Derdriu told Naoise every night what the steward had said to her by day. Naturally the wooing failed, so the steward and the King decided to send the sons of Uisnech into extremely dangerous and risky battles in the hope that they might get killed. But they were of course champion warriors – it was once said that if the whole province of Ulster came at them at once, they could stand together and not be beaten. It was only a matter of time before the King realized that this second strategy was also destined to fail. After consulting his nobles he decided to muster the men of Scotland to kill the sons of Uisnech. However Derdriu, gifted in the art of prophecy, foresaw this, and told Naoise that they must leave immediately or face certain death. So that night Derdriu and the sons of Uisnech departed and went to an island off Scotland.

News of their situation reached Ulster and the Ulstermen were sad that the sons of Uisnech should die in a strange land because of what they saw to be the influence of a bad woman. They urged Conchobhar to forgive and protect them, since they thought it unacceptable that one of their own warrior kin should die at the hands of their enemy in a foreign land. Conchobhar agreed and said, 'Let them come to us then.'

The news was conveyed to Naoise and his brothers, who welcomed it but insisted on a guarantee of their safety. They suggested Fergus Mac Róich, Dubhthach and Conchobhar's own son Cormac as guarantors, to which Conchobhar agreed. However he still wanted Derdriu for himself, and secretly ordered Fergus to make sure that, when he returned to Ireland with Derdriu and the three brothers, all of the household came directly to Emain Macha, on no account were they to eat or drink anywhere else first. At the same time, unbeknown to Fergus, Conchobhar ordered a chief named Borrach, whose fort lay on the road to Emain Macha, to prepare a lavish feast in Fergus's honour. Now Fergus had a *geis* upon him that he must never, on pain of death, refuse to attend a feast that had been prepared in his honour.

When Fergus, Dubhthac and Cormac arrived on the island, Fergus let out a great shout and Naoise exclaimed, 'That is the shout of an Irishman.' But Derdriu quickly denied it, saying it was the shout of a man from Alba. Fergus repeated the shout twice more, with Derdriu each time denying that it was the shout of a man from Ireland. However after the third shout Naoise decided to send his brother to investigate. At this, Derdriu confessed to Naoise that she had known all along it was Fergus, and Naoise asked her why she had denied it. Derdriu explained that she had had a dream the previous night in which three birds had come from Emain Macha with three drops of honey in their beaks, left the honey and taken away three drops of blood. This was a prophecy: no matter how sweet the message of peace and reconciliation from Conchobhar, the three drops of blood represented the blood of the three sons of Uisnech, whom Conchobhar was planning to kill. But in fidelity to the honour of the warrior class Naoise disputed Derdriu's interpretation and rejected her warning out of hand. He asserted that Fergus and the other two warriors were the guarantee of safety and an indication of Conchobhar's good faith.

So the next morning they put out to sea and Derdriu looked back at the coast of Alba and lamented:

'Dear the land, the land in the east,
Alba with its wonders,
Never would I leave it
But that I must go with Naoise.'

Shortly after they arrived in Ireland, as they proceeded towards Emain Macha, the party came across Borrach, who invited Fergus to attend a feast that he had set up in his honour. Fergus was caught between two sacred bonds, one to protect Derdriu and the sons of Uisnech and the other never to refuse a feast in his honour. As the latter *geis* was the more long-standing and therefore the more powerful, Fergus turned to Naoise and Derdriu and told them of his dilemma. Derdriu was furious: 'Abandon the sons of Uisnech if you must, yet to abandon them is a high price for a feast.' Disturbed and distressed, Fergus offered to send his own son Fiacha as a guarantor of their safety.

Derdriu, again divining the dangers that lay ahead, tried to persuade the sons of Uisnech to delay their trip to Emain Macha and wait until the feast was over, but again they rejected her advice. They saw Derdriu's prophecy as a slight against their warrior honour and told Derdriu that Fergus would never have come for them just to bring them back to be destroyed.

With this they set off again, but Derdriu fell behind for a rest, during which time she fell asleep. Naoise turned back to find her just waking, and asked her what had caused her to fall behind. She replied that sleep was on her and that she had had a dream, 'a sad vision that has shown me four tall, fair, bright companions with a head of each taken from them'. Naoise chided her for having such dark thoughts and again reassured her that the King would never break his word. So they continued, until Derdriu looked upwards and showed Naoise a cloud over Emain Macha that was cold and deep red like blood. She urged the three brothers not to go to Emain Macha that night but to wait for Fergus and the others who were feasting with Borrach. But by now Naoise was becoming extremely annoyed with Derdriu and her prophecies, and angrily told her that as warriors they had no fear and they would not take her advice.

Derdriu fell silent for some time and then as they approached Emain Macha she said, 'Sons of Uisnech, I have a sign that I will tell you whether Conchobhar is planning treachery or not.' 'What is that?' said Naoise. 'If you are invited into the house where Conchobhar sits surrounded by his nobles to eat and drink then that means no ill, for no man will injure a guest that has partaken of food at his table,' said Derdriu. 'But if you are sent to the house of the Red Branch warriors then you can be sure he is bent on treachery.' When they came to Emain Macha they were directed to the Red Branch warriors' house, and again Derdriu asserted that it would have been better not to come, and that it was still not too late to leave. But again the three sons rejected her pleas, seeing any move to leave as an admission of cowardice, a violation of their oath of honour as warriors (death was far preferable to disgrace, since the entire clan would be disgraced by any acts of cowardice).

Conchobhar in the mean time sent Lebarcham over to the Red Branch house to report back on Derdriu's beauty. On her way Lebarcham saw a large troop of armed warriors, none of whom she recognized. Eogan, son of Durthacht, a long-standing enemy of Conchobhar's, had come on his father's behalf to make peace with the King of Ulster. Conchobhar, seeing his opportunity, had agreed to peace on condition that Eogan kill the sons of Uisnech. Lebarcham, although having no conscious knowledge of this deal, sensed danger, and out of fondness for Derdriu and Naoise she warned them of the impending danger. 'Beloved children, evil is the deed that is to be done this night in Emain; for the three torches of valour of the Gaels will be treacherously assailed, and Conchobhar is certainly resolved to put them to death.'[13] Lebarcham advised Naoise to put his warriors on guard and bolt and bar the doors in an attempt to hold out until the morning, when Fergus and his companions would arrive. With that she left, weeping uncontrollably as she went. She returned and told Conchobhar that Derdriu had lost much of her youthful form and beauty. At first Conchobhar was relieved and his jealousy temporarily abated, but as the evening progressed his obsessive jealousy of Naoise returned and he became increasingly suspicious of Lebarcham's assessment. He called upon Tréndorn, a lesser chief whose father had been slain by Naoise, and asked him to go and spy on Derdriu and the troops in the house of the Red Branch.

Tréndorn of course found everything locked up and barred, but he managed to climb up and peer through a high window, where he saw Derdriu, who at that very moment glanced up and saw Tréndorn. She alerted Naoise, who flung a chess piece at Tréndorn, penetrating Tréndorn's eye. Tréndorn hastily retreated to Conchobhar and declared that Derdriu was indeed the most beautiful woman he had

ever seen, a woman for whom there was no peer in Ireland.
Conchobhar flew into a jealous rage and reaffirmed his resolve to kill
the sons of Uisnech. Eogan led Conchobhar's soldiers in a furious
battle against the sons of Uisnech and Fergus's son. The numbers
against them were great and whilst they held out for some time finally
Naoise said they must leave the house and fight their way out to a place
of safety. They made a close fence of shields and spears around Derdriu
and marched out of the house, slaying three hundred men in one
onslaught. Conchobhar panicked and called upon Cathbad to put an
enchantment upon the sons of Uisnech, guaranteeing that he would not
harm them but only seek agreement with them. Cathbad believed his
king and put an enchantment on them that created an illusion that they
were in a dark sea, and Naoise put Derdriu on his shoulders. Their
weapons fell from their hands and thus the sons of Uisnech were
captured. Conchobhar then asked Eogan to kill them, and he willingly
thrust a great spear through Naoise, breaking his back. The others
were also slain and Derdriu was brought to Conchobhar with her
hands tied behind her back.

News of the betrayal was conveyed to Fergus, who immediately
proceeded to Emain Macha where another great battle erupted.
Following the battle Fergus, disgusted by Conchobhar's betrayal of his
trust, departed Ulster and joined forces with Conchobhar's enemies
Queen Medb and King Ailill of Connacht. This explains how Fergus is
found fighting for them against Ulster in the next story.

Derdriu spent the following year as a captive of Conchobhar, during
which time she neither laughed nor smiled and ate very little. She never
lifted her head, and if they sent musicians to her she would recite the
following poem:

'Fair to you the ardent warriors
Who march into Emain after an expedition;
More nobly did they march to their dwelling
The three very heroic sons of Uisliu

Sweet to you the fine mead
That battle-glorious Conchobhar drinks;
But often I had before me, across the ocean,
Food that was sweeter.

Melodious to Conchobhar, your king,
His pipers and trumpeters;

> Sweeter to me – fame of hosts –
> The singing of the sons of Uisliu.'

After several more similar verses praising Naoise and the sons of Uisnech, Derdriu concluded with the following three verses of grief:

> 'I do not sleep now,
> Nor do I brighten my nails,
> There is no joy for me
> Since the son of Tindell will not come.
>
> I do not sleep
> But lie awake half the night;
> My thoughts flee from these hosts,
> I neither eat nor smile.
>
> I have today no cause for joy
> In the assembly of Emuin – throng of chieftains –
> No peace, no delight, no comfort,
> No great house, no fine adornments.'

Whenever Conchobhar tried to comfort Derdriu, she would respond:

> 'Conchobhar, be quiet!
> You have brought me grief upon sorrow;
> As long as I live, surely,
> Your love will be of no concern to me.
>
> You have taken from me – a great crime –
> The one I thought most beautiful on earth,
> The one I loved most.
> I will not see him again until I die.
>
> . . .
>
> Break no more my heart today –
> I will reach my early grave soon enough.
> Sorrow is stronger than the sea
> If you are wise – Conchobhar.'[14]

Conchobhar became increasingly frustrated, and one day asked her, 'Of all that you see, Derdriu, what do you hate most?' Derdriu replied instantly, 'I hate you, Conchobhar, and I hate Eogan who killed

Naoise.' Grasping an opportunity to punish Derdriu, he replied, 'If that is how you feel then you can spend a year with Eogan.' The very next day Conchobhar handed Derdriu over to Eogan and all three set off in a chariot for an assembly in Emain Macha, with Eogan in front and behind him Conchobhar with Derdriu alongside. Derdriu could not bear to have any eye contact with her tormentors and her lover's killer so she kept her eyes cast down. 'Well, Derdriu,' said Conchobhar tauntingly, 'here you are where you can eye us both, like a ewe between two rams.' They were travelling fast at this point and Derdriu spotted a large boulder ahead of her on the side of the road. As they approached it she flung herself out of the chariot, hitting the rock so hard that it shattered her head. So ends the story of Derdriu.

This story, along with Da Derga's hostel and the fate of Conaire Mór, confirms that in fairy tales Eros triumphs and in myths Thanatos (death) triumphs. The entire plot of this story is given to us in the opening moments, when Cathbad prophesies Derdriu's future. There are several points in the story when fate could have been altered, but on each occasion the male heroes choose to reject the feminine wisdom of Derdriu, preferring instead the heroic, masculine values of loyalty, action and bravery.

At the broadest thematic level, the story of Derdriu plots the fate of the feminine in the heroic age. This is a theme that is just as relevant today as it was around the time this story may well have found its origins, in the first century AD. The sovereign queen was clearly the dominant force in the Mythological Cycle, in such figures as Morrígan and Macha, but when we move into the heroic Ulster Cycle we begin to witness some changes in the relationship between the warrior/king or male figure and the sovereign queen or goddess. The ascendancy of male values over feminine appears, and the abortion of the heroine's journey by the dominance of masculine values. As part of her heroic journey Derdriu separates from the patriarchy and joins the appropriate personal masculine in the figure of Naoise, only to be finally rendered submissive to the patriarchy again.

Within the modern myth, Derdriu is an unequivocal *anima* figure. She is clearly a heroic figure in this sense, since the role of the hero (in this case the heroine) is to mediate between gods and men, i.e. the unconscious and conscious worlds. Derdriu's birth conforms in part to the heroic biography, since her shriek from the womb portends an unusual birth, and the prophecies that accompany her birth further attest to her not being entirely of our mortal world. That she is claimed by a king/hero figure, her life is threatened and she is fostered out, conforms also to the heroic pattern. Her gifts of prophecy and her ability to place a *geis* upon Naoise alert us to druidess qualities in Derdriu.

Derdriu's power is partly derived from her association with the divine world of the goddess, since like a sovereign queen she chooses her own mate. And the old King needs renewal in the form of the sacral marriage, or remarriage, to the divine feminine if this rule is to continue to be harmonious and productive. As we have seen so often, Irish feminine figures possess real power. However this power is viewed as bad, destructive. Does this point to the intense fear men have of women? A fear that a woman separating from the dominance of patriarchal power will in turn seek to dominate? A fear that is perhaps generated from the strength of men's own longing to return to the womb on the one hand and on the other the envy of women as the source of fertility, life and nurturance. Much as men like to fantasize that they are triumphant and powerful, there is I believe an unconscious recognition of the power of women to create, sustain and destroy life. Her womb is the dark secret and the mystery of creation itself, the mystery of the cosmos repeated on a micro-scale. If women can produce life then maybe they can also take it away.

Derdriu stands out amongst other Irish mythic females as having the power to challenge the strict honour code of masculine values. She is the initiator, pitting her power against the code and winning, thus triggering the jealousy of the rejected King. In the end however her power cannot prevail and the wrath of the jealous King, a symbol of patriarchal power, combined with Naoise's attachment to his warrior honour, forces her to succumb to male dominance. At this point in the story we can clearly witness the unsolicited abortion of her heroic journey. As a heroic figure she personifies the archetypal pattern of seeking awareness, and connection between the conscious and the unconscious realms. Her fate is the fate of this seeking. Our relationship with the archetypal figure of the hero/heroine plays a vital part in determining the quality of our relationship with the central core of our being, the self. How we orientate ourselves to the unknown is in my view a reliable indication of the relationship that exists between our ego and the unconscious aspects of psychic life. Do we reel away from the unknown, fear it, denigrate it, reject it, triumph over it, embrace it, fall into it, intellectualize it, idealize it, theologize it? The one thing we seem to find difficult is to accept and maintain a relationship with the unknown or invisible world. The heroine or hero is the mediator between these worlds and thus heroic myths depict various patterns of being, of this relationship between the ego and aspects of the self. In the story of Derdriu the heroine, the figure who derives her power from the association with the goddess is initially perceived as powerful but comes to be perceived as destructive. The sacral marriage is degraded into lust, as we see in King Conchobhar's behaviour. The power of Eros is reduced to physical desire, whereby the woman becomes an object of lust and not the mysterious and necessary partner of the *hieros gamos*, or sacral marriage, that ensures fertility and growth. This of course is precisely the fate of the *anima* in so many men today, where the fear of the feminine is sexualized, and the phallus becomes the instrument of control over the power of women. Lust and dominance replace the desire for union, and penetration replaces the experience of being together.

If we now return to the story we can trace this change in relationship between ego and self as it is played out by the figures of Derdriu, Naoise and Conchobhar. The king can be seen to symbolize the ruling principle in the psyche, the behaviours and values that the conscious ego, our sense of 'I', identifies with. As the story unfolds we see that the feminine principle, the archetypal *anima*, does not choose to be appropriated and dominated by the ego. There is the telling moment in the story when Derdriu sees the slain calf in the snow and expresses her desire for a man who would incorporate the three colours of black, white and red. A familiarity with alchemy will immediately reveal the parallel between Derdriu's desire and the three colours that depict the three stages. Black signifies the *nigredo*, or dark phase, white the *albedo* or union of opposites, sometimes referred to as the chymical wedding, and red is the colour of completion, the philosopher's stone. The colours represent the stages involved in moving towards some sense of integration and wholeness.

An archetypal wise old woman, in the figure of Lebarcham, knows that Derdriu needs a young male lover, a vibrant masculine energy, to continue her heroic journey and to sustain her move towards individuation. In Jungian terms, she needs the personal *animus* to initiate the process of being in the world and to free her from the grip of the archetypal father/king that up until now has dominated and controlled her. Such is her desire that she declares she will remain ill until she has him. Do we take this 'illness' to mean mental illness? Does this lie behind some young women's self-destructive behaviour, such as anorexia? The feminine needs Logos and the masculine energy to be in the world, to be known. So Derdriu compels Naoise to relate to her by imposing a *geis*, forcing him to choose against the traditional male values of heroism. She forces a choice between personal honour, which we might take to mean personal feeling, and the collective honour represented by his warrior oaths of loyalty. She frees the masculine energy from imprisonment in the stereotype and personalizes it, an outcome that is equally important for Naoise as for Derdriu.

The grabbing by the ears forces him to listen, but the ear is more significant than that, since it is sometimes associated with the process of birth itself. There is a version of the Christian tale of the immaculate conception in which the Virgin Mary is impregnated by the Holy Spirit in the form of a dove entering her ear. One could perhaps say that the birth that occurs through the ear is the word of creation and the Holy Spirit is the *animus* that fertilizes the womb of Mary, the feminine spirit. In grabbing Naoise's ears Derdriu is calling him to choose to listen to his feminine self, his feelings. How many women have not felt like grabbing a man by his ears and forcing him to listen to what he feels? If we are not too literal and see the ears as not simply physical but also metaphorical, then we can appreciate that it is through listening that we conceive new growth. It is through the metaphorical ears that we hear the calling of individuation and respond to the alchemical opus. Naoise does hear, and at this point in the story the power of the feminine is honoured. The feminine, in the figure of Derdriu, acquires masculine energy as the first step in freeing herself from the control of the patriarchal forces that reside both within and without her. Naoise is freed from over-identification with traditional male values, and gains the opportunity to form a relationship with his feminine aspects.

That there are three brothers is of some significance, although Naoise is the only one who is clearly differentiated. Three plus one makes four, which Jung reminds us is the number of wholeness, underlining the need of the masculine to incorporate feminine values.

But this wholeness is permanently under siege from the masculine world and patriarchal values, first in the figure of King Conchobhar and then in Naoise and his brothers. Wholeness is a transitory state, and it is forever under threat of dissolution from the demands of the ego and the outer world. The patriarchal values threaten any sense of integration since they devalue the feminine, devalue connectedness and want to possess, not have union. So as the story unfolds we see the erosion of this moment of wholeness when the feminine power is acknowledged as masculine and feminine come together.

Naoise as the masculine figure in this story needs Derdriu in order to learn to love, to immerse himself in feeling. Falling in love is a sensitizing experience that opens the ears, often enabling a man to hear his own feelings for the first time in his life. When a man is preoccupied, or over-identified, with power then Eros cannot exist, since power and love are mutually exclusive. Derdriu's *geis* upon Naoise binds him to discover the nature of love and to hear the feminine call for union. It is hard, if not impossible, to hear this call when surrounded by the noise of traditional masculine values such as power and status.

All goes well at first, male and female together protected by other kings in Ireland, but finally the threat of Conchobhar, the power-driven ego, grows too strong and the lovers retreat. Symbolically we might take this to mean that in the early phases of any union between the masculine and the feminine, whether a man with his *anima* or a woman with her *animus*, there is an initial powerful sense of connection but it is not long before it is threatened by existing values and retreats to the unconscious. We see on several occasions in this story how Naoise begins to doubt and then finally to dispute Derdriu's prophecies, her (or his own) feminine intuition.

In Conchobhar's trickery we can see the determination of the ego to triumph over any possibility of change or renewal. Our habitual and comfortably familiar ways of being in the world are enormously resistant to any change.

In reflecting on this story from the viewpoint of the feminine heroic journey what we can see is that Derdriu achieves the first important task, with the help of a wise old woman, of separating from the control of the father figure. In other words she rejects being defined by the patriarchy and exercises conscious individual choice when she commands Naoise to join her. At this point in the story she is engaging an appropriate level of masculine energy to enable her own development to take place out in the world. The taking of a lover represents the beginning of a relationship with her personal *animus* and at the same time a differentiation from the collective *animus* or patriarchy. However as the story unfolds she is unable to sustain this relationship with her personal masculine aspects and gradually they drift back into the control of the collective masculine values. This is symbolized by

Naoise's regression to the warrior code when he no longer hears Derdriu. Naoise is a symbol of Derdriu's personal *animus* with which she is initially able to have a satisfactory union when it is freed from the control of the father and the collective masculine values. At a psychological level we might consider that Naoise's regression represents the fact that the *animus* was not adequately internalized, leaving a woman vulnerable to overt patriarchal control of her identity and well-being. The end result of this breakdown in internalization of her masculine aspects is a return to 'the father', and the destructive pattern of masculine values determining her sense of worth. The final cost of this disconnection is death of a sense of self.

11

CÚ CHULAINN

Cú Chulainn, who has appropriately been compared with the Greek Achilles and the Germanic Siegfried, is the epitome of the superhuman hero of the heroic period. Typically he is destined to have a short but brilliant life, to be covered in glory and admired for his deeds long after his death. Cú Chulainn fulfills the criteria of living in order to win eternal fame, and he is unsurpassed in battle, young, exceedingly handsome and of superlative strength. He is closely associated with the gods, is of supernatural origins, and has strong associations with the otherworld during his short life.

The principal tale concerned with Cú Chulainn is the aforementioned 'Táin Bó Cuailnge' ('The Cattle Raid of Cooley'). It is believed that the story was committed to writing around the middle of the seventh century by a poet who was acquainted with the Latin learning of the monasteries and wished to record the native heroic tradition. In the twelfth century an unknown author is said to have composed the coherent and comprehensive version of the story which is preserved in *The Book of Leinster* and also in a sixteenth-century manuscript in the Royal Irish Academy.

Although the story of the cattle raid is the central one of the Tain, there are associated stories that play an important part in establishing the biography of Cú Chulainn. His birth, youth, adult life and death, and the major transitions of life, all accord with the International Heroic Biography.

As is typical of mythological stories, there are two versions of the conception and birth of Cú Chulainn. I have decided to rely on the version translated by Thomas Kinsella in his *Tain*,[1] although some reference will be made to the alternative version, since both appear with regularity in the Irish mythological literature.

One day, when King Conchobhar and his chieftains were gathered at Emain Macha enjoying a feast, a flock of birds landed on the fertile plains on the outskirts of Emain and grazed so forcefully that they ate all the plants and grasses, even the roots. The men of Ulster were shocked to see their fertile land in ruins and took off in rapid pursuit of the birds. Conchobhar was accompanied by his sister (some say daughter) Dechtine, who drove his chariot. All the pursuing party were enchanted by the beauty of the birds' flight: they were in nine flocks of twenty, and each pair of birds was linked by a silver chain. As daylight started to fade the Ulstermen noticed three birds break away and fly towards Bruig na Bóinne, the most famous fairy dwelling in Ireland, the home of the Dagda and Oenghus. When they were near Bruig na Bóinne, night fell and they decided to stop and seek some accommodation for the evening. Conall and Bricriu came across a solitary, newly built house in which they found a couple who made them very welcome. But there was little space and little food, and when they returned to the others Bricriu said that they would have to bring their own food and even then the accommodation was going to be meagre enough. Nevertheless, snow had begun to fall, and the group decided to go to the house, and with great difficulty they squeezed inside. It was not long before they found the door to the storeroom, and in no time they were partaking of food and ale in the manner to which they were accustomed.

Later in the evening the man of the house told the gathering that his wife was in labour, and Dechtine went to help her. At the very moment the boy was born, a mare gave birth to two foals outside, which the man of the house gave to the baby as a gift. In their usual drowsy and drunken state the Ulstermen retired, but in the morning when they awoke there was no sign of the house, the birds or the couple, and all that remained were the newborn infant and the two foals.

According to the second version of the story Dechtine herself had previously mysteriously disappeared with fifty of her companions and the Ulstermen had been seeking them for three years. It was she and her companions who had taken on the form of the birds and flew to Emain in order to lure Conchobhar and the Ulstermen to Bruig na Bóinne.

In both versions the newborn child is given to Dechtine to rear and in the first version the party left this mysterious place that had now disappeared and returned to Emain Macha with the infant. Dechtine loved the child and cared for it tenderly, but after a short period of time it became very ill and died. Dechtine's grief was immense and on returning from her lamentations she felt extremely thirsty. She was brought a drink in a copper vessel, and as she placed it to her lips a tiny creature slipped into her mouth and she swallowed it along with the liquid. That night she had a vivid dream that a man came and spoke to her, saying she would bear a child by him, that it was him that had fathered the child at Bruig na Bóinne and that he had lured her there in the first place. He told her that he was the god Lugh, that she was now pregnant by him and that the boy child to be born was to be called Sétanta. He went on to tell her that the two foals born at Bruig na Bóinne were to be reared for Sétanta.

When Dechtine became pregnant, and there was no obvious father, the men of Ulster began to suspect that Conchobhar had had an incestuous union with his own sister. In self-defence he betrothed Dechtine to the warrior Sualdam mac Róich. But Dechtine was so ashamed of her condition that she had a miscarriage. She subsequently married Sualdam and became pregnant by him; this time the child lived and was named Sétanta. Tradition says it was the same child that she had adopted and conceived, so Sétanta is called 'son of three years', because he is born three times.

In the ancient Celtic world, a child had to have foster-parents; the bond created by fostering was regarded as more sacred and binding than that to the natural parent. While most children would have only one set of foster-parents, an élite or royal child required several foster-parents, to equip him for his future role as an eminent representative of the community. There was much argument over who should foster Sétanta, with Conchobhar wanting his sister Finnchaem to rear him, while Sencha the sage laid claim to him, citing his capacity to teach the child wisdom. The rich nobleman Blai Briuga said he should have Sétanta as he could provide for his material needs better than anyone else. Fergus the warrior also laid claim, attesting to his capacity to instruct Sétanta in warrior skills. Amairgen the poet said he was the most worthy foster-parent to bring up Sétanta. Finally the judgement was made: the child should be given to Finnchaem as she was Conchobhar's kin, but Sencha should instruct him, Blai Briuga provide for him, Fergus teach him martial arts and Amairgen teach him poetry and eloquence. Some say the druid Cathbad was also engaged to teach the child druidic knowledge. In this manner Cú Chulainn (Sétanta's later name) was taught all the skills that befit a hero. With the matter of fosterage resolved Sétanta was given to Finnchaem and reared away from Emain Macha at Imrith Fort on the plains of Muirthemne.

Cú Chulainn's conception and birth are of course no ordinary mundane biological event. The triple birth witnesses a progression from divine through to human: at first the father is completely unknown, then he is known as the god Lugh, and finally the human Sualdam. Indeed, some suggest that the point of the second birth is to convey the knowledge that Cú Chulainn is in fact the reincarnation of Lugh. Jesus Christ in Christian mythology was of course also the son of a god and the son of a mortal, and also a heroic figure who interceded between man and god. In psychological mythology the triple birth could perhaps be seen as the emergence of the ego from the mists of antiquity that constitute the collective unconscious, where the forces are divine or archetypal and therefore impersonal, through into the personal realm.

We can regard the two figures in the isolated house at Bruiġ na Bóinne as folk from the otherworld, Tuatha Dé Danann. Indeed the house itself is an otherworld hostel, a *bruiden*, which miraculously appears in a snowfall and equally miraculously disappears.

The birth of the hero is also often heralded by signs in the natural world, and in Cú Chulainn's case we have the portent of dying fields, the snow, and finally the simultaneous birth of two foals. The coincidental birth of animals is not unusual in the heroic biography; Christ, for example, was born in the company of oxen in the stable. The association with animals, in addition to embodying the hero's links to the animal world, also draws our attention to the belief that the hero represents a state of unity before animate and inanimate, plant and animal, man and beast, were separated out. In a psychological sense perhaps this is the period before a conscious sense of 'I' emerges, when 'I' and 'not I' are one, in a state of undifferentiation. It may also be seen as symbolizing the continuum that is believed to exist between psyche and matter and not the split between these worlds which dominates our current thinking. Death itself may well be a return to this state of unity.

The hero, as mediator between the supernatural and mortal worlds, is also the container of a unity, or continuum, which he must uphold. In psychological terms the hero is the archetypal pattern of integration of the unconscious mind with the conscious mind and represents an approach that maintains a relationship between these two worlds. Sétanta, or Cú Chulainn as we will come to know him, was thus distinguished at birth and destined for greatness by the two features that mark his birth as sacred. First he is the child of a god, the god Lugh, and conceived mysteriously by swallowing a creature. Second he is associated with the birth of animals.

The boyhood deeds of Sétanta form part of the Táin proper when during a battle Queen Medb of Connacht anxiously seeks knowledge about Cú Chulainn before going into battle against him; and Fergus mac Róich, who had defected from Ulster over the death of Derdriu and the sons of Uisnech, told her of Cú Chulainn's youthful exploits. (He of course was uniquely poised to do so since he had at one time been one of Cú Chulainn's foster-parents.)

A hero's youth usually includes some form of exile, separated from his natural mother. The child usually also displays from a very early age extraordinary strength, courage, cunning, knowledge and a wide range of skills. The Greek hero Heracles is a clear example of these qualities when at the age of eight months he strangles the serpents that are sent to attack him by the goddess Hera. Just as there is an auspicious time for the conception or birth of the hero, so also there is often an auspicious time for his initiation into manhood, his separation from society and his ultimate return. Frequently the hero acquires a second and final name in the course of childhood, usually as a consequence of some meaningful event.

Sétanta was reared by his foster-parents on the plains of Muir-themne, and at the same time received instructions from his various other foster-parents. When he was five, he heard rumours about the warrior apprentices at Emain Macha and how King Conchobhar spent one-third of his day watching them perform their various tasks and sports, one-third playing *fidchell* (a chess game), and one-third drinking until he fell asleep. He also heard that there was no great warrior in Ulster, because Fergus had been driven into exile over the issue of Derdriu. Sétanta begged his mother to let him join the boy-warrior troop, but she said he could not go until there were some Ulster warriors to go with him. He complained bitterly, exclaiming that he wanted to go now, only he did not know the way to Emain Macha. His foster-mother eventually gave in, and gave him directions to Emain Macha, explaining at the same time that it was a long and dangerous journey. But Sétanta was undaunted and headed off carrying a toy javelin, a shield and his hurley stick and ball. These he then used to entertain himself and pass the time on the journey, throwing his javelin ahead of himself and then catching it before it hit the ground.

When he reached Emain Macha he enthusiastically and naïvely went straight to join the boys without first meeting the ritual requirement of seeking a guarantee from them that they would protect him, as was the custom of the time. Since he had broken the rules of admission, the boys attacked him, flinging javelins at Sétanta, all of which he stopped with his toy shield. They then drove all their hurley balls at him, but he caught all 150 of them. Finally they threw their hurley sticks at him, but he dodged them all with great skill and agility.

Then Sétanta entered a strange state called *riastradh*, a sort of battle fury.

> Then his riastarthae came upon him. You could have thought that every hair was being driven into his head. You would have thought that a spark of fire was on every hair. He closed one eye until it was no wider than the eye of a needle; he opened the other until it was as big as a wooden bowl. He bared his teeth from jaw to ear and he opened his mouth until his gullet was visible. The warrior's moon rose from his head.[2]

Thus charged with the heat of his battle fury, Sétanta laid low fifty of the boys on the spot. He then chased several others, following them through the hall where Conchobhar was playing chess. Sétanta leapt over the chessboard, scattering some pieces as he went. King Conchobhar was not impressed; he grabbed Sétanta by the wrist and said, 'You are handling these boys roughly and your treatment is not fair.' 'Oh yes it is fair,' declared Sétanta. 'I left my mother and father to join their games and they treated me roughly.' 'Whose son are you?' Conchobhar asked. 'I am Sétanta, son of Sualdam and your sister Dechtine, and I didn't expect to get hurt here.' Conchobhar asked him why he hadn't put himself under the boys' protection as was the custom, and Sétanta replied that he knew nothing of such procedures, but there and then asked Conchobhar for his protection, to which the King agreed, and Sétanta continued his chase. Later in the day he returned to Conchobhar and suggested that he himself undertake the protection of the boys, and Conchobhar agreed. In no time Sétanta became the King's favourite, often inflicting defeat, even wounds, upon the boys as he defeated them single-handedly at team games.

This moment in the story signifies Sétanta's entrance into the community, setting him on his heroic life path. In some respects one could see this entrance into the community as the beginning of an initiation process that continues throughout Cú Chulainn's youth and one that inevitably involves the facing of a monster or dangerous situation. The first of these initiation tasks came when Sétanta was still only five years of age. The men of Ulster were challenged by Eogan Mac Durthacht and were badly beaten in the battle, so that Conchobhar and his son were both left for dead, piled up in a trench with others. The wailing woke Sétanta and he made straight for the battlefields, armed only with his hurley stick. On the way he met a monstrous man with half a head carrying a corpse on his shoulders. The monstrous man asked Sétanta to carry the corpse for him, but Sétanta refused and immediately a fight erupted, with Sétanta being knocked to the ground. At that moment he heard the voice of the goddess Badb calling from amongst the corpses, 'It's a poor sort of warrior-apprentice that lies down at the feet of a ghost.' Sétanta sprang up, knocked off the monster's half-head with his hurley stick and drove it before him across the battle plains as if it were a ball. As he went he cried out, 'Is my friend Conchobhar on this battlefield?' Conchobhar heard Sétanta and responded to his call. Sétanta found him and Conchobhar said, 'What brings you here to the field of slaughter?' 'To learn what mortal terror is,' replied Sétanta. He rescued Conchobhar and they headed towards a house for food and shelter. Conchobhar was most appreciative but told Sétanta that he really yearned for a cooked pig. Sétanta did not hesitate to meet his king's request and he went in search of one. In the middle of the woods he came across a monstrous, ferocious-looking man who was cooking a pig over a pit. Sétanta charged at him, simultaneously taking off his head with his hurley stick and acquiring the pig.

On their return to Emain Macha Sétanta and Conchobhar came across Conchobhar's wounded son; Sétanta picked him up and carried him on his shoulders back to Emain Macha. Thus Sétanta conquers a phantom and a monstrous ferocious man, fulfilling another of the requirements of the heroic biography.

However, in Sétanta's case the facing of the monster is by no means over. When Sétanta was six, Conchobhar and his chiefs were invited to a feast given by the blacksmith Culann. Sétanta decided to follow on later as he was busy with the other boys. Culann possessed a famous hound, a ferocious beast, which protected all the herds of his master and which, it was said, required nine men to hold it on a leash. As the feasting got under way Culann asked whether anyone was still to come, and Conchobhar said no, forgetting momentarily the arrangement he had made with his foster-son. 'In that case,' said Culann, 'I will release my hound to guard the cattle.'

Not long after this Sétanta arrived, and the hound charged at him. Sétanta hit his hurley ball so hard at the dog that it went straight down the brute's throat. He then grabbed the beast, dashed it to pieces against a pillar and tore its entrails out. The men of Ulster were greatly relieved that Sétanta had survived, but Culann was less than pleased at the death of his guard-dog. Sétanta told Culann that he himself would guard the herd until a pup from the same pack was old enough to take over the task. Cathbad immediately declared that henceforth Sétanta should be known as Cú Chulainn, meaning 'the hound of Culann'. His guardianship of Culann's domain and the change of name symbolize an initiation into his future heroic function as a protector of the land and the people of Ulster.

Some time later Cú Chulainn overheard Cathbad telling a group of students that it was an auspicious day for any warrior who took up arms for the first time. Such a warrior's name would endure for ever in Ireland. Immediately Cú Chulainn went to Conchobhar and demanded weapons. Fifteen different sets of weapons were offered to him in succession, but he smashed all of them and was satisfied only when the King offered him his own weapons. Cathbad then warned that whilst what he said was true and the warrior who took up arms would be famous, his life would be very short. 'Wonderful news', replied Cú Chulainn, 'for, if I am famous, I will be happy even to live just one day.'

The next morning a student of Cathbad's asked what that day would be auspicious for. Cathbad replied, 'Anyone who steps into a chariot on this day will be known to Erin for ever.' When Cú Chulainn heard this he went to Conchobhar and demanded a chariot; a repeat of the scene with the weapons took place, until Conchobhar finally offered Cú Chulainn his own chariot. Thus armed with the King's weapons and driving the King's chariot Cú Chulainn headed out of Emain Macha to the boundary of the province, where the warrior Conall Cernach was keeping watch, and after a short dispute persuaded Conall to let him take over the watch. But Cú Chulainn did not merely keep the watch: he ventured into enemy country, where he confronted the three sons of Nechta Scéne, who between them had killed more Ulstermen than were left alive.

The first son, Foill, had to be defeated with the first thrust otherwise he was invincible; the second son, Tuachell, had never before fallen to any weapon; and the third, Fanall, could traverse water with the ease of a swallow. Cú Chulainn slew them all, beheaded them and turned towards Emain Macha with his prize. On the way back be brought down a flock of swans with two shots from his sling without killing any of them, and tied the flock to his chariot. Then he also captured a stag, subduing it with a mere glance, and tied it behind his chariot.

Thus in grand manner he arrived back in Emain. But the sentry on the walls of Emain was alarmed, since Cú Chulainn was still in the grip of his battle fury, his *riastradh*, which meant that he could not distinguish friend from foe. Cú Chulainn shouted, 'I swear by the god by whom the men of Ulster swear that if there is no man to give me combat, I will shed the blood of all those in the fort.' Conchobhar responded quickly, and ordered the women of Emain to go out and bare their breasts before Cú Chulainn. When Cú Chulainn saw the breasts of the women he turned his face away, since there was a *geis* upon him not to look upon naked women. At that the warriors of Ulster seized him and plunged him into a huge vat of cold water. But he was so heated up by his battle fury that the vat simply burst asunder from the excessive heat. So they plunged him into a second vat, and it too boiled with Cú Chulainn's heat. Finally they plunged him into a third vat which only became warm, and finally cooled Cú Chulainn down. The Queen then came forward and dressed him in a blue cloak with a silver brooch and a hooded tunic, and he was seated between King Conchobhar's two feet, which was his place thereafter.

So by seven years of age our superhuman hero had separated from his home, in his desire to join the boy-troops at Emain Macha; acquired his adult name, in the ritualistic slaying of the monstrous hound of Culann (the change of name itself spells out a change of status, as in some religious rites); and slain the three supernatural sons of Nechta Scéne, which is parallel to the struggle with three monsters or a three-headed monster, such as Cerberus, the triple-headed dog who guards the entrance to Hades. Other monsters of Greek mythology include the many-headed Hydra and the monstrous Nemean lion, both slain by Heracles.

MacCana asserts that the concept of the hero as someone who is fired up with fury belongs to a widespread notion that sacred power is often marked by an intense accession of physical heat.[3] In this sense the battle heat is essentially a magical-religious experience signalling Cú Chulainn's initiation into the warrior class. Cú Chulainn's *riastradh* is described vividly by Marie-Louise Sjoestedt:

> He revolves in his skin so that his feet and knees are behind and his calves and buttocks in front. His hair stands on end and on the tip of each hair is a drop of blood, or in other versions, a spark of fire. His

mouth, wide open so that his gullet is seen, emits a stream of fire. One of his eyes recedes into his skull so far that a heron could not pick it out. The other, as big as a cauldron, protrudes on to his cheek. A strange emanation called the 'hero's moon' rises from his forehead as 'thick as a whetstone'. From his skull rises a stream of black blood as high as the mast of a ship.[4]

In fact several scholars note that there is a direct equivalent of this state in the Scandinavian tradition, in the image of the fierce berserkers, warriors clad in bear furs and characterized by enormous physical strength and uncontrollable fury.

It is interesting that only the intervention of the naked women can reduce the mystical heat of transformation. It is possible that this episode of the women and the vats, coming as it does at the end of the initiatory ordeals, indicates the young man's sexual coming of age. The tribal initiation of young men is often accompanied by scenes and rituals of a sexual character. It is as if the young man, having been initiated as a warrior, is also now eligible to join the class of men to whom sexual relations with women is permitted. Sjoestedt suggests that the cloak that the Queen gives Cú Chulainn after he cools down represents his manly garment, his *toga virilis*.[5]

Within Jungian mythology one might see this intervention of naked women as the role of the *anima* in a man's psyche. The *anima*, or feminine aspect of a man's psyche, plays a vital role in helping him to contain his rage. A man will often respond to any sense of rejection or separation with rage, but as the relationship with his feminine self develops he becomes increasingly able to contain this rage, along with other feelings. Rage, like Cú Chulainn's *riastradh*, prevents one from discriminating friend from foe. This is why a man in a rage can so readily murder, or be violent to, someone he at other times is close to. The role of the *anima* is to enable him to discriminate, name and accept his feelings, which is a little like putting them in a feminine container such as a vat of water. A very underdeveloped feminine side usually results in an overdeveloped masculine side, manifesting itself in over-identification with such qualities as aggression and power rather than persuasion and influence. Men in whom the feminine side is under-developed are also more inclined towards action rather than reflection. The latter attribute requires containment of feelings, not the impulsive acting out of them.

Cú Chulainn's initiation into manhood leads into the next stage of the heroic biography, the transition from boyhood to full manhood. It heralds yet another cycle of separation, initiation and return. Cú Chulainn, apart from being an outstanding warrior, was also a very handsome man, possessing a beauty that was more baroque than classic. His hair it is said was of three colours, brown on the crown, red in the middle and fringed with gold, which formed a triple braid before it fell in ringlets on his shoulders. A hundred strings of jewels decorated his head, and collars of gold glittered on his chest. He also outstripped the other warriors at whatever games or events they undertook. He had many gifts, including the oratory that Sencha had taught him and the foreknowledge that Amairgin had instructed him in. With all these qualities the women of Conchobhar's household were increasingly attracted to Cú Chulainn, so that the other men became jealous and decided it was time that this too daring, too handsome and too gifted young warrior found a wife. Moreover, since it had been foretold that his life would be heroic but short, they felt it would be prudent for him to father a son like himself as soon as possible. In response to the Ulstermen's concerns King Conchobhar sent nine men to each province to look for a suitable woman for Cú Chulainn, i.e. the daughter of a king or chief. But after a year and a day had elapsed not one of them had been able to find such a partner, and Cú Chulainn decided to take the matter into his own hands; he went to a place called the Garden of Lugh to woo a girl he knew there; her name was Emer and she was the daughter of Forgall the Cunning.

On arriving at the Garden of Lugh Cú Chulainn saw Emer on the lawn with her foster-sisters. Emer lifted her eyes and recognized Cú Chulainn, saying, 'May your road be blessed.' 'May the apple of your eye see only good,' he replied. Then they spoke for some time in riddles, for they were both skilled in the art of poetry. After Cú Chulainn caught sight of Emer's beautiful breasts over the top of her dress, he said:

'I see a sweet country. I could set my weapon there.'

Emer answered him by saying, 'No man will travel this country until he has killed a hundred men at each fort from the fort of Scemen to Banchuin.'

'In that sweet country I'll rest my weapon,' Cú Chulainn said.

'No man will travel this country until he has done the feat of the salmon leap carrying twice his weight in gold, and struck down three groups of nine men with a single stroke, leaving the middle man of each nine unharmed,' she said.

'In that sweet country I'll rest my weapon,' said Cú Chulainn.

'No man will travel this country', she said, 'who hasn't gone sleepless from Samain, when the sun goes to its rest, until Imbolc, when the ewes are milked at spring's beginning; from Imbolc to Beltine at the summer's beginning and from Beltine to Brón Trogain, earth's sorrowing autumn.'

'It is said and done,' Cú Chulainn said. And with that he finished his journey and returned to Emain Macha.[6]

The next day Forgall heard of the strange visitor who spoke with his daughter in riddles and immediately declared, 'It could be no one else other than the warped one from Emain Macha.' He recognized that Emer had fallen in love with Cú Chulainn and determined to put an end to the wooing.

He headed for Emain Macha disguised as Gaulish royalty, and upon arrival demanded that Conchobhar speak with the royal messengers from Gaul. Forgall spoke in glowing terms of the Ulster warriors but singled out Cú Chulainn as one who could be even greater if he undertook some further training. He suggested that Cú Chulainn should visit Scáthach, the shadowy female warrior in Alba, and study with her, guaranteeing to Conchobhar that if Cú Chulainn did this there would be no one in the world who could beat him. Forgall knew full well the dangers involved in this journey and hoped that Cú Chulainn would never return. Cú Chulainn accepted the challenge, but before he left for Alba he visited Emer, who told him that it was her father who had visited Emain Macha, disguised as a royal messenger, and that he wanted to destroy Cú Chulainn. At this they took leave of each other, promising to be faithful, and Cú Chulainn headed off to Alba along with Laegaire and Conall Cernach.

At first he trained with Donnall the Destroyer, who after some time advised Cú Chulainn that his training would not be complete until he had visited Scáthach. Scáthach was a mysterious woman warrior, fierce and powerful, who also possessed secrets of war and weaponry that, if imparted to any warrior, made him one of the finest in Europe. This voyage to Scáthach's fort meets all the requirements of the voyage to the otherworld that the typical hero must undertake.

So Cú Chulainn set off for the mysterious land where the border between mortal and supernatural beings is blurred. A short time into the journey Laegaire and Conall were struck with homesickness and decided to return to Emain Macha, leaving Cú Chulainn to undertake the journey alone. Some say that the homesickness was induced by Forgall, others that Donall's daughter had put a curse upon the other two warriors because Cú Chulainn had rejected her love. Cú Chulainn wandered, hopelessly lost, for some time until suddenly there appeared in front of him a large beast like a lion. At first Cú Chulainn was terrified of the fierce-looking creature but as it came closer it suddenly turned around and walked ahead of him. Quickly Cú Chulainn realized that this creature was guiding him. Eventually the creature encouraged Cú Chulainn to leap on to its back, and they travelled like this for four days until they came to the end of the bounds of men. Here there was a small lake; some boys who were rowing on it laughed at the sight of a grown man on the back of a strange-looking creature. At this Cú Chulainn leapt off and the beast left him.

Cú Chulainn continued until he met a young man whom he asked the way to Scáthach's fort. The young man told him the way was across the Plain of Ill Luck that lay immediately before him, but on the near side of this plain his feet would stick fast and on the far side the blades of grass were like knives. But this was no ordinary young man: as is often the case in heroic legends, he was in fact a guide from the otherworld. He gave Cú Chulainn a wheel, telling him to roll it in front of him in the first half of the plain and follow its tracks. He also gave him an apple, telling him to throw it when he was in the second half of the plain and follow it wherever it went, and it would protect him from the knife-like blades of grass. He told him many other things that would happen and how he would win a great name in the future.

Cú Chulainn did as the mysterious youth had told him and eventually came across a narrow valley full of monsters, sent there by Forgall to destroy him. He managed to pass through it safely, only then to have to pass through a terrible wild mountain until he finally came to a camp where Scáthach's pupils lodged. 'Where is Scáthach?' he asked. 'On that island out there.' 'How do I get there?' queried Cú Chulainn. Then the students replied, 'By the pupil's bridge – but no one can cross it unless he is trained in the craft of arms.' This bridge was low at each end and considerably higher in the middle, and whenever anyone leapt on to it it rose from the middle and threw the person off. Three times Cú Chulainn tried to cross it and three times it threw him, and the students jeered. Finally Cú Chulainn became furious and broke into his *riastradh*, then he did the salmon leap demanded by Emer and landed on the middle of the bridge before it could rise to throw him off.

Having overcome many other obstacles, he finally arrived at the door of Scáthach's fort and struck it so hard that the shaft of his spear went through the door. Scáthach knew that only a true warrior could have reached her door and she sent her daughter to see who this champion might be. The moment she set eyes on Cú Chulainn she fell in love with him and at her mother's suggestion she slept with Cú Chulainn that night. The daughter then tended to Cú Chulainn's every need and after three days she told him that if he really wanted to learn heroic deeds he needed to go to the place where Scáthach was training her two sons, perform his salmon leap on to Scáthach, set his sword between her breasts and extract three promises: that she give him a thorough training, that she provide a dowry for his marriage, and that she foretell his future. At the point of death, Scáthach agreed to meet all Cú Chulainn's demands.

So Cú Chulainn lived with the daughter and Scáthach undertook his training. During this time Scáthach was at war with another female chief called Aoife, a warrior so fierce that even Scáthach feared her. A battle broke out one day and in order to keep Cú Chulainn out of harm's way Scáthach gave him a sleeping draught, but it only put him out for an hour, not twenty-four as it would have done for anyone else. Soon Cú Chulainn was in the fray and he overcame Aoife by enticing her to look away, pouncing on her and carrying her off on his back. Again he extracted three promises at the point of his sword: that she should give hostages to Scáthach, that she should spend the night with him, and that she bear him a son to be named Connla whom she would send to Ireland when he was seven. He also instructed her that this son was to reveal his name to no one, was to make way for no man and was to refuse no man combat. These were his *geasa*.

It was not long before Cú Chulainn's training was complete, and before he departed Scáthach fulfilled the third of her promises and told Cú Chulainn of the great perils that awaited him in Ireland. Thus the hero has undergone his initiation, has passed horrendous tests of strength, has shown courage and valour, through sexual union he has made the transition from boyhood to manhood, and finally he has been taught esoteric secrets by his supernatural instructor. Through his terrifying ordeals Cú Chulainn experiences an ecstatic state and is liberated from fear for ever. Initiation involves both humiliation and elevation; it is both terrifying and the means of triumphing over terror. Having achieved all this the hero is ready to undertake the next phase of his journey, the return.

Cú Chulainn, unlike some of the other male figures who journey to the otherworld, manages to return. Some, such as Connla, son of Conn of the Hundred Battles, having succumbed to the fascination of the mysterious otherworld and its female inhabitants, are lost for ever to the world of mortals. In our modern view they are lost for ever to consciousness and live an unconscious life. So within the figure of Cú Chulainn we have the archetypal pattern of the returning hero, the seeker of consciousness, who manages to avoid being obliterated by the unconscious forces. One interpretation that could be made of this section of Cú Chulainn's life is that the union between the masculine and feminine at the personal, or human level (marriage to Emer), is difficult until one has at least faced the great mother, or archetypal feminine, within (Scáthach). Without this recognition one is vulnerable to mistaking it for personal feeling when in fact it is impersonal. The consequence of such a misreading is very often an indiscriminate falling into feeling, into the innumerable 'isms' that are available. The archetypes have both a positive and a negative side, and we could consider Scáthach to be a symbol of the dark side of the great mother archetype. We will see later that the fairy figure Fand with whom Cú Chulainn falls in love is representative of the positive side of this archetype. Cú Chulainn needs to learn about the destructive and dark feelings. He has both to journey to and threaten Scáthach in order to acquire esoteric knowledge. This journey is treacherous; anyone who has undertaken long-term psychotherapy will know only too well the nature of this land and the archetypal figures found therein. Our dreams are another source of this knowing.

In acquiring knowledge of his dark side, Cú Chulainn has faced his shadow. He overcomes fear itself because he no longer worries that negative, repressed material will return to consciousness and disturb his persona. In other words, when we can accept our negative side we no longer need the compromise of neurotic symptoms to ward off the possible return of the repressed, and energy is available to help us be more completely in the world and pursue our destiny with an increased measure of consciousness.

The departure of Cú Chulainn's travelling companions shows that there will always be part of oneself that will resist the facing of our unacceptable aspects. It also shows that the hero's journey is a solitary, not a collective one. The hero is the individual who does his or her own thing. He must, as we know from the International Heroic Biography, undertake a journey to the otherworld and return renewed in spirit to continue the cyclical process of separation, initiation and return. From this journey the hero returns, as Campbell reminds us, 'with the power to bestow boons on his fellow man'.[7] The 'boon' to be bestowed from this part of the journey is some integration of good and bad, black and white.

Cú Chulainn's heroic journey to date has exhibited the essential elements of the heroic life. He separated from his homeland; found his way across the Plain of Ill Luck; received help from magical allies; faced seemingly insurmountable obstacles, monsters and hags; had union with a supernatural woman; and acquired esoteric training from the goddess warrior. All of this could be seen as constituting an initiation process for the next stage, the return to his homeland and the goal of wooing Emer. The theme of difficult tasks to be overcome as a prelude to union with a loved one is a common one throughout mythology. The paternal ogre's refusal to permit life to follow its natural course represents a refusal to allow renewal and his own demise of power.

The negative father-figure image of Forgall could be seen as a superego figure that prevents union between Cú Chulainn's masculine and feminine aspects. Within the Jungian story we might see Forgall as a negative old man, or 'senex' figure, who restricts spontaneity and creativity. Individuals driven by a harsh superego or rigid senex quality display a resentful conformity that generates adaptation at the cost of spontaneity and a sense of self-acceptance. In many women the Forgall figure, in the form of what Jungians call the negative animus, is experienced as a persecuting voice in the psyche that tells her she is hopeless, pathetic, of no value; this often results in a woman dismissing her desire for change as a meaningless whim.

Cú Chulainn, having faced the negative great mother and acquired a sense of differentiation between the archetypal negative feminine and the personal feminine, is still held up by his internal negative father image in the figure of Forgall. This figure symbolizes rigid masculine values which, until challenged, inhibit the development of Eros or connection for both genders.

On his way back to Emain Macha Cú Chulainn slayed an evil hag that he met on a narrow path and also, like the Greek hero Perseus, rescued a maiden named Dervogil from being sacrificed to the Fomorians. Finally he arrived back in Emain Macha and at a great feast in his honour he related all his adventures to the assembled warriors. When he had rested and recovered from his journey he decided to set out for Forgall's fort to reunite with his beloved Emer. Forgall however had gone to great lengths to fortify his fort so that Cú Chulainn could not gain entry. For a whole year Cú Chulainn approached the fort again and again, only to be driven back. Finally he mounted his chariot and charged, then did his salmon leap across the outside walls, landing right inside the fort. Three groups of nine warriors charged at him, but Cú Chulainn dealt them three mighty blows so that eight men in each group fell and the middle one escaped, thereby fulfilling one of Emer's initial demands. Forgall panicked and tried to escape, but as he leapt over his walls he stumbled and fell to his death. Cú Chulainn grabbed Emer and her foster-sister along with their weight in gold, and jumped over the wall of the rampart in yet another dramatic salmon leap. Forgall's warriors pursued them but, in accordance with Emer's demand, Cú Chulainn slew a hundred at every fort between Scemen and Banchuin. By the time they reached Emain Macha, Cú Chulainn had fulfilled all of Emer's demands. She was brought to the house of the Red Branch, where King Conchobhar welcomed her into the assembly, and Cú Chulainn and Emer became man and wife.

Another noteworthy tale recounts a further visit to the otherworld by Cú Chulainn and repeats the theme of the wasting sickness that comes upon a man (or a god) when he falls in love with a woman of the otherworld. 'Cú Chulainn's Sickbed and Emer's One Jealousy' commences one day when the Ulstermen were assembled on the Plain of Muirthemne to celebrate the feast of Samain. While the various festivities and games were going on a flock of birds, of a type that were extraordinarily beautiful and had never been seen in Ireland before, descended on a nearby lake. All the women were enchanted by them and longed to have a pair, one for each shoulder. Cú Chulainn promptly set about meeting this request by catching the birds and distributing them amongst the various women. Having satisfied all the women of Ulster he discovered that he had not provided a pair for Emer, and there were no birds left. He promised her that if more birds did show up then he would immediately catch the most beautiful of all for her. A little while later two birds flew over the lake, linked together by a golden chain and singing a gentle song that put all the other men to sleep. Cú Chulainn rose up to pursue the birds, but Loeg, his charioteer, warned him not to hurt these two birds as they had special powers and they were not to be tampered with. But Cú Chulainn was not about to be put off by such warnings from his charioteer, since after all honour was at stake. He carefully placed a stone in his catapult and launched it at the birds but for the first time in his life he did not hit the target. So he launched a second stone, only to miss his mark once again. Feeling totally dismayed, he angrily threw his spear at the birds; it went right through the wing of one of them, forcing them to fly away. After this humiliating failure Cú Chulainn rested against a standing stone, but before long a strange sleep came upon him. In his sleep he saw two women, who horse-whipped him until he was almost dead, then mysteriously left him.

Some time later Cú Chulainn awoke and requested that he be taken straight to his bed, where he lay for a whole year. By this time Samain had come around and a visitor from the otherworld appeared at Cú Chulainn's sickbed: the brother of the otherworld woman Fand, wife of Manannán mac Lir. He invited Cú Chulainn to come to the otherworld, where his wounds could be healed. Then he disappeared, and Cú Chulainn sat up in his bed and told the men of Ulster about his vision of the previous Samain. Conchobhar advised him to return immediately to the stone pillar where he had the initial vision. No sooner had he positioned himself against the pillar than one of the women of the dream appeared to him. She said her name was Lí Ban, wife of the otherworld chief Labraid the Swift Sword Wielder. She told Cú Chulainn that they had come the previous year as beautiful birds to seek his friendship and assistance, but when he injured them they decided to retaliate and teach him a lesson. She now brought a message from her husband and from her sister, Fand: if he would fight for just one day against Labraid's enemies, he could have the love of Fand, who had been abandoned by Manannán mac Lir, and also have his wounds healed. Cú Chulainn was very wary of the request and decided to send his charioteer with the woman to learn something of her country. She and Loeg duly departed for Mag Mell, the Plain of Delights, where Loeg was welcomed and entertained by Labraid and the women of Mag Mell. Loeg returned to tell Cú Chulainn of the delights and the beauties of Mag Mell. By now Emer had discovered the cause of Cú Chulainn's sickness and she addressed him in no uncertain terms: 'Shame upon thee to lie prostrate for a woman's love, well may this long sickbed of thine cause thee to ail.' But Loeg's description of Mag Mell had been so enticing that Cú Chulainn had made up his mind to go. He and Loeg drove to the island home of Labraid and there Cú Chulainn defeated Labraid's enemies and became Fand's lover.

The original agreement had been that he and Fand would be lovers for a month, but at the end of the month they arranged to meet again in

Ulster. Emer found out about this, and on the day she headed towards the appointed place with fifty women, all armed with knives. Cú Chulainn moved to protect Fand, saying to her:

> 'Though the daughter of Forgall vows war against thee,
> Though her dear foster-sisters she raises against thee,
> Bold Emer will dare no deed of destruction,
> Though she rageth against thee, for I will protect thee.'

Then turning to Emer he declared:

> 'Speak thou, Emer, and say,' said Cú Chulainn,
> 'Should I not remain with this lady?
> For she is fair, pure and bright and well skilled,
> A fit mate for a monarch, filled with beauty,
> And can ride the waves of the oceans:
> She is lovely in countenance, lofty in race,
> And skilled in handicraft, can do fine needlework,
> Has a mind that can guide with firmness.'[8]

But Emer was not deterred and said she found Fand no better than herself. 'All that glitters is fair, all that is new is bright, all that is lacking is revered, all that is familiar is neglected, until all be known.' Then with sadness in her heart she turned to Cú Chulainn and said, 'Once we dwelled in honour together and we would so dwell again, if only I could find favour in thy sight.' This honest and mature expression of feeling moved Cú Chulainn to reply, 'By my word thou dost find favour and thou shalt find it as long as I am in life.'

At this point the two women both expressed their willingness to give Cú Chulainn up. Finally Fand asserted that it was she who must leave and she sang a lament, part of which is as follows:

> It is I who will go on a journey,
> I give assent with great affliction;
> Though there is a man of equal fame,
> I would prefer to remain.
>
> . . .
>
> O Emer! the man is thine,
> And well may thou wear him, thou good woman –

What my arm cannot reach,
That I am forced to wish well

. . .

Woe! To give love to a person,
If he does not take notice of it;
It is better for a person to turn away
Unless he is loved as he loves.[9]

In the mean time Manannán mac Lir had heard that Fand was faced with fifty armed women, and that she was about to be deserted by Cú Chulainn. He came to seek Fand and asked her whether she was coming with him or waiting for Cú Chulainn. Fand returned to Manannán, at which Cú Chulainn became inconsolable and took off to the mountains of Munster, where he wandered for a very long time. Finally the druids were able to catch up with him and give him a draught of forgetfulness so that he lost all memory of Fand. The druids also gave Emer a draught so that she in turn forgot her jealousy. The god Manannán himself then helped out by shaking his magical cloak between Cú Chulainn and Fand so that they would never meet again.

With some very minor changes this story is just as relevant today as it was long ago. Cú Chulainn, pursuing masculine heroic values, succumbs to the power of the otherworld woman who first appears to him in a vision after he has failed to hit the two birds with his sling. The whipping that follows is a self-flagellation that symbolizes how the *anima* is capable of turning anger in on a man and plummeting him into depression.

Our approach to the unconscious plays a substantial part in what occurs in the journey. In the story the heroic ego is humbled because it approached the archetypal feminine in a dismissive, domineering manner. For a man used to unquestioned competence the first major experience of incompetence, which often occurs around the mid-life period, can be sufficient to propel him into depression (wasting sickness).

The women of the otherworld initially came in friendship, seeking connection, only to be spurned and triumphed over. This is often how the modern masculine hero responds to his entire feeling life, with contemptuous scorn. But the great hero is laid low by the power of the *anima*, acquires a case of wasting sickness and is finally seduced into a relationship in an attempt to heal himself. How many powerful, down-to-earth, modern men have fallen prey to such sexual desires, often as a defence against the intolerable prospect of getting depressed? Sex is one way that men defend against feelings of disconnection. The power of the *anima* is in inverse proportion to the extent to which she is denied at the conscious level. This is why our modern-day heroes are often undone by inappropriately falling in love, because their personal feeling life is so underdeveloped that they cannot exercise any measure of conscious discrimination or judgement. In short they fall into the grip of an archetypal feminine energy in the infantile hope that the possibility of bliss will be fulfilled and their painful feelings of disconnection will go away.

That Fand is an archetypal figure can be seen by the company she keeps, none other than the god of the sea. It is the power of the feminine archetype that can teach men about Eros, love and relationships, but this very same power can seduce him with the fantasy of blissful fusion, or a symbolic return to the womb, unless he can develop a personal relationship to the feminine realm. So Emer is a symbol of the personal feeling life that enables Cú Chulainn to reject the seduction of the archetypal feminine. Consciousness is a precarious state and in many respects requires the knives of fifty women to defend it and the draught of repression to separate us and establish a boundary between the two realms of the unconscious and the conscious. It is the establishing of this boundary that allows Cú Chulainn to make yet another return, this time from the collective feminine to the personal, from the archetypal realm of perpetual delights to that of the uneven human reality of personal feelings and relationships.

We can gain another view of this story if we see it through the figure of Fand herself and her interaction with Emer. Fand represents collective or stereotyped positive feeling. Some women over-identify with this figure, an over-identification that has been substantially encouraged by the New Age phenomenon. It is not uncommon to find these women exhibiting a very idealized view of the world that does not tolerate any negatives, and men are often seen as the enemy, personifying the negative. Their dreams often show that behind the very positive façade lies a terrifying level of rage. It is this feeling that is being defended against in the over-identification with the positive archetypal Fand. On the other hand the figure of Emer represents the development of personal feeling life to the extent that one can challenge the masculine heroic values. Emer is a symbol of an evolved, conscious level of the feminine that allows her not only to assert her essential worth as a woman but also to bring consciousness to bear upon the archetypal feminine and to appeal to the *reality* of the relationship she has with Cú Chulainn and not the fantasy.

Táin Bó Cuailnge

Without doubt the most dramatic and unequivocal statement of the heroic ideal is to be found in the central tale of the Ulster period, the 'Táin Bó Cuailnge' or 'The Cattle Raid of Cooley'. Here the ideal qualities of a society of aristocratic warriors are personified in the figure of Cú Chulainn. This story tells of a great conflict between Ulstermen on the one hand and Queen Medb and the Connachtmen on the other. Whilst the story does not conform perfectly to the stages of the heroic biography, in so far as Cú Chulainn is not banished from his homeland, it can nevertheless be seen as depicting the hero returning, and in this sense the battle is the conclusion to his return from the shadowy land of Scáthach. It is also in accordance with Joseph Campbell's stage of the hero returning and serving the community, which Cú Chulainn does as protector of the tribe.

The actual story is the work of many hands over many centuries, and hence it is long and at times riddled with inconsistencies. It is not possible to tell the complete story here, but anyone who is interested in a comprehensive retelling could do no better than to read the translation by Thomas Kinsella, *The Táin*.

The Queen of Connacht, Queen Medb, had at one time been married to Fergus mac Róich, when he was King of Ulster, before Conchobhar displaced him. Because he felt his honour had been violated when Conchobhar tricked him into abandoning his guarantee of Derdriu's safety, Fergus had left Ulster and finished up in the service of Queen Medb, but not as her husband this time. Instead she had married Ailill of Connacht, because he was fearless and generous and without jealousy. This was important, since as a sovereign queen and goddess figure Medb needed to be promiscuous in order to secure the fertility of the land.

The story opens with what has become known as 'pillow talk', with Medb and Ailill lying in bed and talking about their respective wealth. They compared their lands, flocks, dwellings, furnishings, jewellery, concluding that in all things they were equal – with one exception. Ailill's herd included a magnificent bull, called white-horned, *Finn-*

bheanach. Medb had no such animal, but she had heard that a farmer in Cooley, which lay in the southern part of Ulster, had a magnificent bull that would easily match Ailill's. This was Donn Cuailnge or the Brown Bull. Medb was determined to get it, so she sent her messengers to the farmer, seeking a loan of the bull for a year. But the farmer was not interested. Medb decided that this was not good enough and that she would take the bull by force. She mustered her army, along with some troops of Leinster and Munster and Fergus mac Róich, who knew the territory and the enemy very well. Before she set off she consulted her druid, who prophesied that she at least would return alive, which was hardly an optimistic forecast. She had not gone very far before she came across a strange woman who rode on the shaft of a chariot, and sought her prophecy. The woman answered ominously, 'I see crimson, I see red.' Four times Medb appealed against this oracle, but each time the answer was exactly the same. Then the prophetess chanted a poem in which she foretold the heroic deeds of Cú Chulainn. But Queen Medb was not a woman to give up easily, and she ventured on with Fergus, guiding her army towards Ulster.

Although Fergus yearned for revenge for the betrayal by Conchobhar, he still felt a pang of longing for Ulster and he delayed his progress long enough to send warnings of the impending attack to the Ulstermen. But the Ulstermen were stricken with a mysterious sickness which came upon them at times of danger and greatest need. (Recall that Macha Wife of Crunnchu had placed a curse upon the warriors of Ulster that for nine times nine generations they would suffer the sickness of childbirth in the hour of greatest danger. This curse came to be known as 'the Novena of the Ulstermen' and debilitated all adult males of the province for five nights and four days at a time of danger.) Cú Chulainn, being from Muirthemne, was exempt from the curse, so he alone was left to face Queen Medb's warriors. It was he alone who could, and indeed had to, defend the tribe of Ulster.

At Ard Cuillen Cú Chulainn cut an oak sapling with a single stroke and, using one arm, one leg and one eye, shaped it into a hoop on which he wrote a message in ogham before fixing it to a standing stone. When the Connacht army reached Ard Cuillen, Fergus read the message, which said that any man who advanced further that night would be slain by Cú Chulainn unless he made a hoop in the same manner. They decided to avoid the challenge that night and the next day Cú Chulainn found them at Cnobga. There he cut off the fork of a tree and rammed it into the earth so that two-thirds of it was buried.

Then he came upon four Connacht warriors and their charioteers, and promptly beheaded them. He stuck their heads on the branches of the tree and sent the horses and chariots back to the Connacht camp with the headless bodies. This sent the Connacht men into a panic, and they feared that the entire Ulster army must be nearby. They sent one of the other defectors from the Derdriu period to check the situation out, assuming that the Ulstermen would not kill one of their own kind. The scout was Cormac, son of Conchobhar, who advanced with three thousand men, but he found only the tree with the four bleeding heads. When Fergus caught up with the advance party he explained to them that there was a *geis* against crossing the ford until one of them could remove the fork with one hand without dismounting from his chariot, because that was the manner in which Cú Chulainn had placed it. Medb asked Fergus to do it himself, but he failed seventeen times until finally he used his own chariot and succeeded. Ailill and Medb wondered who could have killed four men so suddenly, and Fergus told them it was Cú Chulainn, his own foster-son. Fergus then related the youthful biography of Cú Chulainn to Medb and Ailill.

The next day the army moved eastward, but Cú Chulainn pursued and harassed them, killing a hundred men at a time. Medb pleaded with her troops for someone to stand up to Cú Chulainn but no one would, so finally she sought a parley with him; but Cú Chulainn refused to accept any conditions and for the next three nights he killed a hundred men each night. Medb sent a further messenger to Cú Chulainn, who replied that they should send a single warrior to fight him each day and the army could only advance while that combat lasted. Medb decided to accept the proposal, but of course few single combats lasted very long with Cú Chulainn. Medb became increasingly frustrated at the slowness of her army's progress and as a result she reneged on the agreement and marched north. Cú Chulainn was hard-pressed to defend Ulster alone; and one of Medb's contingent managed to capture the Brown Bull of Cooley and take it away.

By now Cú Chulainn was exhausted, and his divine father Lugh came to his assistance and held the fort for him, allowing his son to sleep for three days and nights. Lugh also administered herbs to his wounds so that they healed while he slept. In the mean time the boys of Ulster, who were not affected by the curse, fought three battles against the Connacht army and killed three times their number, but were finally all obliterated by the Connachtmen. When Cú Chulainn awoke he learnt of this tragedy, which immediately evoked his *riastradh*, and he took off, seeking vengeance for the boys of Ulster. He went on a wild rampage, slaying all he came across, until Medb prevailed upon Fergus to oppose him. This put Fergus in a dreadful dilemma, since he was being asked to fight his own foster-child. Fergus arrived unarmed, and the two agreed that Cú Chulainn would flee before Fergus now, on the understanding that Fergus would yield to Cú Chulainn in the final battle.

Medb meanwhile persuaded a renowned warrior, Fer Diad, to oppose Cú Chulainn. Fer Diad was most reluctant to fight Cú Chulainn, because they had both trained together under the tutorage of Scáthach and therefore regarded each other as foster-brothers-in-arms. However Medb tricked Fer Diad by telling him that Cú Chulainn had claimed superiority over him, and challenged his honour. This was a challenge that any heoric warrior could not decline. The harrowing battle that followed between these two friends lasted for three days without either warrior gaining the ascendancy. Each night Cú Chulainn sent leeches and herbs to heal Fer Diad's wounds, and he in turn sent a share of his food to Cú Chulainn. On the fourth day the choice of weapons lay with Cú Chulainn and he called for his *gae bolga*, a spear which exploded into thirty separate spear points when it entered the body. Cú Chulainn alone had learnt the art of this weapon from Scáthach, and in choosing it he was also choosing to kill his friend, for no one survived a wounding from the *gae bolga*. As Fer Diad was dying Cú Chulainn clasped his arms around him. Fer Diad looked up at Cú Chulainn and uttered his last words:

> O Cú of grand feats
> Unfairly I am slain
> Thy guilt clings to me
> My blood falls on thee
>
> . . .
>
> My rib's armour burst
> My head is all gore;
> I battled not well;
> I am smitten, O Cú!
> Unfair, side by side,
> To come to the ford.
> 'Gainst my noble ward
> Hath Medb turned my hand![10]

Loeg, Cú Chulainn's charioteer, became impatient with him and feared that Fer Diad's death would provoke a major attack. But Cú Chulainn was frozen in his grief and uttered the following words:

> Ah, Ferdiad, betrayed to death,
> Our last meeting, oh, how sad!
> Thou to die, I to remain.
> Ever sad our long farewell!
>
> When we over yonder dwelt
> With our Scáthach, steadfast, true,
> This we thought, that till the end of time,
> Our friendship would never end!
>
> Dear to me thy noble blush;
> Dear thy comely, perfect form;
> Dear thine eye, blue-grey and clear;
> Dear thy wisdom and thy speech.[11]

Cú Chulainn himself was badly wounded from the battle and utterly exhausted, and his human father Sualdam had sensed his son's distress and sought him out. But Cú Chulainn would not allow any sympathy and instead instructed his father to return instantly to Emain Macha and rouse the Ulstermen, for by now the curse upon them would have passed. This Sualdam did and an advance party was sent to rescue Cú Chulainn, and the remainder of the Ulster army followed on, attacking the Connachtmen and their allies with great fury. Cú Chulainn rose from his sickbed when he heard the noise of the battle and rushed forward, yielding his chariot as a weapon. Seeing him approach, Fergus fulfilled his part of the agreement and led his company away from the battle. The men of Leinster and Munster followed, and the Connachtmen stood alone to face Conchobhar and the Ulstermen. Queen Medb intervened at this point and appealed to Cú Chulainn to spare her army, to which he consented, and they retreated in disgrace.

However Medb was not that easily defeated: she had already dispatched the famous brown bull to her herd in Cruachan, where the two big bulls met. A ferocious contest ensued, and by nightfall the noise of the white bull and the brown bull goring away at each other could be heard all over Ireland. In the morning the brown bull was seen passing by Cruachan with the mangled carcase of its rival on its horns.

On reaching its own homeland the brown bull's heart burst and the great bull of Cooley expired.

Thus ends 'The Cattle Raid of Cooley', with the death of the two bulls that started it in the first place. Clearly they were not ordinary bulls, and we should bear in mind the divine status of bulls in ancient religion. Some have suggested that the names of the bulls are indirectly derived from two earlier figures, Find and Donn, who may be viewed as opposites. Find, according to Daithi O'hOgain,[12] was sometimes pictured as a divine child who symbolized wisdom. At his birth Find emerged from mystical waters physically mature, symbolizing the existence of a mystical wisdom and the ability to penetrate the future, present and past. The parallel between this figure and another of Jung's archetypes, the miraculous child, is striking. Donn was the warrior who refused to pay homage to the goddess of Ireland and was therefore cursed to drown and never set foot on Erin's shore. He went instead to inhabit the island of the dead known as Tech Duinn and, as the name itself suggests, is associated with endings, the dark side of human nature and the shadowy realm of the dead. Donn could then be seen as symbolizing the opposite of Find, and 'The Cattle Raid of Cooley' as depicting the conflict between these two opposite aspects of being, the dark and the light.

A further clue to the divinity of these bulls is found in accounts that they underwent several metamorphoses. In ancient Irish tradition, as in other mythic traditions, this is an attribute of deities. There is a ninth-century tale in *The Book of Leinster* entitled 'The Quarrel of the Two Pig Keepers', in which Friuch and Rucht, two otherworld pig keepers, quarrelled and cast spells on each other's pigs. Their otherworld masters, learning of this, dismissed them both from service, whereupon they turned themselves into birds of prey, fish, stags, warriors, phantoms and dragons, fighting each other all the time. Finally they turned into maggots; one of them went into a spring in Cooley and was swallowed by a cow belonging to a farmer called Daire. The other was swallowed by a Connacht cow belonging to Queen Medb and her husband. These two cows then bore two bull calves which became the brown bull of Cooley and the white bull of Connacht.

There has been some suggestion that 'The Cattle Raid of Cooley' indicates the existence of an Irish version of the Mithraic cult, involving the sacrifice of a bull. Certainly the divination rite of *tarbhfeis*, which was used to determine who should be king, involved the killing of the bull and the drinking of its blood. However I think it is perhaps more useful to see the bull as a complex symbol which over time has symbolized both the female earth goddess and the masculine solar god. The Mithraic cult itself seems to reflect the masculine solar principle penetrating the feminine principle, resulting in the fertilization of the earth by the sun. So within the seasonal mythology of Ireland the two bulls may symbolize the cyclical struggle between the darkness of winter and the fertilizing quality of spring and summer. The question that then arises is why Queen Medb felt disadvantaged in not having the bull of Cooley. It is also possible that Medb, who personifies the feminine divinity, is attempting in this story to retrieve the power that has slowly been eroded by the masculine divinity with the rise of an aristocratic warrior class.

The Táin itself is perhaps also a story of transition from a lunar-based, feminine divinity to a solar, masculine one. Certainly Cú Chulainn has been seen in some circles as a personification of a solar hero, particularly since his father the god Lugh is very often associated with the sun. Cú Chulainn aids the conquering of the feminine form in the symbol of Queen Medb, and in this way the hero transcends his role as mediator between the worlds and becomes instead temporarily triumphant over one of them. This is of course precisely what is occurring in our modern world, where the ego has identified itself with the hero of rationalism and 'forgotten' that it is merely part of the plot. In psychological terms the ego's over-identification with the hero archetype leads to a sense of ego-inflation, which results in a severing of contact with the feminine or inner world. The wider consequence of such an inflation, in which Logos becomes rampant, is the trampling of the feminine values of Eros, connection and feeling, manifested in social concern. But just as the earth needs the sun to fertilize its seed, so does the feeling life need Logos to facilitate the expression of feeling in the outer world. It is all a question of balance, the holding of the opposites, not the triumphing of one over the other.

So, our hero has now triumphed over his enemies, received help from the otherworld, chooses between friendship and honour, draws upon his learning from the otherworld and finally emerges as the archetypal protector of his tribe. However the hero must inevitably face his death, and this as we know from the International Heroic Biography is usually as dramatic as his birth and life.

The death of the hero is the final significant event of his biography and is characterized by two features: the hero dies young, and the death has some magical or miraculous qualities about it. Just as there was a propitious time for each of the stages of the hero's life from conception on, there is also an appointed time for his death. Druids, seers or people from the otherworld often prophesy the nature of the hero's death, and there are frequently omens or portents of it. Within Irish mythology the death regularly occurs at Samain, symbolizing the beginning of the darkness of winter. The hero's invincibility means that his death can only be brought about by supernatural forces in combination with the violation of his personal *geasa*. Once dead, within Irish myth, the hero is truly dead and unlike the divine figures does not continue. This reminds us that the hero is not of the divine world but of the mortal one, and that his uniqueness lies in his capacity to mediate between the worlds.

By the time Cú Chulainn was in his twenties he had made many enemies. The chief amongst these was Queen Medb, who continued to harbour resentment at the humiliation her troops had experienced during the cattle raid of Cooley. Another much-feared enemy were the children of the magician Calitin. Cú Chulainn had slain Calitin and twenty of his sons, and at the same time his wife had given birth to six children, all monstrous and misshapen. Medb took them as foster-children and instructed them in sorcery. To advance their knowledge she sent them away to a mysterious land in the east and upon completion of their training they conjured up a fierce wind and rode it back to Queen Medb's fort at Cruachan. With these powerful allies she decided it was time, once again, to raid Ulster and specifically to destroy Cú Chulainn. King Conchobhar heard of the plan and called Cú Chulainn to Emain Macha, ordering him to remain there until the war was over. When Medb arrived at his fort she found that he had gone. Infuriated, she set fire to it and destroyed all the remaining inmates. The children of Calitin then promised Medb that they would kill Cú Chulainn within three days.

Conjuring up another magical wind, they went to Emain Macha and used their sorcery to create an illusion of a raging battle in which there were vast armies of warriors furiously fighting and attacking Emain Macha. Cú Chulainn heard the noise and rushed to get his weapons, but the druid Cathbad grabbed him and told him it was a mere illusion. Cú Chulainn momentarily heeded Cathbad's advice, but before long the noise of battle came again, and again it stirred him into action. Eventually Cathbad was able to persuade Cú Chulainn to resist the illusion and he returned to the company of Emer and another woman, Niamh. While he was asleep, Cathbad and the women decided to take

Cú Chulainn away to the Glen of the Deaf until the three days had passed. Again Cú Chulainn resisted, but he was finally persuaded by Emer to go with Cathbad and Niamh to the glen.

But the children of Calitin were not to be deterred, even though they realized that Cathbad's magic was more powerful than theirs. They called up their enchanted wind and flew all over Ulster and then into Donegal, searching every glen, wood and mountain for Cú Chulainn. Finally they spotted his two horses, the ones that were born at the same moment as Cú Chulainn. One of the daughters of Calitin took on the shape of Niamh's attendant and tricked Niamh and the rest of the company into leaving the hostel. They then threw a magical mist between the women and the hostel, temporarily obscuring it from view. The daughter then changed herself into Niamh's form and told Cú Chulainn that it was now high time he put on his weapons and faced the enemy. Cú Chulainn did not need a second invitation and in no time he was donning his battledress. But just as he went to attach his gold brooch to his cloak it sprang straight out of his hand, piercing his foot as it fell. Cú Chulainn knew this to be a bad omen but he chose to ignore it.

Cathbad and Niamh pursued him, yelling at him that it was all a trick, but by now the adrenalin was running in Cú Chulainn. Meanwhile Loeg, his charioteer, could not harness one of the horses, the Grey of Macha, who kept bucking away until Cú Chulainn coaxed it into its harness. But as he did so it shed great black tears of blood which fell at Cú Chulainn's feet and raised the dust. Again he knew this to be an omen but he declared that he had never shirked a battle and repeated the heroic dictum that fame outlives life.

On his way to the battlefield he came across three old hags, each blind in the left eye, bent over a cooking fire. Cú Chulainn saw that the animal being cooked was a dog, and there was a *geis* upon him that he should never eat the flesh of a dog, since he had killed the hound of Culan. The three hags offered him a piece of meat, but there was another *geis* upon him that he could never pass a cooking hearth without partaking of the fare. At first he refused, but one of the hags berated him for refusing a meal. So he submitted, taking the portion she offered him in his left hand, eating a little then placing it under his left thigh. At this instant both the left hand and the left thigh lost their strength. Shaken, he quickly departed and rode on to the Plain of Muirthemne where the enemy were to be confronted.

Next he came to a ford where he observed a young woman washing bloodstained clothes and sobbing uncontrollably. Cú Chulainn watched and then saw that it was his clothes she was washing. She was the Washer of the Ford, the daughter of Badb, goddess of war and death. Loeg pleaded with him to turn back before it was too late, since the Washer at the Ford was a portent of impending death. But the warrior fury was upon Cú Chulainn and he raced towards the plain. By now he had violated his *geasa*, death was imminent and so he fatalistically advanced towards the Plain of Muirthemne where the sons of Calitin had been joined by two of his old enemies, Lugaid and Erc.

Although now virtually undone by his *geasa*, Cú Chulainn was still a formidable warrior, killing many of his opponents, and his enemies resorted to the weapon of sorcery. Erc selected three pairs of his champions and positioned a druid beside each couple of warriors. As Cú Chulainn approached the champions started a mock battle, and the druid called on Cú Chulainn to separate the fighters. Cú Chulainn promptly did this by killing them both in one blow. The druid then demanded that Cú Chulainn forgo one of his three spears, but Cú Chulainn refused. The druid replied, 'I shall revile you if you do not give it to me.' Cú Chulainn, exclaiming that he had never lost his good name by refusal, flung the spear towards the druid with such force that it passed through his head and killed the nine men that stood behind him. Lugaid picked the spear up and asked, 'What will fall by this spear?' The sons of Calitin replied, 'A king will fall by that spear.' Lugaid cast the spear, which killed Loeg, the king of charioteers.

This scene was repeated a second time, with the druid threatening to revile Ulster if Cú Chulainn didn't hand over his spear after killing two more mock combatants. Warrior honour demanded that Cú Chulainn hand it over to protect the good name of his tribe. Erc picked it up and threw it, striking Cú Chulainn's horse, the Grey of Macha, the king of steeds. A third time Cú Chulainn encountered two combatants in a mock fight, killed them both, and yielded his spear to the druid under the threat of satire. This time Lugaid picked it up and hurled it back, striking Cú Chulainn so that his entrails were exposed. At this his second horse panicked and broke away from the chariot, leaving Cú Chulainn, the king of warriors, lying alone.

But still his enemies were wary of the great warrior and kept their distance. Cú Chulainn broke the impasse by yelling to his enemies that he was thirsty and desperately needed a drink from the nearby lough. They conceded to the request, so he gathered up his entrails and dragged himself to the lake. As he took a drink an otter known in Irish as a water dog, came to drink his blood. Cú Chulainn cast a stone and killed it, and now he knew he must die, for it had been prophesied that his last heroic deed, like his first, would be to kill a dog. On the shore he saw a stone pillar and struggled towards it. He fastened himself to the stone with his breastplate so that he would die standing up, for he had sworn that he would meet his death 'feet on the ground, face to the foe'.

Lugaid finally decided to move towards Cú Chulainn and drew his sword. Suddenly the noise of pounding hooves was heard and the Grey of Macha, covered in blood and sweat, charged at them and routed the gathered warriors, scattering them far and wide. Having achieved his final feat the noble horse retreated and died.

Some say that for three more days the enemy warily watched Cú Chulainn while the raven of death, the Morrígan in her bird form, hovered overhead. Finally she descended on to Cú Chulainn's shoulder and this signalled the moment at which he finally expired. As he did so he let out an enormous sigh and the stone pillar split in half. Lugaid now approached Cú Chulainn and bared his neck for decapitation, but at that very moment Cú Chulainn's sword fell from his hand and severed Lugaid's wrist. Then Cú Chulainn's head was cut from his body and borne to Tara as a trophy, leaving his body still tied to the cracked pillar.

Thus the great Ulster hero's life ends as extraordinarily as it began. Even the great hero must submit to the forces beyond his control, as symbolized by his *geasa*. It is as if a hero is safe from harm so long as he does not violate his *geasa*, but as fate would have it such a violation is inevitable; the forces that govern *geis* are more powerful than the heroic ego. This is simply because it is the otherworld that lays the *geis* upon a mortal, and determines the process of violation. The *geasa* thereby serve as a symbolic reminder of the permanent presence of the otherworld. So also in our modern psychological myths, the unconscious and various internal objects, or figures of the otherworld, exert their influence, waylaying the best of our ego-based plans and revealing the power of life beyond our conscious horizon.

1 2

THE FENIAN CYCLE

Around the second century AD, King Cathaer Mór, Cathair the Great, ruled from the traditional seat of the High King at Tara. In the service of King Cathaer Mór was a famous druid called Nuada who sought from the King an allotment of land in Leinster. Cathaer willingly gave the land to Nuada, who built a beautiful white-fronted fort, and his wife Almu requested that the hill upon which it was built be named after her.

> Almu – beautiful was the woman!
> Wife of Nuada the great son of Achi;
> She entreated – the division was just –
> That her name should be on the perfect hill.[1]

When Nuada died, his gifted son Tadg took over his role as a druid to the King. His wife bore him a daughter, known as Muirne the Fair Neck. She grew into a most beautiful young woman and the sons of kings and the lords of Ireland sought her hand in marriage. Among one of these ardent suitors was Cumall mac Trénmór, the leader of the King's band of warriors. Conn of the Hundred Battles and Cumall's father were half-brothers (the wife of Tuathal, the High King of Ireland, had eloped with Cumall's father, who was at that time the dashing and courageous chief of the King's warriors, and to him she bore three sons, Cumall, Crimall and Aed Ollan). Conn and Cumall's relationship as kinsmen put obligations upon both of them.

Where all the suitors for Muirne's hand had failed, Cumall was not so easily dissuaded. Yet he represented a serious threat to Tadg, who believed that if Cumall was successful then he would not only lose his daughter but also his land. But his flat rejection of Cumall as a future son-in-law only served to strengthen the warrior's determination and, not being able to acquire her legitimately, he went ahead and abducted her. Tadg was so enraged by Cumall's actions that he went to Conn,

185

who by now had become King, demanding that he order Cumall to return Muirne to Almu. He further reminded him that as a kinsman he had an obligation to do so.

Conn immediately dispatched a messenger to Cumall ordering him to return Muirne to her family. Cumall told the messenger to convey to the King that he would give anything in compensation to Tadg, but would not return his daughter.

This defiance left Conn no choice other than to fight Cumall, so he mustered support from the chiefs of Leinster and Connacht and the soldiers of the Clan of Morna. From Munster in the south Cumall gathered men loyal to his clan of Baoiscne. The armies faced each other at Cnucha (now Castlenock in Co. Dublin) and a fierce battle followed, with Cumall's soldiers greatly outnumbered by the king's troops. During the battle Luchet struck Aed, one of the sons of Morna, in the face and blinded him in one eye. From this time on he was always known as Goll mac Morna ('goll' means 'blind' or 'one-eyed'.) But Goll was a furious fighter: he killed Luchet, and his followers routed the Clan Baoiscne, killing Cumall, who had been badly wounded by a warrior who stole the *corrbolg*, the bag in which Cumall kept the treasures of his clan.

Muirne was pregnant, and now, with Cumall dead, she returned to her father's house, but Tadg disowned her because she was pregnant. He indeed had gone so far as to order his people to burn her, so she fled to the King's fortress at Tara and sought Conn's protection and advice. He advised her to seek refuge in Leinster with Fíacal, the husband of Cumall's sister, the druidess Bodbmall. Shortly after her arrival Muirne gave birth to a boy who was given the name Demne.

Conn in the mean time had rewarded Goll mac Morna by appointing him head of the *fían* (warrior band) in place of Cumall's heir, and from this position Goll mac Morna pursued both Muirne and her child with the intention of killing both of them. He was particularly determined to kill Cumall's son, who he knew would one day seek his rightful position as head of the *fían*. Muirne decided that the only chance Demne had of surviving lay in her giving him over to Bodbmall and another druidess-warrior known as the Grey One of Luachair. These two women, being *benfénnid* (female warriors), knew how to survive in the wild and were able to rear the child in complete secrecy and safety in the woods and valleys of Slíab Bloom, a mountain range on the boundary between Leinster and Munster. Muirne escaped to the south of Ireland, where in due course she married a king.

When Demne was six years of age his mother, who had pined deeply for the boy, secretly came to visit him. The two women recognized her and warmly welcomed her. They led her to where the young boy was asleep and she lifted him up, holding him to her bosom, and gently spoke to him, finally rocking him to sleep and then taking leave of her son. As she left she thanked the women for the care and love they had provided for him and asked them to look after him until he was able to fend for himself. She then left, secretly weaving her way through the woods and wilderness until she arrived safely back in her own territory in the south of Ireland.

As Demne grew his foster-mothers taught him many things about nature, the seasons and the animals, and how to live in the woods, and he became skilled in many crafts. One day he saw a flock of wild duck flying overhead and he struck one of them a fatal blow with his catapult. As his confidence grew from this first hunting experience he ventured further and further afield. However this meant he became more visible, and it was not long before there was talk about the fair-haired boy seen hunting so skilfully in the forests around Slíab Bloom.

Goll mac Morna heard the rumours and suspected that this was Cumall's son, so he sent his trackers to seek him out. However the druidesses intuited the danger and sent Demne off in the company of three craftsmen. He remained with them for some time, but they treated him extremely poorly and he became mangy and lost his hair for a while (and thus for a short period he was known as Demne the Bald). One night the craftsmen were killed by a robber, who captured Demne and took him south to be a slave in his own house. But the druidic foster-mothers learnt of the kidnap, and sought him out. They forced the robber to hand Demne over and made their way back with him to the safety of the mountains of Slíab Bloom.

One day he came upon an open plain on which there was a large fort and a group of boys playing hurley. Demne joined in the game, and very quickly established that he was both the fastest and the most skilful of all the boys there. The next day he returned to play again; he first played against a quarter of them and won, then against a third of them, winning again, and finally he competed against them all and still won. The boys were astonished and asked him his name. When they recalled the event to the chief of the fort, he found it hard to believe what he was hearing. 'What is his name?' he enquired, and they replied, 'Demne.' 'What does he look like?' the chief asked, and the boys replied that he was tall and his hair was very fair. 'Then,' said the chief, 'we will call him Fionn,' meaning 'fair-haired'.

Amazement and admiration quickly turned to envy and hatred, and when Demne appeared the next day they all threw hurley sticks at him. Demne grabbed a stick and charged the troop, knocking seven of them down and scattering the rest. Sometime later he was going for a swim in a nearby mountain lake when he heard noisy shouting from the water. It was the same boys he had beaten at hurley, and they challenged Demne to come and wrestle in the water, planning to drown him the moment he entered the water. Just as they tried to grab him he whirled around and held nine of them underwater, drowning them. The remaining boys panicked and fled back to the fort to tell of the latest drama involving the fair-haired boy. It wasn't long before word of these exploits spread, so that his foster-mothers began to doubt whether they could keep him safe much longer. The matter came to a head shortly afterwards, when they came across a fierce herd of wild deer; both women expressed regret that they were not able to catch one of the deer, but Demne ran after the deer, caught two of them and brought them back to the bothy.

The women realized that Demne was now at the stage where he could fend for himself, and the promise they had made to his mother had been honoured. They told Demne that it was now time for him to leave, as they could no longer guarantee his safety. Sadly Demne left his foster-mothers and headed towards the south of Ireland, finally stopping at Bantry, where he offered his services to the local king. Of course it was only a short time before his outstanding prowess as a hunter made the King wonder who this youth was. Because Demne had kept his identity secret the King decided to trick him into revealing it and one day he said to him, 'I would have sworn you were the son of Cumall because you are so like him, except I know he left only one son who I believe is in military service with the King of Scotland.' Demne did not take the bait, but he decided to leave the King of Bantry and headed to Kerry, where he undertook further service with another king. This time it was Demne's skill at *fidchell* (a form of chess) that jeopardized his anonymity. After Demne had beaten the King seven times in a row, the exasperated and bewildered King asked him who he was. Demne replied that he was the son of a peasant from Tara. The King did not believe him: 'No, you are not. You are the son of Muirne and Cumall, and you cannot stay here any longer because Goll mac Morna is out to kill you and I do not want you to be slain under my protection.' Demne now made his way east, to another chief who was loyal to his own clan, and sought protection from him. This chief had a blacksmith named Lóchán, who had a very beautiful daughter called Cruithne. She fell in love with Demne and Lóchán, not even knowing who Demne was, agreed to give his daughter to him. Lóchán then made Demne two spears to protect him from a fierce wild boar that had been terrifying the local people. One day, after taking leave of Lóchán, he encountered the wild boar in a narrow mountain pass; it charged towards him and with no escape possible he hurled one of the spears, which went right through the huge beast, killing it instantly. Demne then brought its head back to Lóchán as a gift for giving him his daughter. The mountain in Munster where the boar was slain is to this day known as Slíab Muicce, the Mountain of the Pig. After a while, restlessness took hold of Demne and he set off to Connacht in search of his uncle Crimall.

On his way there he heard the loud wailing of a woman, and as he went towards her he noticed that her tears were of blood and blood gushed from her mouth. 'Why are your tears of blood and your mouth red with blood?' said Demne. The woman replied that her only son had just been killed by a huge warrior. Demne responded as any true hero would and immediately went after the murderer, challenging him to a fight. A furious battle followed in which Demne slew the tall warrior; then he noticed a strange bag beside the body, which he took.

He continued his journey westward, to the desolate area where Crimall and the last remaining followers of Cumall had taken refuge. Crimall was delighted to receive his nephew and instantly noticed the strange bag that he carried, and Demne explained how he had come by it. Crimall told Demne that the warrior he had slain was Líath Lúachra, who had wounded Demne's father at the Battle of Cnucha and then stolen the *corrbolg*. The craneskin bag had originally belonged to Manannán mac Lir of the Tuatha Dé Danann, and it contained magical objects from the god. Crimall regarded the recovery of the bag as a good omen and prophesied to Demne that his clan would once again become leaders of the *fían*. But he went on to tell Demne that his leadership, and indeed his own safety from the death threats of the Clan Morna, would only be achieved when he was as accomplished a *fili*, or poet, as he was a hunter.

Demne took his uncle's advice and travelled to the banks of the River Boyne where there lived a poet and teacher named Finnéces. This poet, whose name literally means 'Fionn the Seer', had been waiting by the

Boyne for seven years to catch the salmon of wisdom from a pool called the Linn Féic. Whoever ate the salmon of Linn Féic would be all-knowing and nothing would remain unknown, because the salmon ate the hazelnuts of wisdom that fell from a magic tree overhanging the pool. When Demne arrived, Finnéces had just caught the salmon; he entrusted the cooking of it to Demne, but gave him the strictest instructions that he must not, under any circumstances, eat even the smallest morsel of it. Demne built a fire and cooked the salmon, but just as he lifted it off the spit the hot skin of the fish burnt his thumb and instinctively he placed it in his mouth to ease the pain. He then brought the cooked fish to Finnéces, who realized that Demne had a different aura about him. 'Are you sure you have not tasted the fish?' he demanded. Demne replied that he hadn't, but that he had burnt his thumb and put it into his mouth to ease the pain. Finnéces let out a long, loud groan of disappointment, and then asked, 'What is your name, boy?' 'My name is Demne,' the boy replied. 'No,' said Finnéces, 'your name is Fionn, since it was prophesied that a fair-haired person would eat the salmon of knowledge and it is you for whom this prophecy has come true.' Finnéces explained to Fionn that he could now acquire wisdom and knowledge whenever he needed it by simply putting his thumb into his mouth. Fionn was then taught the three things that defined a poet, that is, knowledge which illuminates (*imbas forosnai*), the chewing of the pith (*teinm laída*) and incantations from heads (*díchetal dí chennaib*). At the same time he acquired the power of saving the life of any sick or wounded man by giving him a drink of water from his cupped hands. From Finnéces he proceeded to Cethern, son of Fintin, to master the twelve books of *fili* lore. (The filid were not only seers and poets, but were also experts on the rights and duties of kings.)

At the time all the men of Ireland were pursuing a beautiful otherworld maiden called Éile. One man at a time would come to her fairy fort, but the wooing could only be done at Samain (1 November), when the *sídhe* opened up and the barrier between the visible and the invisible worlds was temporarily dissolved. However every time a man attempted to woo Éile one of his company would be killed. Cethern had decided it was his turn to attempt to woo the beautiful otherworld maiden, and Fionn, concerned for his welfare, decided to accompany Cethern along with three bands of nine men. However just as with every other previous attempt to woo Éile one of the number, Oircbél the poet, was mysteriously slain. Following this, Cethern's company disbanded and Fionn returned to the home of Fíacal. Here he expressed his sorrow about the companion who had been slain at the fairy fort of Éile, and his desire to seek revenge for the death, to honour the warrior responsibility of putting a wrong right, even if that wrong had been perpetrated by the folk of the otherworld. The ledger always had to be balanced between the otherworld and those outside it, and the role for a *fénnid*, or warrior, was to restore the balance.

Fíacal advised Fionn to go and camp at the Two Paps of Anu. He arrived at Samains and the magic mist that normally protected the fairy kingdoms from view dissolved. This allowed Fionn to see the two strongholds of the fairy kingdom. The first thing he saw was two great fires, one in each *sídhe*. He then overheard a conversation between two figures, one asking the other whether there was anything that needed to be brought from one *sídhe* to the other in order to facilitate a feast. Next, Fionn witnessed one man emerging from a *sídhe* carrying a cooked pig, a cooked calf and a bunch of garlic for a Samain celebration. The man of the otherworld did not see Fionn and as he went past Fionn threw a spear he had got from Fíacal, saying to himself, I think I have avenged the death of my companion. Fionn then fled for his life, as a great wailing came from the *sídhe*:

> By the spear Birga on the Barrow River
> Aed, son of Fidach, has fallen
> With the spear of Fíacal, son of Codna.
> Fionn has slain him beyond the dwelling.

Fíacal then joined up with Fionn and asked him whom he had slain, to which Fionn replied that he had no idea. At this point they both heard more lamentations from the *sídhe*:

> This spear is poisoned,
> The one who owns it is poisoned
> And it is the poison of anyone who throws it,
> It is poison for whomever it strikes.

Fionn then seized a woman of the otherworld as a hostage, since he wanted to guarantee that his spear was returned. She promised that if he let her go she would have the spear returned. Fionn let her go and she kept her promise by throwing the spear out and saying at the same time:

> The spear is poisoned,
> The hand that threw it is poisoned;
> Unless it is thrown out of the Síd,
> Plague will seize the land because of it.[2]

Fíacal told Fionn that he had indeed slain the otherworld man who had killed his companion, and that this man had killed everyone who came to woo Éile because he was in love with her himself. Fíacal then gave the spear to Fionn to acknowledge his achievement. Having avenged the death of Oircbél, and learnt the art of poetry, Fionn set off for Tara to reclaim his rightful role as leader of the *fían* of Conn, who was now the High King of Ireland.

When he arrived at Tara it was the eve of Samain, and the King and his court were holding a feast. Conn was seated on his throne in the great hall of his palace with his son Art beside him and Goll mac Morna, the leader of the *fían*, in a privileged position nearby. With the banquet in full swing Fionn walked into the hall where the King, taken aback to see the youthful intruder, asked him who he was. He replied, 'I am Fionn, son of Cumall, your former leader of the *fían*, and I have come to make peace with you and put myself at your service.' Conn replied, 'You are the son of a friend and trusted servant,' and welcomed Fionn into the court of Tara. Fionn swore his allegiance to Conn, who responded by placing him next to Art. The feasting and entertainment continued until the merriment was suddenly stopped by the sound of the King's horn. Conn spoke to the assembled group, reminding them that at this time of the year no feuding or revenge could take place amongst mortals, and also that Tara itself was attacked every Samain by an otherworld figure. This was Aillén, who first lulled everybody to sleep with his music then burnt Tara down with fire spewed from his mouth. Conn told all those gathered that anyone who could defend Tara against the destructiveness of Aillén would be awarded his birthright, no matter how humble or important. The group remained silent, since they all knew the irresistible soporific power of the music that Aillén played on his harp. Then into the silence came the voice of Fionn: 'If I save Tara who will guarantee my heritage?' Conn replied that he would, as would all the druids and poets gathered at the festival. Fionn of course was gambling on achieving the return of his rightful place as head of the *fían*.

Now amongst the many warriors gathered at Tara celebrating Samain was Fíacha, who had been a close and much-trusted friend of

Fionn's father Cumall. He quietly pulled Fionn to one side and offered to help him in return for a third of Fionn's profits he gained and becoming one of this three most trusted advisers. Fionn asked in return in what way Fiacha would help him, and Fiacha said he would give him a certain magical spear that never missed its mark. The youth and the old warrior agreed, and Fiacha brought the spear to Fionn. In giving it to him Fiacha said that as soon as he heard the first note of Aillén's enchanted music he had to put the spear up against his forehead, to protect himself from the spell of the music so that he would be able to stay awake.

Fionn retreated from the festivities and took up his position outside the fort to await the arrival of Aillén. It was not long before he heard the first alluring notes of the harp, and instantly he placed the spear against his forehead. The plaintive and enchanting music filled the halls of Tara and every man and woman was lulled to sleep by the magical sounds. Thinking he was now safe, Aillén blew out a great burst of fire, but Fionn held up his purple-fringed cloak and deflected the fire down on to the ground, where it scorched the earth. Aillén was shocked that his powers had been resisted and took flight back to his otherworld dwelling, but just as he was about to enter the hilltop cairn Fionn hurled the magic spear at him, killing him instantly. He then beheaded Aillén and returned triumphant to Tara, impaling the head on a pole for all the assembly to see when they woke from their sleep. When Conn saw the head of Aillén he asserted that the son of Cumall was to claim his rightful heritage as the Rígfénnid, or head of the King's *fían*. He turned to Goll mac Morna and offered him the choice of accepting Fionn as the Rígfénnid and serving under him or leaving Ireland altogether. Goll did not hesitate to give his loyalty to Fionn.

Fionn led the *fían* to great notoriety and glory, undertaking many, many heroic adventures throughout Ireland. The *fían* produced three great poets, Fionn himself, his son Oisín, and Caílte. Their adventures included visits to the otherworld, hunting, fighting as élite militia on behalf of their king, extracting justice for people, collecting fines and writing poetry about the beauty of nature, to which they remained very close. Throughout the summer months they lived in the forests, and during the winter they were billeted in the towns and villages. During these months they worked for the King, assisting in the imposition of justice and order.

In addition to his bravery, Fionn is frequently described as an extremely generous figure who was renowned for his hospitality.

Unlike Cú Chulainn's one marriage to Emer, there are tales of Fionn's many marriages and relations with women, including two of Cormac mac Art's daughters, Gráinne and Ailbe, a Scottish princess called Aine, the otherworld woman Scáthach and Sadb, the mother of the great Fenian Oisín. He is invariably portrayed as an outstanding hunter and often he is out hunting deer or pig when he finds himself and his men in an otherworld place where they enjoy a great feast. One story tells of Fionn and five companions spending an entire year in a fairy fort and fighting a battle on behalf of their fairy host.

Another story tells of a female visitor from the otherworld to Almu. This was Bodb Derg's daughter, who had come to stir up trouble at Almu. She challenged the women present to put on her cloak, knowing that it would only completely cover the woman who was pure. None was completely covered by it, and Fionn cursed her and ordered her to leave. Some say she was perhaps the same otherworld woman who tricked Fionn into diving into a magical lake to reclaim a bracelet she had dropped in. As soon as Fionn entered the water he was transformed into an old man and his comrades didn't recognize him at first. They then attacked the fairy fort nearby and demanded that the father of the otherworld woman give Fionn a rejuvenating drink. Fionn was thus restored to his original age, but his hair remained grey.

Of all the stories of Fionn's contact with otherworld women the one involving the birth of his son Oisín is the most significant and perhaps best known. Fionn and his party were returning from a hunt when a beautiful deer appeared in front of them and began to run as fast as the wind towards the fort of Almu. When his two favourite hunting dogs, Bran and Sceolang, finally caught up with the deer, instead of attacking it they began to lick and frolic with it. Fionn knew by this that this was not an animal that could be harmed, so he returned to Almu; the doe followed on their heels, and was given safe quarters for the evening.

That evening, when Fionn retired to his room, a most beautiful woman walked in. She told him that she was the deer he had spared earlier in the day; her name was Sadb and she had been transformed into a deer by an evil spell cast upon her by a dark druid because she refused to love him. She knew that the spell could be broken if only she could get inside a warrior band's fortress. Fionn's hunting dogs had not attacked her because they too had once been humans who had been transformed into animals by a curse, and they recognized her for who she was. Fionn fell deeply in love with Sadb, but one day reluctantly had to leave her because the King had asked him to defend the country from invaders. The moment the battle was over Fionn returned to Almu and to his utter despair he found that Sadb had gone. His servants told how in his absence an evil druid had created the illusion that Fionn himself was outside the fort calling Sadb. Despite their attempts to tell her that it was an evil trick, she ran out to meet him. She threw her arms around the man she thought was Fionn, only to be struck by the wand of the evil druid and once again transformed into a deer.

For fourteen long years Fionn and his two dogs searched for Sadb. Then one day, out hunting near Ben Bulben in Co. Sligo, they heard a great clamour coming from the dogs. They rushed to where the noise was coming from to find Fionn's two faithful hounds holding the other dogs at bay and preventing them from attacking a handsome, long-haired youth. As soon as Fionn called off the other dogs Bran and Sceolang licked the boy and showed delight at being with him. Fionn approached the youth and recognized in him the features of his beloved Sadb. The boy confirmed that he had been reared by a gentle deer, and Fionn realized that when Sadb had been tricked into leaving Almu she was pregnant and that this was his son, whom he named Oisín, meaning 'little deer'. His mother had finally been enchanted by the evil druid who had cast a spell upon her before, and then forced her into leaving the boy and following him. Oisín went on to become a famous Fenian poet he and Caílte miraculously survived for two to three hundred years and lived to tell the tale of Fionn and his *fiana* to St Patrick, a tale that is told in the twelfth-century compendium entitled *Acallam na Senórach*, meaning *The Colloquy of the Ancient Men*.[3]

Fionn, like the other heroic figures of Cú Chulainn and Conaire Mór, dies as a result of transgressing his *geis*. Fionn must never drink from a horn, but once he took a drink in his horn from a spring at a place called Ardharca Iuchbha (the Horn of Iuchbha). Then he put his thumb into his mouth and was able to foresee his own imminent death in a battle that was shortly to follow on the banks of the River Boyne in an area controlled by his enemies. They slew him and brought his head back to their camp, where they proceeded to cook fish. As they were cooking the head suddenly spoke and asked for a morsel of fish. Thus ended the heroic life of Fionn mac Cumhaill.

The story of Fionn forms the central theme of the Fenian Cycle (sometimes known as the Ossianic Cycle, after Oisín). It is concerned with a period around the third century AD and follows directly on from the Ulster Cycle. However, unlike the Ulster Cycle, the Fenian material does not appear to have been written down until around about the twelfth century, perhaps because it was not recited by the *filid* before then. The stories were well known by the simple folk, told around firesides in the country. This, according to such scholars as Gerard Murphy, accounts for the fact that the *fíanna* tales have survived strongly into contemporary Irish folk tales,[4] whereas the gods and Cú Chulainn are scarcely represented in the folk tales, if at all. However the *filid* gradually began to incorporate the tales of Fionn into their repertoire. Beginning around the twelfth century, a succession of poets developed a form of ballad literature, as opposed to the prose style of the mythological and Ulster tales, so that by the sixteenth century Fionn emerged as a far more prominent figure in Irish literature than his predecessors such as Lugh and Cú Chulainn. These poets wove the figure of Fionn into the mythic history of Ireland, so that the Fenian Cycle was conceived as the cycle that followed the Ulster.

The embellishment of the Fionn cycle culminates in the last quarter of the twelfth century with the composing of the *Acallam na Senórach*. This may have had an original single author but has been added to over time and is a kind of reservoir for a diverse range of tradition incorporating folk motifs, mythological and warrior motifs, quasi-history, *dinnshenchas* (mythical geography, also known as the lore of place), lyric and ballad poetry. Above all else the *Acallam* fixes the character of Fionn and narrates his adventures. These as mentioned previously are told by his son Oisín and foster-son Caílte, whose narration of the adventures to St Patrick is the means by which the tales are given authority. Oisín survives to tell St Patrick of his father and the *fíanna* because, having been enticed there by Niamh, he survived in the otherworld of Tír na nÓg, a place where no one grew old or died.

The *Acallam* represents a coming together of pagan and Christian Ireland, and intially tells of how Caílte led St Patrick to a well, which was used to baptize the people of north Dublin and Meath. One of its tales is central to grasping a distinguishing characteristic of the *fíanna*. Caílte tells the assembled nobles of Ireland that there was once a king of Ireland who had two sons, Tuathal and Fiacha. When he died his sons divided Ireland between them (thereby replicating the theme of the division made by the Sons of Mil and the Tuatha Dé Danann). One of the sons took the treasures, the herds and the fortresses; and the other the cliffs and estuaries and the fruits of the forest and the sea. The nobles interrupted Caílte to object to what they saw as a very uneven division. 'Which portion would have preferred?' Caílte asked them. They unhesitatingly replied that they would prefer the first portion, the one which included herds and fortresses and all that came with that choice. 'The part that is despised', replied Caílte, 'seems more precious to us.' The second choice was made by the younger brother, who succeeded to the throne on the death of his older sibling anyway. Initially he chose to be a *fénnid* (a warrior) and live in the wilds of nature, the land of the landless, not the landed gentry. The *fianna* are heroes of the warrior-bard kind, but they are heroes who live outside the tribe, in the forest, and on the margins of organized society. They inhabited the wilderness, which places them close to the many entrances of the otherworld. Thus a *fénnid* would have many encounters with the folk of the *sídhe*, and was in constant contact with the mysterious powers of the people of the otherworld whom they variously fought for and against.

The story of the boyhood deeds of Fionn establishes his credentials as a hero. His conception does not appear to involve a divine father, but it does feature a virgin as his mother, in the person of Muirne. Whilst the mortal Cumall is considered to be his only father, Fionn's maternal grandfather's fort at Almu was also the fairy fort, or *sídhe*, of the god Lugh. Indeed some writers such as O'Rahilly assert that Fionn is a latter-day form of Lugh, since Fionn means 'the fair one' and Lugh 'the bright one'.[5] Another parallel is that they fight a one-eyed monster, Balor and Goll mac Morna respectively. Further, in the *Acallam na Senórach* Tadg, Muirne's druidic father, is considered a member of the Tuatha Dé Danann tribe and he acquires a residence that is said to have been built by the god Nuada himself. So one way or another a divine father was present, thereby confirming the first part of the heroic biography of Fionn mac Cumhaill.

His birth in the wilderness is another feature of the typical hero's life, and a threat to his life (by exposure or by a figure seeking to kill him) because of some prophecy is also present. Although he is not reared by animals, he is reared by two women who live in the wilderness, close to animals, and educate him in the ways of nature. This is akin to the regular heroic theme of being raised by shepherds or other figures who live on the perimeter of organized society. Just as Cú Chulainn did, Fionn asserts his prowess and strength very early, in competing with the young boys. He further fulfils the heroic pattern in his initiatory experiences with the poet Finnéces by the River Boyne. Here Fionn conforms perfectly with the first two stages of Campbell's paradigm of separation and initiation. The initiation by the poet is preceded by his inevitable separation from the two foster women and his venturing out into the world where, following the initial chess confrontation with the King, he wins himself a maiden, the daughter of the blacksmith Lóchán, and slays the monster, in the form of the huge pig that has been ravaging Munster.

Whereas Cú Chulainn learnt martial arts in his time with the female warrior Scáthach, Fionn takes a different path, choosing to learn the craft of poetry. The experience with Finnéces at Linn Féic initiaties him into the world of the *fili*, or poet-seer, and he acquires invulnerability not through military prowess but through his capacity to receive *imbas forosnai*, the knowledge that enlightens or illuminates. He also acquires his new name, Fionn, and at this point he is initiated into the adult life of a hero. This is followed by contacts with the otherworld and the slaying of an otherworld figure with Fíacal's spear. At last Fionn returns to Tara to reclaim his rightful position as head of the *fían*. So from whence the hero was banished in his youth he returns victorious over his opponent (Goll mac Morna). Finally his death is as unusual or miraculous as his life. In Fionn's case the consistent Irish theme of transgression of a *geis* is present, plus the miraculous event of the severed head speaking and requesting a morsel of fish.

Thus Fionn conforms to the heroic paradigm. However he is profoundly different from Cú Chulainn in one fundamental aspect and that is, as Marie-Louise Sjoestedt points out, that Cú Chulainn is a hero of the tribe and Fionn is a hero outside the tribe.[6] The *fianna* lived outside tribal institutions (and were in fact the living negation of the spirit that sustained such tribal institutions). Indeed the two mythologies, the Ulster and the Fenian, present two independent notions of the hero.

The *fianna* lived as semi-nomads under the authority of their own leaders. During the winter, from Samain to Beltaine, they lived like billeted troops in the villages, but from Beltaine to Samain they spent their time hunting in the wilderness. They were not a race as such, nor were they tribes, and one was not born a *fénnid*: one acquired admission to the *fían* by choice, after undergoing various stages of initiation and selection. First, the candidate had to have an advanced liberal education and be versed in twelve traditional forms of poetry. Next, the applicant underwent a series of initiation tests. First, a hole was dug in the ground and the applicant placed in it and buried up to his waist. He was then given his shield and a stick of hazel as long as his arm. With these he confronted nine warriors, who threw their javelins at him simultaneously. If one javelin should touch him he was not accepted into the *fian*. If he survived this initiation, he then had to braid his hair and make his way through the forest, with the warriors pursuing him and trying to wound him. If he was caught, if his weapons trembled in his hand, or even if a dead branch cracked under his foot or a live branch disturbed a single braid of his hair, then he was not accepted into the *fian*. Third, he had to be able to draw a thorn out of his foot while running and not slowing down at all. Finally he had to be able to leap over a hurdle as high as his forehead and pass under one as low as his knee. If he fulfilled all these requirements then he was accepted into a *fian* and became a *fénnid*.

However it was also necessary for the members of his clan to pledge that they would never seek compensation for his death or any injury that he may receive. This rendered him clanless (*écland*), with no kin or social group other than the *fian*. As a clanless person he was also deemed to be landless (*dithir*). So, no longer protected by law or family, he acquired the right to secure justice for himself and for others. However his clanless and landless state did not mean that he was without privileges or recognition. The *fianna* were counted amongst the institutions necessary for the prosperity of the tribe, and could make certain claims on the community, such as the right to live off the people during the winter and to choose amongst the women of the tribe: no female could be given in marriage until she had first been offered to the *fian*. (It was this privilege that is said to have contributed to the final downfall of the *fianna*. King Cairbre wished to marry his daughter to a prince but the *fian* objected, claiming the girl for themselves. The furious King refused and went into battle with the *fianna*, inflicting lasting damage upon the movement. This was said to have occurred around AD 280.)

Because a *fénnid* lived in the wilderness he was not only in contact with the supernatural but also very close to nature, so that there was no rigid distinction between the animal kingdom and the human. One of Fionn's wives, of course, is a deer. Sadb was told that her child would be human so long as she did not lick it when it was born, otherwise it would turn out to be a fawn. However she could not completely control her instincts and when the child was born she licked it on the forehead and as a consequence Oisín had a tuft of fur on his forehead. Fionn's two dogs, Bran and Sceolang, were in fact his nephews, whose mother had been changed into a bitch by jealous rivals.

In a psychological sense we could consider this to symbolize a comfort with one's instinctual nature. Animals are often depicted in people's dreams, and the manner in which one relates to the animal in the dream portrays the type of relationship one has to one's own instinctual life. For example, do you face the animal, befriend it, attack it, kill it, run away from it . . . ? To analyse such a dream one needs to ascertain what this particular animal means to the dreamer and then elaborate on the characteristics of the animal itself. This usually provides an understanding of the nature of the instinct that the dreamer is dealing with.

Whilst the initiation rituals and the renunciation of clan and land suggest permanent *fian* membership, this was not necessarily so. It seems that there were two different types of *fénnid*. One sort, of which Fionn Mac Cumhaill is the prototype, was a *fénnid* throughout his life; another sort merely spent a formative period as a member of a *fian*. The young Prince Fíacha who forwent the castles, land and treasures for the wilds of nature is one example of a temporary *fénnid*, since he later returned to claim the kingship. Other motives than vocation prompted a person to join a *fian*. Fíacha has been said to have redirected the tension between himself and his royal brother by leaving and joining the *fian*. Another motivation is to be found in the story of Creidne, who had three sons by her own father, the King of Ireland. Creidne's stepmother, the King's wife, resented her as a sexual rival and pressured the King into expelling Creidne and her sons from the kingdom. No doubt the three ill-begotten children were also a source of shame and embarrassment to the royal family. Creidne and her sons were placed in an anomalous position by the banishment, since they were without kin and land and their social status and individual identities were thrown into uncertainty. But in this problematic situation she is perfectly poised to join a *fian* and became a *benfénnid*, a female warrior. In joining a *fian* she achieved the task of avenging the wrong her father had done her, since one of the roles of a *fénnid* was to seek retribution. For seven long years she fought as a *benfénnid* on sea as well as land, and wore her hair in the traditional braids. The King was ultimately forced to grant his estranged sons and daughter their rights and their land. Creidne then left the *fian* and took her place back in organized society just as Fíacha had done. Choosing to become a *fénnid* can symbolize a reaction to tension, social conflict and transition. This transitional aspect of the profession of a *fénnid* is captured in the text 'The Instructions of King Cormac mac Airt':

'Everyone is a *fénnid* until he has settled own. Everyone is a hireling until he has a dwelling.'[7]

In addition to his warrior capacity the other distinguishing feature of a *fénnid* is competence in poetry. It is this seemingly unusual combination of warrior and bard that distinguishes the main figures of the Fenian Cycle from those of the other cycles. Although it is accurate to say that this combination of skills is also present in the other cycles, for example in the Ulster Cycle when Cú Chulainn woos Emer with a piece of poetry, it is in the Fenian that this combination of skills is fully articulated and becomes the distinguishing characteristic of the main figures.

The poet, or *fili*, was one of the most important and honoured figures in ancient Ireland. It was a role that combined several functions: proclaimer of truth, upholder of tradition, seer and possessor of otherworld knowledge. Possibly the *fili* stepped into the vacant role left by the druid, and his role has a certain sacred quality about it. Both druid and poet are characterized throughout Irish mythology as possessors of special knowledge and power derived from the otherworld. Indeed the poet, or wordsmith, still remains the most enduring symbol within the Irish psyche. The Irish exhibit a unique capacity for story-telling, an invaluable asset in contemporary Western culture, with its emphasis on the singularly boring story of economic rationalism. The 'poet' as writer, painter or musician, sustains the imaginative life, the necessary antidote to materialism and the pervasiveness of banal secularity.

So the *fénnid* represents a combination of both military and sacred power, and Fionn Mac Cumhaill encapsulates this role. Along with this he is sometimes seen to be a blacksmith and also a physician; here we see the overlap between Fionn and the god Lugh, who was referred to as a *samildánach*, master of all arts. The word '*fili*' has as its root the verb 'to see', so the poet is one who sees, not only the present but also the past and the future. He has many qualities which suggest that he is akin to a shaman, and both *fili* and shaman are able to communicate with figures of the otherworld. In this way the *fili* is an archetypal hero, a mediator between this world and the otherworld. But his mediation is not so much as a warrior (although he does triumph over otherworld adversaries), but rather as a seer. Via specific ritualistic practices, Fionn obtains enlightened knowledge, or *imbas forosnai*, when he sucks his thumb. Fionn's sucking is a form of an established divinatory rite that involved the poet-seer chewing a piece of raw cat, dog or pig meat, then taking the morsel out of his mouth, placing it behind a door and offering it to the gods. The *fili* would then cover his face with his hands and sleep until what he sought to know was revealed to him. Another divination ritual was termed *díchetal dí chennaib*, 'an incantation from the tips', and this involved the poet using the tips of objects – skulls, hazel branches, bones, etc. – to receive information. A further ritual consisted of the *fili* lying on hurdles made of mountain ash and covered with the skins of sacrificed bulls. The seeker of knowledge then partook of new ale, invoked the gods and awaited revelation. According to MacCana, every master poet might enjoy equal honour with the King of Tara provided he was expert in the three arts of *imbas forosnai*, *díchetal dí chennaib* and *teinm laída* (chewing pith).[8]

O'Rahilly asserts that the omniscient otherworld god was often represented as a salmon, giving Fionn's fish an extra significance.[9] The story of the salmon finds its parallel in other traditions, such as the Welsh, where Ceridwen was boiling her cauldron of inspiration for her son, and employed Gwion Bach to stir it. Three drops of the magic boiling potion spilt on to his fingers, and when he put them into his mouth to ease the pain he gained the capacity of foresight. He was later reborn as the famous Welsh poet Taliesin, recalling the Irish poet-seer tradition. There is also the old Norse story of Sigurd, who was an apprentice smith to Regin. Having slain a dragon, he roasted its heart for his master and, like Fionn and Gwion, burnt his finger while cooking it. He put his finger into his mouth and at once understood the language of birds. From the birds he learnt that his master was actually his enemy and further that whoever ate the heart would become the wisest of men. Thereupon he slew Regin and ate the heart himself. So Fionn Mac Cumhaill's acquisition of seer knowledge via sucking his thumb conforms to a regular mythological theme that is probably related to the primitive notion of partaking in the flesh of a god to acquire wisdom. This type of belief persists to the present day in the Catholic practice of taking the host to be the body of Christ.

When one looks at all the known characteristics of the *fénnidi*, one sees that their defining characteristic is marginality, or liminality. They are, as Marie-Louise Sjoestedt asserts, the heroes outside the tribe. Joseph Nagy, in his book *The Wisdom of the Outlaw*, uses this idea of liminality as his major explanatory notion in his analysis of the *fianna*. He argues that the seeker of knowledge, the poet-seer, acquires his knowledge in liminal situations via liminal means.[10] The word 'liminality' comes from the Latin word '*limen*', meaning 'doorway' or 'threshold'. It is a place of transition, flux and ambiguity. Little is fixed in liminality, and consequently it generates a sense of vulnerability. Within the Greek mythological tradition liminality is Hermes', the guide of souls', territory. In the rites of many cultures the ambiguous quality of liminality is seen as a sacred state, perhaps because it is a transitional state that connects this world to the otherworld.

The raw meat chewed to gain *imbas forosnai* is seen by Nagy as a liminal object, in so far as it was probably taboo, the meat somewhere between the categories of edible and inedible. Being betwixt and between is of course a distinguishing feature of liminality. He also argues that its being chewed and not swallowed is a liminal act, the food being in the state between eaten and not eaten. Finally the placing of the chewed meat near a door as an offering to the gods locates the meat in a liminal space.

There are other stories of how Fionn Mac Cumhaill acquired *imbas forosnai* that further highlight this link between liminal space and access to the source of enlightened knowledge. One story tells of an otherworld figure called Cúldub who used to come and steal food from the *fíanna* every time they cooked it. He was so fast that even Caílte and Oisín, the fastest of the *fénnidi*, could never catch him before he escaped into his *sídhe*. However he met his match when it was Fionn's turn to cook and guard the food. Cúldub emerged as usual from his *sídhe*, stole the food and took off swiftly. Fionn caught up with him and slew him at the door of his *sídhe*. There was a woman at the door, holding a vessel with some liquid in it. She hurriedly slammed the door to prevent Fionn from entering the otherworld, but in so doing she jammed his finger in it, spilling some of the liquid on it at the same time. Fionn managed to extricate his finger from the door; to ease the pain he put it into his mouth, and immediately acquired enlightened knowledge. The liquid spilt on this thumb was the magical draught of the otherworld.

This version of enlightenment serves to highlight the liminal space of a doorway, a space between this world and the otherworld, as the location for the acquisition of illuminated knowledge. Fionn doesn't get his knowledge by actually entering the otherworld, but at the boundary between the worlds. The sacred poet-seer knows the truth because he is an in-between figure who has access to both categories of existence, this world and the other. His heroic status is determined by this capacity to mediate between the worlds as a seer-prophet, but unlike Cú Chulainn he does not reside permanently in the community, is not a hero inside the tribe but outside. He is a hero of liminality.

In our modern psychological myth we have considered the unconscious to be merely another name for the otherworld, and in this context we can see that Fionn Mac Cumhaill as a hero outside the tribe is a hero who lives closer to the unconscious life than the conscious life. Cú Chulainn is in a way a hero figure at the ego level and Fionn a hero figure of that ambiguous space between the ego, conscious level and the unconscious. Whilst it is going way beyond the actual stories themselves, I think it is useful to consider the idea that Cú Chulainn, with his heroic and triumphant conquering in the outerworld, may well symbolize the first half of life and Fionn Mac Cumhaill, living in the liminal space between the outer and inner worlds, may symbolize the second half of life. Cú Chulainn achieves his power through physical force. He is a societal man, a hero who reflects society's view of what constitutes success. Perhaps he is our present-day businessman, lawyer or politician. Fionn on the other hand derives his power from insight, reflecting the unique psychic life of the individual and the consciousness that is derived from life outside the mainstream. Marginality begets creativity and individualism, as opposed to mimicry and conformity.

Whilst the heroic biography provides a model for approaching and managing transitions, Fionn Mac Cumhaill provides a model of the transitional space itself, facilitating the development of others who temporarily visit it. He is perhaps the hero who is constellated when we are feeling disconnected in our conscious lives. He is the archetypal soul-guide who is evoked whenever the ego is unable to identify itself with a fixed image (or images) that has previously sustained a sense of identity. These images and sense of identity have more often than not been derived from external social values, that is, tribal values. Liminality, a crossing into a state of ambiguity and uncertainty, occurs when we are disconnected, by whatever means – individual development, trauma, divorce, societal changes – from a fixed sense of who we are. The *fénnid*, you will recall, is both clanless and landless and has no fixed identity. When a woman moves into the state of motherhood she enters a liminal space, a period of unclear boundaries, unbounded time and an uncertain sense of who or what she is. Divorce, separation, the death of somebody close to us, a child leaving home, are all experiences that plummet us into liminal space. A person made redundant, particularly a male who has embodied his identity in a work role, is catapulted into liminality by the separation from previously fixed ideas of who he is. Mid-life is an archetypal liminal space, a period of transition from the first half of life to the second. It is a transition that brings with it profound uncertainty and ambiguity about one's identity. Mid-life often involves a shift from the ego being over-identified with the outer image, the tribally approved and sanctioned image, to deriving a sense of identity from within the self. The hero or heroine of the first half of life is slain and there is a crumbling of defences. It is at this time that 'Fionn Mac Cumhaill' is evoked from the collective unconscious.

At such times of uncertainty we are more open to messages and images from the unconscious life to knowledge derived from the edges, which brings with it the risk of inflation and grandiosity, as seen in some self-appointed gurus. In the worst possible scenario this knowledge can also induce psychosis. At times of transition we live closer to the entrances to the otherworld and increase the probability of encounters with the figures that reside there. So the dreams of people in mid-life have rich and complex plots, with a variety of characters representing repressed and previously unconscious aspects of themselves.

Unlike Fionn, however, we cannot stay permanently in liminality, for if we did we would risk being maladapted and immature, qualities that Jung embodied in the *puer eternus*, the eternal youth. It is a space for initiation into new insights and knowledge about oneself, followed by a return to the world. But if the ego over-identifies with any one archetypal figure (whether the great mother, the wise old man or the liminal Fionn Mac Cumhaill) then mental disturbance is the result. In many respects Fionn serves as a symbol of an archetypal pattern of tolerance of not-knowing, as opposed to the knowing that is exhibited by the hero of the tribe, i.e. conscious, Logos-based factual knowledge.

This liminal space characterized by ambiguity and uncertainty as opposed to the ego demand for clarity and categories, is the space from which creativity is born. In modern psychoanalytic mythology Donald Winnicott, the paediatrician and psychoanalyst, has done much to articulate this space. He termed it the transitional space, an area of experience that commences in infancy but forms the basis of imaginative and creative life in adulthood.[11] But the poet Keats, more than anyone else, most clearly stated the vital link between liminal space and creativity. In a letter to his brother in December 1817 he says that he has come to understand the essential quality of creativity, specifically literary creativity. He calls this quality 'negative capability'; 'that is where man is capable of being in uncertainties, mysteries, doubts, without any irritable reaching after fact and reason'.[12] Fionn Mac Cumhaill could be seen as providing, amongst other things, a paradigm for negative capability. It is negative capability that allows us to tolerate not-knowing long enough to actually know. Its presence in a person is perhaps the factor that determines whether someone merely accumulates knowledge, or actually has understanding that leads to wisdom. But the opportunity for this development in a person is unlikely to occur much before mid-life, since the first half of life is predominantly tied to the outerworld. Jung, using the analogy of the sun to refer to the first half of life, says, 'For a young person it is almost a sin, or at least a danger, to be too preoccupied with himself; but for the ageing person it is a duty and a necessity to devote serious attention to himself. After having lavished its light upon the world, the sun withdraws its rays in order to illuminate itself . . . We cannot live the afternoon of life according to the programme of life's morning; for what was great in the morning will be little at evening, and what in the morning was true will at evening have become a lie.'[13]

The need to go beyond the extroverted and material characteristics of the first half of life and begin the process of reflection and acquisition of inner knowledge finds its mythic parallel in the Fenian Cycle. It is the poet-seer who fulfils a sacred role in his capacity to communicate with the otherworld and to seek knowledge from that world. Georges Dumézil proposed three essential functions in society: sovereign, warrior and cultivator, to deal with the themes of the sacred, force and nurturance. The emergence of the poet-seer is a significant addition to the warrior role. The *fili* sees beyond and through the material world in which the warrior is more comfortable. So when we have conquered some aspects of the outerworld, it is time to add a more reflective, creative aspect to our lives. Resistance to liminality can only lead to stagnation within the personality, since the border crossing of mid-life provides the opportunity for further ego development incorporating an inner and outer perspective. To refuse this opportunity is to stay a hero or heroine of the tribe and to restrict oneself to living extensively out of the persona, the archetype of conformity.

Whereas the Mythological Cycle was dominated by the gods and magic and the Ulster Cycle by aristocratic warriors, the Fenian Cycle is dominated by liminality. The three cycles perhaps symbolize psychology's divisions of the collective unconscious, the ego and the personal unconscious respectively.

Diarmuid and Gráinne

Any discussion of the Fenian Cycle would be incomplete without the romantic and tragic story of the elopement of Diarmuid and Gráinne ('Tóraigheacht Dhiarmada agus Ghráinne'), generally regarded as the greatest tale of the Fenian Cycle. It is first mentioned in a tenth-century listing of sagas in *The Book of Leinster*, and was incorporated into the Fionn saga at a later date. My abbreviated version of the story has been derived from P. W. Joyce's rendition of Standish O'Grady's translation,[14] from Cross and Slover's version in their *Ancient Irish Tales* and from Myles Dillon's succinct summary in his *Early Irish Literature*.[15] It is generally believed that the story of Diarmuid and Gráinne is the prototype for the later Arthurian story of Tristan and Iseult.

The story returns to the theme of the rivalry between the ageing suitor and a young lover for the love of a beautiful woman. The romantic tragedy usually results in the young lover dying, often at the hands of the jilted old suitor. We have already seen this in the story of Derdriu, where Naoise is finally tricked and killed by King Conchobhar. In both stories it is the woman who initiates the relationship by giving the hero a more compelling reason than his warrior vows of loyalty. The figure of the beautiful young woman (as an earth goddess) is a vehicle for the transference of power from the old to the new and as such encapsulates the theme of a seasonal mythology.

One fine morning Fionn Mac Cumhaill rose early and went out to sit alone on the grassy plain surrounding his fort at Almu. Shortly Oisín and the druid Diorruing followed him out. Oisín asked if there was anything worrying Fionn that had caused the early-morning rising. Fionn replied that since his wife Maighnéis had died he was lonely and restless: 'For a man without a worthy wife is not wont to sleep well and that is why I have risen early.' Oisín was somewhat taken aback by his father's sadness and quickly assured Fionn that 'There is not a woman in Ireland on whom you would set your eye that we would not bring to you by favour or by force.' Then Diorruing chipped in: 'I know where there is a woman who would be suitable for you in all respects.' This was Gráinne, the daughter of King Cormac mac Art and the granddaughter of Conn of the Hundred Battles. Fionn rebuked him: 'You know that I have been in conflict with Cormac mac Art for some time now, and I will not give him the satisfaction of refusing me the hand of his daughter in marriage; but if you insist then I suggest that the two of you go off and do the bidding on my behalf.' Oisín and

Diorruing readily agreed and set off for Tara with this purpose, insisting that all was to be kept secret until they returned.

When they arrived the King of Tara was hosting a feast for his chiefs and nobles. He made Oisín and Diorruing very welcome and, sensing the importance of their unexpected visit, he temporarily delayed the celebrations to allow time to meet with them. Oisín explained how they had come on Fionn Mac Cumhaill's behalf to seek his daughter's hand in marriage. The King said, 'In all of Ireland there is scarcely a young prince or noble who has not sought my daughter's hand in marriage and she has refused them all.' He told them that in every instance he had been blamed for the refusal and been perceived as a difficult and controlling father, and he insisted that they meet Gráinne in person and hear her reply directly.

He then accompanied the warriors to Gráinne's sunroom, a room he had built especially for her. In response to her father's explanation Gráinne gave the very surprising reply that if Fionn was considered by her father to be a worthy son-in-law then she would consider him a worthy husband. The two messengers returned to Almu with the news and the instruction that King Cormac wanted to meet Fionn at Tara in a fortnight's time.

So Fionn with his retinue travelled to Tara, to be welcomed by the King and the nobles of Ireland. A great feast was set up in the banquet hall and the guests were seated around the King in order of social status. Cormac's wife and daughter were immediately on his left, and Fionn was placed on the right next to the King. A druid called Dáire sat next to Gráinne, who asked the druid why Fionn Mac Cumhaill was here. The druid replied, 'If you do not know then it is little wonder that I don't.' But Gráinne persisted, saying, 'I want to know from you.' 'Well,' replied the druid, 'he has come to seek you for his wife.' Gráinne fell silent for a long time, and finally said, 'If indeed Fionn had sought me for his son Oisín, or for the youthful Oscar, then there would be nothing to wonder at, but I am astonished that he seeks me for himself seeing that he is older than my father.' Again she fell into a long and deep silence, only emerging from it by looking across the festive table at the various figures who were accompanying Fionn. 'Tell me,' she said to the druid: 'who is that warrior on the right of Oisín?' 'That is Goll mac Morna, a ferocious warrior.' 'And who is that next to Goll?' 'That is Oscar, Oisín's son,' replied the druid. 'And beside him?' 'Caílte, the fastest runner in the *fianna*,' replied Dáire. 'Tell me, druid,' said Gráinne, 'who is that freckled, sweet-talking warrior on Oisín's left hand?' 'Ah, that', replied the druid, is 'Diarmuid O Duibhne of the white teeth and radiant face, the best lover of women in Ireland.' She then asked the druid who was sitting next to Diarmuid, and Dáire informed her that it was Diorruing, Fionn Mac Cumhaill's druid. Gráinne murmured that it was indeed a very interesting group of people, and summoned her handmaiden, instructing her to bring a gold drinking horn from her chambers. Gráinne filled it and told the maid to take it to Fionn, telling him that she had sent it. Following Gráinne's directions, the maid arranged for the gold goblet to be passed around the group anticlockwise. In itself this should have informed the party that something was untoward, since to pass things around in an anti-clockwise direction was an omen of bad fortune in ancient Ireland.

In no time, Fionn and all who partook of the drink from the cup were fast asleep. Gráinne then crossed the floor to seat herself between Oisín and Diarmuid, who along with Oscar and Diorruing had refused the drugged drink. Gráinne turned to Oisín and asked him to accept her love, which he promptly refused, declaring he could never accept the love of any woman who had been promised to Fionn. Then she turned to Diarmuid and asked him the same question, and he too refused on the same grounds as Oisín. But Gráinne confronted him: 'Then I put a *geis* upon you of danger and destruction unless you take me from this house tonight before the King and Fionn wake from their sleep.' Diarmuid was shocked and pleaded with her not to put the *geis* upon him, asking why she had chosen him to put the curse upon. Gráinne told him that she had first seen him from her window, playing hurley on the lawns of Tara, and she had so admired his outstanding play that she had instantly fallen in love with him there and then. (Others say that Diarmuid had a magic love spot on his forehead (*ball seirce*) and that any woman seeing it instantly fell in love with him. He usually wore a cap to cover it up but during the fateful game of hurley his cap was dislodged.)

Torn between his masculine warrior honour to his leader and the bond of a woman, Diarmuid turned to his companions for advice. Each said the same thing: that he had no choice but to honour the *geis* put upon him. Diorruing told him: 'Follow Gráinne, for you have no choice, but I pity you, for she will be the cause of your death.' With tears in his eyes and a heavy heart, Diarmuid left his companions and joined Gráinne outside the walls of the fort, still pleading with her to change her mind before it was too late. But she resolutely refused to do so and they set out westward until they came to a forest in Connacht called Derry Da Both, where Diarmuid built a hut and a wooden enclosure in which he constructed seven doors.

The next morning when Fionn awoke and discovered that Diarmuid and Gráinne had eloped, he was instantly consumed with rage. But then he placed his thumb in his mouth and was able to ascertain where they were hiding. He summoned his troops and headed westward and it was not long before they had surrounded Diarmuid and Gráinne. Oisín and Oscar, still loyal to Diarmuid, became increasingly alarmed for his well-being, as they could observe the vengeful rage that was now obsessing Fionn. Oscar sent Fionn's hound Bran into the hut, where he placed his head on the sleeping Diarmuid's chest. Diarmuid instantly understood the warning and told Gráinne what it meant. She pleaded with him to leave immediately but he refused, since he felt compelled to uphold his honour as a warrior. Then miraculously it was revealed to Oenghus, Diarmuid's foster-father, that his foster-son was in grave danger. He flew on a magical wind to Derry Da Both, where he agreed to take Gráinne to safety under his cloak, leaving Diarmuid to face Fionn. When Fionn and his warriors arrived at Derry Da Both Diarmuid went from one door to the other asking who was there, and at the first six doors were friends of Diarmuid's who refused to block his way or harm him in any way. Finally at the seventh door he found Fionn himself, who threatened him with death. But Diarmuid had a magical trick: he took two javelins and vaulted high into the air, over the wall and the heads of his enemies, taunting them with his escape, and reunited with Oenghus and Gráinne at Ros Dá Shoileach. Gráinne was overjoyed to see Diarmuid and they ate their full of wild pig in celebration of their escape. The next morning Oenghus took his leave, but not before offering his advice to his foster-son on how to outwit Fionn. He instructed Diarmuid never to go into a cave with only one entrance, or to an island with one approach, not to eat food where he cooked it, nor to sleep where he ate it, and in the morning not to rise from the same bed that he had settled in the night before. Following these instructions Oenghus departed and Diarmuid and Gráinne set out on their travels, wandering throughout Ireland and having many adventures.

One of these included meeting up with a young warrior, Muadan, who entered into service with Diarmuid, offering him protection day and night. During this period under the protection of Muadan, Diarmuid confronted a group of green-cloaked seafaring warriors who had been sent by Fionn to kill him. Diarmuid killed many of them through various tricks, finally tying up the three leaders in a manner that only Oisín or Oscar were able to undo. However both of these warriors were under a *geis* never to untie anyone whom Diarmuid had bound. So when, along with Fionn, they discovered the three seafaring warriors they were unable to free them. Following this adventure Muadan told Diarmuid it was time for him to leave; the lovers reluctantly let him go and recommenced their journey alone.

Up until this point Diarmuid had not consummated his relationship with Gráinne, and in order to communicate this fact to Fionn he would leave raw meat or salmon at each of their campsites as a symbol of their non-consummation. However, one day, not long after Muadan had left them, Gráinne was walking beside Diarmuid when some water splashed on her leg. At this she began to tease Diarmuid, telling him that the trickle of water was more adventurous than he was when it came to love. That night he made a bed of birch boughs and fragrant rushes and for the first time on their travels, they lay together as man and wife.

In the mean time, Fionn Mac Cumhaill was sitting on the hill at Almu when he observed a band of warriors coming towards him. At its head were two tall men who introduced themselves as champions of the Clan Morna, whose fathers had been slain at the battle of Cnucha, in which Fionn's own father had been killed. They sought permission to become members of Fionn's *fian*, and he agreed on condition that they compensated him for his father's death at the hands of their clan. They asked Fionn what would be required by way of compensation and he told them that he wanted the head of Diarmuid or a fistful of berries from the rowan tree of Dubhros. These were magical berries that protected a person from all sickness and injury and made a hundred-year-old feel like a thirty-year-old. The tree had grown from a berry from the Land of Promise that had been inadvertently dropped by the Tuatha Dé Danann as they passed by the place. In order to guard its magical qualities they had sent a huge one-eyed giant called Searbhán Lochlannach to guard it. He was a fearsome figure, burly and strong, with a great club tied by a chain to an iron girdle around his body. There was no way to kill him other than with three blows of his own club. By day he sat at the foot of the tree and at night he slept in a hut high amongst the branches. He was so ferocious that no one dared approach the tree or any of the surrounding land for miles. It was into this area that Diarmuid had ventured, knowing full well that Fionn and his warriors would not come near. Diarmuid boldly approached the giant and sought his permission to hunt for food in the area around the magic berry tree. The giant had agreed that Diarmuid could do this on condition that he did not take or eat any berries from the magic tree. Diarmuid accepted, and he and Gráinne lived in harmony alongside the one-eyed Searbhán.

Despite the dire warnings of peril that Oisín and Oscar gave, the two chiefs of the Morna clan refused to be deterred, and set out to acquire one or other of the compensations demanded by Fionn. They travelled west until they found Diarmuid's hut. They declared their identity and their intention and Diarmuid asked them to choose whether they wanted to fight him or seek the berries from the fearsome giant Searbhán. They chose the former, and they all agreed to fight with their bare hands. The two warriors were no match for Diarmuid and in no time he had overpowered both of them and tied them up.

When Gráinne heard Diarmuid explaining to the two warriors about the magic berry tree, she pleaded with him to get her some berries since she was pregnant and needed them especially. Diarmuid did not want to break his pact with the giant, but the two warriors offered to help him if he would set them free. Diarmuid was contemptuous towards them, declaring that just one glimpse of the one-eyed giant would scare them to death, but nevertheless he set them free and the three of them set off for Dubhros.

The giant stirred from dozing at the foot of the tree and asked Diarmuid whether he had come to break his pact. Diarmuid replied that he didn't want to but that the daughter of the King of Ireland was pregnant and was craving some berries. The giant answered, 'I swear that if the princess and her child were now dying and that one of my berries could save them I would not give it!' Diarmuid was infuriated by Searbhán's reply and shouted at him, 'By fair or foul means I'll get one of those berries.' The giant jumped to his feet and struck Diarmuid three blows, injuring him, but when he lowered his club Diarmuid leapt at him, catching him off guard and hurling the giant to the ground. Seizing the club he dealt him three blows, dashing his brains out with the final one. After recovering from his ordeal, he, Gráinne and the two warriors all ate the berries that Diarmuid picked and the two sons of Morna returned to Almu with a handful. Fionn examined and smelt the berries: 'I smell the skin of Diarmuid on these berries and I know it was him, not you, who slew Searbhán Lochlannach and gathered the magical berries.' He refused them admission to the *fían*, but had of course now ascertained where Diarmuid was; he gathered his troops and headed for Dubhros.

When he arrived at the tree he rested, knowing full well that Diarmuid was up the tree, and challenged Oisín to a game of chess. Fionn played a skilful game and finally had Oisín cornered, leaving him only one move to make, which Fionn was confident Oisín would not be able to work out. Diarmuid had a bird's-eye view of the game from his treetop position, and was frustrated that he could not help Oisín, since he could see the very move that needed to be made. He threw a berry at the chesspiece that Oisín needed to move in order to win. His aim was perfect and Oisín moved the piece and won the game. This situation was repeated twice, Fionn turned angrily to Oisín saying that he had not won fairly but because Diarmuid had helped him out. Oisín disputed his father's suggestion, claiming that Diarmuid would not be so silly as to stay in the tree while Fionn waited for him at the bottom. Fionn looked up into the tree and shouted, 'Which of us is right, Ó Duibhne?', to which a voice from the treetop responded, 'You, Fionn, have never yet erred in your judgement, for indeed I am here, with Gráinne in the hut of Searbhán Lochlannach.' With this he made himself visible to Fionn, and at the same time took Gráinne into his arms and kissed her three times. Fionn was enraged and vowed that Diarmuid would pay with his head.

Fionn ordered all the men of his *fían* to form an unbroken ring around the tree and promised great honour to anyone who could bring him Diarmuid's head. The opportunity for such honour was of course irresistible to any hero and in no time there were volunteers to climb the tree to behead Diarmuid. But at the very moment that the first *fénnid* began to climb the tree Oenghus again sensed the danger to his foster-son and again appeared beside him. As the *fénnid* reached the treetop hut Oenghus transformed the warrior into the shape of Diarmuid, and the real Diarmuid kicked him down to the ground. He looked so like Diarmuid that the surrounding soldiers immediately beheaded him, but as soon as they did this the warrior's original shape returned and they were shocked to recognize that they had beheaded one of their own. Nine other men climbed the tree and each suffered the exact same fate, until Fionn was forced to call off the attack. As on the previous occasion when Diarmuid was confronted with Fionn at Derry Da Both, Oenghus whisked Gráinne away wrapped in the magical mantle of his cloak and Diarmuid used his javelins to make a magical leap over the heads of the warriors surrounding the foot of the tree.

After several further attempts to capture Diarmuid, Fionn, through Oenghus's mediation, finally agreed to reconciliation. Diarmuid's terms included the granting of his father's territory, and that Fionn and the members of his *fían* be forbidden from hunting around the land that had been granted to him. Second, he required that Gráinne be granted her own territory in County Sligo, far away from her father and Fionn. The terms were agreed too; some say for up to sixteen years. Diarmuid and Gráinne settled down peacefully at Rath Gráinne in Keshchorran, where they had four sons and a daughter and enjoyed a prosperous life.

One day Gráinne said to Diarmuid, 'It is surely a thing unworthy of us, seeing the greatness of our household and our wealth, that we should live in a manner so much removed from the world, and it is unbecoming that the two most illustrious men in Erin have never been in our house, namely my father the King, and Fionn the son of Cumall.' It was true that Gráinne had not seen her father since the fateful night that she had eloped from Tara with Diarmuid. At first Diarmuid was unwilling, but she persuaded him that it was long overdue that they win back the friendship and love of the two famous men. Thus the household prepared for a feast and both the King and Fionn were invited. The King arrived with his full retinue and Fionn with his chiefs and warriors, and they all stayed at Rath Gráinne, hunting and feasting for a whole year.

On the very last night of the festive year Diarmuid was awoken by the cry of a hunting dog. He voiced his bewilderment to Gráinne that he should hear such a sound in the middle of the night. Gráinne told him, 'It is the Tuatha Dé Danann who are bewitching you, despite the protection of your foster-father Oenghus, so lie down, ignore it and go to sleep.' But it was not very long before he heard the cry a second time and finally, just before daylight, a third time. He could no longer ignore it and exclaimed to Gráinne that he had to find out why the hound cried in the middle of the night. Gráinne anxiously consented but advised Diarmuid to take with him the sword that the god Manannán had given him and the spear that his foster-father Oenghus had provided him with. But Diarmuid scoffed that he had no need for such powerful weapons since after all he was only going to investigate why the hound was crying. He opted for a smaller sword and spear, and also took his own hound, called Mac an Cuill, leading him on a chain.

Diarmuid ventured forth until he reached the summit of modern-day

Ben Bulben, the mountain five miles north of Sligo made famous by the Irish poet W. B. Yeats. On the summit he found Fionn. 'Have you organized this chase?' he asked. Fionn told him that a company of men and dogs had chased a wild boar during the night and that they were foolish because the boar had killed many men before. 'What's more,' said Fionn, 'if you look you will see that the wild boar is heading our way and the sooner we get out of his way the better.' But Diarmuid, being a heroic warrior, chose to face the wild boar. Fionn became agitated and told Diarmuid that there was a *geis* upon him never to hunt a wild boar. This was the first that Diarmuid had ever heard of this *geis* and in response to his look of utter bewilderment Fionn went on to explain its origins.

Diarmuid's father had killed the child of a steward whose son was in fosterage with Oenghus at the same time as Diarmuid. Diarmuid's father resented the fact that the steward's son was more popular and more loved by all the members of the household, and as a result of this killed the steward's son. The steward had changed his dead son into a boar and put a *geis* upon it that its life should last as long as Diarmuid's and that finally Diarmuid should be killed by the boar:

> By this magical wand,
> By the wizard's command
> I appoint and decree
> For Dermat and thee
> The same bitter strife,
> The same span of life:
> In the pride of his strength,
> Thou shalt slay him at length;
> Lo, Dermat O-Dyna
> Lies stretched in his gore;
> Behold my avengers,
> The tusks of the boar!
> And thus is decreed,
> For Donn's cruel deed,
> Sure vengeance to come –
> His son's bloody doom;
> By this wand in my hand,
> By the wizard's command![17]

But Diarmuid still resolutely refused to leave the hillock and stood his ground while Fionn retreated. Diarmuid regretted that he had not taken Gráinne's advice concerning his weapons, and wondered whether Fionn had set up the whole scene. 'I fear me indeed, that thou has begun this chase hoping that it would lead to my death. But here I will await the event; for if I am fated to die in this spot, I cannot avoid the doom in store for me.'[18]

It was not long before the boar came rushing up the hillside, charging at Diarmuid and frightening his hound away. Diarmuid hurled his small spear at the beast and although he hit it in the middle of the forehead the beast was unharmed and continued to charge ferociously. Next he drew his sword and dealt the beast a severe blow to the neck, but all this achieved was that the sword split in two. The boar now rushed at Diarmuid, impaled him on its tusks and then raced around the countryside with Diarmuid on its back, finally returning to the summit of Ben Bulben. There it flung Diarmuid off and gored him. In one last valiant heroic effort Diarmuid lurched at the boar with the hilt of his broken sword and bashed the beast's brains out; it fell dead beside the fatally wounded Diarmuid.

Soon Fionn and his warriors came rushing up the hill and found Diarmuid, bleeding profusely and close to death. Fionn then revealed his true hatred for Diarmuid: 'It likes me well, Dermait, to see thee in this plight; only I am grieved that all the women of Erin cannot see thee also. For now, indeed, the surpassing beauty of thy form, that they loved so well, is gone from thee and thou art pale and deformed.'[19] To which Diarmuid replied, 'Alas, oh Finn! Those words surely come from thy lips only, and not from thy heart. And indeed it is in thy power to heal me even now if thou wilt.' He reminded Fionn that when he had tasted the salmon of knowledge at the River Boyne he had also received the special power to heal anyone who drank from water held in his hands.

Fionn of course knew this, but replied that Diarmuid did not deserve to be healed because he had so humiliated him on that evening in Tara. Oscar, who was standing near by, could no longer tolerate the situation and exhorted his grandfather to give Diarmuid a drink from his palms. Fionn resentfully conceded to his grandson's request, but as he slowly walked back from a nearby well he opened his fingers and let the water slip through. At another request from his grandson, Fionn returned again to the well, only to repeat the event: as soon as the thought of Gráinne entered his head the palms of his hands opened and the water spilt out. This time Oscar threatened that either he or Fionn would not leave the place alive if he did not give Diarmuid a healing drink. A third time Fionn returned with the water held in his hands, but as he arrived beside Diarmuid the warrior took his last breath and expired.

When the *fían* saw that their fellow warrior had died they all let out three great sorrowful shouts. Oscar, Oisín and Caílte all stayed for a while beside the body of their companion and then they sadly went down the mountain to Gráinne's rath. When she heard the news she let out three long cries of anguish which were heard for miles and miles around. She sent the members of her household to Ben Bulben to recover the body and they arrived at the same time as Oenghus. Together Gráinne's warriors and Oenghus's people raised their voices in lament and sent three great anguished shouts up into the heavens that were heard over the five provinces of Ireland. Oenghus insisted that the body had to come with him back to Bruig na Bóinne, where he would bring Diarmuid back to life for a short period each day and talk to him. Gráinne knew she had no choice but to accept the authority of the god, and the body was carried back to Bruig na Bóinne. Some say that Gráinne exhorted her sons to seek revenge against Fionn and that she mourned Diarmuid's death until the day she died. Others say that, because of the slaughter that occurred when the sons vengefully attacked Almu, Fionn and Gráinne were reconciled and peace established between the families. This resulted in Fionn giving the sons of Diarmuid their rightful place in the *fían*.

The story of Diarmuid and Gráinne is true to the Fenian tradition: the geography is sufficient to alert us to this fact, since the lovers wander in the forests, mountains and valleys. This we already know is *fianna* territory, which symbolizes a liminal space. A further important quality of this story is its romantic tone, in addition to the characteristically warrior-heroic quality of the Ulster Cycle. The romantic quality can be explained in part by the fact that the Fenian stories came to prominence during the period of the troubadours and the Arthurian romances. But the Irish stories differ from this tradition in the involvement of divine figures in the life of the hero. For now, let us concentrate on the romantic triangle of an ageing suitor, a beautiful young woman and a handsome young lover. In this theme we can see the repetition of the motifs of the sovereign queen as the land of Ireland, and sacral marriage. The power of the feminine in this story is unequivocal. She chooses her mate and places him under a *geis* so that he cannot reject her.

These thoughts are further developed by focusing on the names of the leading figures, Diarmuid, Gráinne and Fionn. Diarmuid's full name as we have seen is Diarmuid Ó Duibhne: the surname translates as 'dark' or 'brown', and Diarmuid is considered to be the son of Donn, host of the House of Death. So Diarmuid is linked to the darkness of the otherworld; yet he is also described as beautiful, with a magnificent radiant face and striking white teeth. The dark and the light coexist in the figure of Diarmuid. This is also the situation with Gráinne, whose name, despite the claims for her beauty, is a variant form of the modern Irish word '*gránna*' which means 'ugly', 'unsightly' and 'displeasing to the senses'. She embodies the two qualities of beautiful and ugly and can be equated with the ugly hag, or loathsome crone, who is transformed by sacred marriage into a beautiful maiden. As a sovereign queen figure she is inevitably a symbol of the earth and fecundity itself; indeed, her name is also considered to be derived from the Irish word '*grán*', which means 'grain'. Just as the earth can be barren and desolate, so also can the sovereign queen appear ugly. She is transformed, and the land restored to life, when united with her young lover and not with the ageing King. So each of these figures, whilst not truly divine, is clearly linked to that realm. There is also Diarmuid's strong link to the divine through his foster-parentage by the god Oenghus, who plays such a pivotal role in the story.

Fionn is also seen as having a strong link to the divine world. Some scholars, as already mentioned, have seen him as a later version of the god Lugh.

The plot reflects the persistence of a seasonal rather than societal mythology. The figure of Gráinne, the crone/beautiful woman, is symbolic of the earth, and places a *geis* upon the dark, handsome young lover to elope with her. He is irresistible, because of his love spot, so there is something inevitable going on: in symbolic terms the earth wants to be mated with a male energy in order to fertilize itself and be renewed. The whole story is set in the wild, so we can safely assume that it is summer, in accordance with Fenian tradition. The ageing Fionn could be seen as symbolizing the fading sun that heralds the coming of winter, during which time nature dies and awaits renewal. So the play between the figures can be considered to symbolize the seasonal changes, when winter must yield to the fertilizing quality of spring and the fruitfulness of summer. Indeed, there exists some folklore concerning Diarmuid and Gráinne which confirms their connection to fertility. The dolmens, the ancient burials portals consisting of a flat stone raised on top of two other stones, which are so common throughout the Irish landscape are known as the Beds of Diarmuid and Gráinne. The lovers slept on these and it is said that if a childless woman sleeps on one of them she, like Gráinne, will conceive.

If Diarmuid and his union with the earth represent spring and summer, then the uncertainty about the ending of this story makes sense if one allows for Gráinne's returning to Fionn. This would mean that the seasonal cycle is continuing and the earth must be paired with the autumn and winter to await the next elopement. The story then does not really have an ending, since each union is destined to impermanence. It is only the recurring cycle of light and dark, life and death, summer and winter, that is permanent. In eating the magic berries Diarmuid and Gráinne become immortal, i.e. the process of seasonal change is immortal and governed by the otherworld that lies beyond mortal sight.

Parallels to other mythologies, particularly the Greek, readily present themselves. The most obvious one is the parallel between Diarmuid and Adonis. Both could be seen as vegetative gods, since Adonis is derived from the earlier Egyptian god Tammuz, whose death and resurrection symbolize the death and renewal of vegetation. Adonis encapsulates the change in nature by the fact that he spends half the year in the underworld with Persephone and the other half in the upper world with Aphrodite. Here we have the death of nature in winter and its regeneration in summer.

Adonis and Diarmuid are both killed in an identical manner, that is by a boar. Some say that Aphrodite's estranged lover Ares disguised himself as a boar and killed Adonis. Diarmuid knew that it was the vengeful Fionn who had set up the hunt in which the boar killed him. So the ageing autumnal sun will always seek revenge on the vibrancy and renewal of spring and summer.

There is a Welsh version of the Tristan story of which, as already mentioned, Diarmuid and Gráinne is an earlier prototype, in which Iseult's husband King Mark of Cornwall complains to King Arthur about Tristan eloping with his wife. King Arthur intervenes and suggests a compromise whereby one of the rivals can have Iseult while the leaves are on the trees and the other while the trees are leafless. King Mark, the husband and older man, chooses the leafless period because the nights are longer. Thus Mark identifies himself with winter and Tristan with the summer and the open-air freedom of the woods. Again the old king is associated with winter and the young virile lover with the spring and summer, with Iseult being a later Welsh version of an earth goddess or sovereign queen.

What then can be made of this story if it is viewed from the perspective of our modern psychological mythology? The answer depends partly on which figure it is viewed through. Each of the main characters lend themselves to psychological reflection. In Gráinne, we again see the power of the feminine to entice a warrior to break his honour code, just as in the story of Derdriu. But a noticeable difference here is that Gráinne initially complies with her father's wishes, submissively agreeing that if her father considers Fionn to be a suitable husband for her then she will accept him. The heroine totally under the control of the patriarchy is the equivalent of a modern woman being totally unconscious of her masculine self, which would leave her with little sense that she had a legitimate place in the outerworld. Furthermore she would be prone to a passive acceptance of the male viewpoint, a phenomenon we witness when Gráinne simply accepts her father's decision. However there is a moment of dramatic change when she asks the purpose of the festival she is attending and is shocked to find out that it is in honour of her impending marriage to Fionn. Consciousness breaks through and Gráinne literally wakes up to herself. She hears her own needs and forms her own ideas as to what she wants, and with this emergence of consciousness she is able to disconnect from the control of the father. The action that follows reveals that when a woman can challenge the inner voice of the father, the partriarchal values, she can begin the process of developing a relationship with her personal *animus*, or masculine principle. Within Jungian mythology this means she can develop a sense of being somebody in the world, with a legitimate place and contribution. Gráinne grasps her new-found sense of self with zest, and demands that the masculine join her on her terms when she places a *geis* upon Diarmuid. Elopements within Irish mythology depict the power of the feminine to set the hero's agenda, a pattern that is so clearly seen in modern men at mid-life. By way of contrast, wooings, such as that by Cú Chulainn of Emer, depict the male taking the initiative, though the enemy is usually again a father figure. In this situation the *animus* sets the agenda for a woman to be free of the control of the father or the patriarchal values.

So Gráinne is freed to embrace her personal *animus*, as Emer did with Cú Chulainn. Gráinne appears to be a more evolved figure though, in so far as she symbolizes the integration of her dark and light sides. In a psychological sense this suggests that she has a level of awareness of her shadow aspects. Without this awareness, a woman is more vulnerable to male control, since her own rage is more often than not turned in upon the self, where it can damage her self-worth. Gráinne's adventures and union with Diarmuid could be seen as the story of a woman's journey with her *animus*. The outcome appears in the main to be positive, in so far as it is a fertile relationship and results in her acquiring her own territory separate from her father/king. Women who develop a conscious relationship with their *animus* acquire their own territory in the form of their own psychic space, and a sense of self-worth that is relatively independent of the need for male approval.

The end of the story however reveals the tragedy of her attempt to reincorporate the patriarchy in her life when she invites her father and Fionn to visit. In doing this she sets up the scene for the death of her *animus* in the figure of Diarmuid, who is lured back into the traditional warrior code; resulting in his death. Perhaps this symbolizes how easy it is for a woman to fall back into the power of the patriarchy and how difficult to hold to a conscious relationship with her *animus*. Part of the power of the patriarchy is derived from a woman's yearning for approval, which originates in her early relationship with her father. Separation is an essential step in any psychological development, and in the case of the *anima* and the *animus* a separation is required within the person from the parental figures. Gráinne initially achieves this, only to undo it by inviting the father back into her psychic house. However the end of the story is ambiguous; death in the psyche means being lost to consciousness, going underground, so to speak: winter is followed by spring. The ambiguous ending points to the possibility of another cycle of reclamation. Whether this occurs or not depends in part on the level of conscious awareness of loss that a woman can bring to bear on the situation.

By reflecting on the major female figures that we have been discussing, we can see an evolution of the feminine. Étaín was relatively powerless in relation to the masculine figures. Derdriu shows some improvement in this respect, but the later and essentially human figures of Emer and Gráinne depict a much stronger and more developed sense of one's own authority and capacity to influence male figures, both internal and external. This movement indicates an ever-emerging *animus* quality in these female figures with a matching quality of being able to be themselves in the world. Within Jungian mythology it also points to the evolution into consciousness of the personal *animus* in the figures of Emer and Gráinne, out of the collective unconscious where the gods reside and the patriarchy asserts its presence without challenge. A woman in this situation finds it difficult to hold on to her values and sense of self.

Diarmuid displays the typical male heroic pattern of being seduced by the feminine in order to learn about feelings, in particular love. The feminine is able to challenge the strict male code that involves the exclusion of the feminine and feeling. Diarmuid displays the resistance that most men do when they are required to give up the security of a male group and peer approval. The difference from Derdriu's lover Naoise is that Diarmuid manages for the most part to resist falling back into the power of the male honour code, as Naoise does when he naïvely believes the guarantee offered by King Conchobhar. Diarmuid shows far more discrimination and one might conclude that this is because he has a more developed relationship with the personal feminine in the figure of Gráinne. As part of his reconciliation with masculine authority he negotiates a separate territory for the feminine, rather than naïvely returning to the fatherland as Naoise does. When a man has developed such a relationship he brings his conscious awareness of feelings to bear on his judgements and does not rely entirely on logic and facts; nor does he naïvely fall into some regressive idealization emanating from the archetypal feminine. The relationship with Gráinne also allows him to conquer monsters and to taste the fruits of immortality; this could be seen as the equivalent of a voyage to the otherworld which gave the hero a glimpse of the invisible reality within which this material world is suspended, a glimpse of the eternal cycle of birth, life and death. From this experience, and his relationship with Gráinne, Diarmuid rises above the strictly male warrior code. This code is a primitive means of preserving and consolidating male power and excludes the feminine. Such a code finds its origins in adolescence, and much of today's literature on men (which forms part of the men's movement) reflects this same primitive preoccupation with bonding. In this sense it is stereotypically heroic and essentially anti-feminine. A recent example of this is the quasi-religious American movement called the Promise Keepers, which is blatantly anti-feminine and unequivocally patriarchal. The men's movement by and large has all the hallmarks of a blacklash against feminism and as such encourages a regression to a primitive level of heroic honour. Diarmuid symbolizes a more evolved level of honour than Cú Chulainn, since he not only responds to the feminine call from within but honours it. It is perhaps only by integrating the feminine that a man can develop his sense of individual identity separate from the group, and in so doing honour the self and not the ego. In this process one can observe the gradual shift from a need for power to a sense of acceptance and compassion, attributes that one can readily recognize as being derived from the feminine aspects of the psyche. It is also of interest to note that Diarmuid's foster-father is Oenghus, the god of love, and that Oenghus protects the feminine whenever it is under threat from the warrior force. So we might say that Eros protects a man from losing contact with the feminine self. However, for far too many men, Eros is under-developed and remains at a specifically sexual level and it is not uncommon for Eros to be appropriated into the service of power; thus male sexuality becomes an exercise in power, not an expression of connection. Regrettably at the end of the story the archetypal masculine aspect still wins out, when Diarmuid is unable to resist the call to hunt and unable to accept the feminine advice not to go.

Consciousness and integration are always precarious, and from the depths of a man's psyche the call to arms and power always beckons. It is an archetypal force that men have to struggle constantly to integrate. This same call to arms, however, can be the source of energy for heroic acts of social justice and compassion. The integration and consequent maturation are very different from a regressive yearning for male bonding, no matter how positive we make it sound in the language of the New Age.

And finally, what, within the mythology of psychology, can we make of Fionn, the symbol of liminality, in this story? Essentially he is possessive, envious and vengeful, attitudes that most of us would prefer not to know about in ourselves. But in a liminal space we come across both positive and negative attributes of the shadow. The psychic life is composed of dark and light, and the task is the integration of these opposites. Self is forged out of an awareness of ambivalence, and the capacity to hold it and not regress into splitting. Liminality often introduces us to parts of ourselves that have hitherto been denied. Fionn reveals much of his dark side in this story, serving to remind us of our own darkness which resides in liminal spaces in our psyche.

13

CONCLUSION

The final cycle of Irish mythology, which we will not be discussing in the present work, is the Cycle of Kings or Historical Cycle. It is generally seen as covering a period of time around the seventh or eighth century AD, and brings us into the factual world, since it contains stories of presumed historical kings and queens.

We could perhaps consider the four cycles as paralleling the development of consciousness in an individual. The cycles commence in the vast unknown and non-human realms of the collective unconscious, symbolized by the world of the gods. Then through the emergence of the heroic ego a sense of individual separateness and mastery over the world develops, a process personified in the Ulster Cycle. Finally one returns at mid-life to the liminal space of the personal unconscious to forge some integration of opposites, as a prelude to returning to the outerworld with a sense of being rooted more in the self than in the ego. The Historical Cycle symbolizes this return to the world, where the marriage with the sovereign queen has occurred and fertility of the psychic land is attained. All this takes place within the pervasive and dominant presence of the eternal cycle of birth, life and death. An emergent period in outer life, a time mastery over the world, is followed by the experience of liminality and reimmersion in the inner world, which in turn is followed by a return to the outer. This is the heroic journey of the human soul, not a straight line but a recurring spiral.

It is to the eminent French anthropologist Claude Lévi-Strauss that I turn for the concluding words.

> The constant recurrence of the same themes expresses this mixture of powerlessness and persistence. Since it has no interest in beginnings or endings, mythological thought never develops any theme to completion. There is always something left unfinished. Myths like rites are interminable.[1]

PRONUNCIATION GUIDE

The spelling of Irish names and places is notoriously variable. This is because the stories extend over a vast period of time, and there are also extensive regional variations. It is my belief that one of the major barriers to people becoming acquainted with the rich world of Irish mythology is the difficulties that are presented by the spelling and pronunciation of the names.

Because of the antiquity of many of the stories, I have decided to use Old Irish spelling wherever possible. Apart from being truer to the times, the Old Irish spelling is visually less complicated than modern Irish and is no more difficult to pronounce. However there are situations in which it is neither possible nor advisable to use Old Irish, either because the story has been compiled well after the relevant period and no Old Irish word exists, or because through common usage the modern Irish word is well established and it would be sheer pedantry to insist on Old Irish. The word *'sidhe'* is an example of this, where the Old Irish word *sid* is less familiar. Other words exist in an Anglicized form, for example Tara, and again because of familiarity there is little justification for altering them.

There did seem to be merit in attempting to provide some guidelines to the pronunciation of the main names and places referred to in this book. Representing sound by words is at any time going to be an imprecise exercise, an exercise that is rendered even more imprecise when trying to represent Irish sounds. What follows can only be regarded, at best, as an approximation, and readers are encouraged to consult publications that provide more precise guidelines by using the International Phonetic Alphabet. Daithi O'hOgain's *Myth, Legend and Romance*, which has been of considerable assistance in developing this pronunciation guide, is one very valuable resource.

There are both vowel and consonant sounds in Irish that do not exist in English, but the following list attempts to illustrate some of the more difficult vowel sounds.

'a' as in the English 'cat'	
'aw'	'awe'
'ai'	'bait'
'ee'	'feel'
'e'	'bed'
'o'	'hot'
'ou'	'flour'
'oa'	'coat'
'oo'	'cool'
'ôô'	'put'
'u'	'gun'

Emphasis in Irish is usually on the first syllable.

Irish Name	English Approximation
Acallam na Senórach	*og*-ul-uv nuh shan-*aw*-rukh
Aed ollam	ai *oll*-uv
Aes sídhe	ays shee
Ailill·	al-il
Aillén	*al*-yayn
Almu	*al*-môô
Amairgin	our-gin
Anu	*aw*-noo
Aoife	*ee*-feh
Aobh	eev or ayv
Badb	bive or bahv
Balor	boll-ur
Baoiscne	*bweeshk*-nuh
bean sídhe	ban shee
Beltaine	*bal*-tin-uh
benfénnid	ban-fay-nee
Biróg	*bee*-roag
Boann	*boa*-un
Bodb Derg	*bove dyarr*-ug
Bodbmall	*baw*-vul
Borrach	*bor*-ukh
Bres	brass

Bricriu	*brik*-roo
Brigit	bri-yid
Brí Léith	bree lay
Blai Briuga	blwee broo
Bruig na Bóinne	*broo* nah *boan*-yuh
Bruiden	broo-yuhn
Caer	kwair
Cailleach Bhéarra	koll-yukh vai-ruh
Caílte	*kweel*-tyuh
Cairbre	*kar*-bruh
Calitin	*kal*-ityin
Cathaer Mór	*koheer more*
Cathbad	*kof*-uh
Cessair	*kess*-ir
Cethern	*kay*-hurn
Cian	*kee*-un
Cnobga	k-*now*-uh
Cnucha	k-*nukh*-uh
Connla	*kon*-luh
Conall Cernach	*kun*-ul *kaar*-nukh
Conaire Mór	*kun*-er-eh *more*
Conchobhar Mac Nessa	*kunna*-khoor mok *nassa*
Cormac mac Art	*kurmok* mok art
Credne	*krai*-nuh
Crimall	*kriv*-uhl
Crunnchu	*kron*-ukh-ôô
Cú Chulainn	koo *khul*-inn
Culann	*kul*-un
Cúldub	*kool*-dôôv
Dagda	daye
Danu	*don*-u
Dáire	*daw*-ir-eh
Dechtine	*dekh*-tin-eh
Derdriu	*dair*-dir-eh
Demne	*dem*-nuh
Diancecht	*dee*-un keckt
Diarmuid	*deer*-ur-mwid
díchetal dí chennaib	*dyee*-khyet-ul dyee *khyen*-uv
Diorruing	*dyir*-ing
Donn	doun/dun

Dubhros	*doo*-ros
Dubhthach	*duff*-ukh
Éile	*ai*-luh
Emer	ai-vur/ai-mur
Emain Macha	e-vwin vw*okh*-uh/
	evin-*mokh*-uh
Ériu	*ai*-ryoo
Eochaid Airem	*ukh*-i-*arr*-uv
éric/éiric	*ai*-rik
Eogan/Eoghan	*oa*-un
Ethal Anbual	e-hul on-uh-vôôl
Étaín	*ai*-deen
Ethniu	*eh*-noo
Eterscél	edur-skhayl
Fer Diad	*farr*-deea
Fedlimid	*fay*-lim-i
fénnid	*fay*-nee
Fergus mac Róich	*farr*-ees mok *roe*-ikh
Fíacail	*fee*-uh-kul
Fiachna	*fee*-ukh-nuh
fían/fíanna (pl)	*fee*-un/*fee*-un-uh
fili/filid (pl)	fill-ee/fill-i
Finnéces	*fin-yay*-gus
Fionn Mac Cumhaill	f-*yun* mok *koo*-il
Fir Bolg	fir bull-ug
Fódla	*foa*-luh
Forgall	*for*-gul/for-ee-ul
Fúamnach	*foo*-um-nukh
gae bolga	*gwai boll*-ug-uh
Geis/geasa (pl)	gesh/gas-sa
Goibniu	gwiv-new
Gráinne	*graw*-in-yuh
imbas forosnai	*eem*-us for-*os*-nuh
imbolg	*eem*-bol-ug
Ingcél	*eeng*-kayl
Labraid	*lour*-ee
Laegaire	*lai*-ur-eh
Lebor Gabála	*lyou*-ur guh *vaw*-luh
Lebor na hUidhre	*lyou*-ur nuh *hwee*-ruh
Lebarcham	*lev*-or-khum

Lí Ban	*lee*-bon
Lir	lir
Lóchán	loe-kh*aw*n
Loeg	lway/lay
Luchta	*lukh*-tuh
Lugaid	*loo*-i
Lugh	loo
Lughnasa	*loo*-nu-suh
Macha	*mokk*-uh
Mac Cécht	mok-*kyay*-ukht
Mael Dúin	*mwai*-ul *doo*-in
Mag Mell	moy mell
Maighnéis	*moyn*-yaysh
Manannán mac Lir	monn-un *awn* mok *lir*
Mes Buachalla	mas *boo*-ukh-ul-uh
Medb	mwai-uv
Midir	*mee*-er
Morrígan	moer-*ee*-en
Mag Tuired	moy *tu*-ruh/moy *twir*-uh
Muiŕne	*mwir*-nye
Mag Muirthemne	*moy* mwir-*hev*-ne
Naoise	*nwee*-shuh
Nechta Scéne	*nyakh*-tuh *shkay*-nuh
Nemain	*nye*-vin/nye-vwin
Nemed	*nev*-eh
Nemglan	*nyev*-glun
Niamh	*nyee*-uv
Nuada	*noo*-a
Oenghus	*ai*-nees
ogham	oam
Ogma	*oam*-uh
Oisín	ush-*een*
Partholón	*por*-hu-lawn
riastradh	*ree*-us-truh
rígfénnid	*ree*-h*ay*-nee
Ruad	*roo*-a
Sadb	sive
Samain	*sou*-in (as in 'south')
samildánach	sou-il-*daw*-nukh
Scáthach	*skaw*-hukh

Sceolang	*shkyoe*-lung
Searbhán Lochlannach	*shar*-uvawn *lokh*-lun-ukh
Sétanta	shay-*dan*-duh
sídhe	shee
Slíab Muicce	*shlee*-uv *mwig*-yuh
Slíab Bladma	*shlee*-uv *blime*-uh
Sualdam Mac Róich	*soo*-ul-duv mok *roe*-ikh
Tadg	*toy*-ug
Táin Bó Cuailnge	*tawn*-in *boe khool*-ing-eh
tarbfheis	*tor*-uh-faish
Tech Duinn	*tyakh* doo-in
Temair	*tyou*-ir
teinm laída	*tye*-nim *lwee*-uh
Tir fo Thuinn	*tyeer* fo *hwin*
Tir na nÓg	*tyeer* nuh *noeg*
Tír Tairngire	*tyeer tar*-ing-gir-eh
Tír Már	*tyeer* moer
Tír na mBan	*tyeer* nuh *mon*
Tír na mBeo	*tyeer* nuh *myoe*
Tréndorn	trayn-doern
Tuachell	*too*-uh-khyel
Tuatha Dé Danann	*too*-a-huh dai *don*-un
Tuireann	twir-un
Ulaid	ôôl-uh
Uisnech	*ush*-nyekh

SOURCES

CHAPTER 1: ANCIENT MYTHOLOGY AND MODERN SOCIETY
1. Sigmund Freud, *Civilization, Society and Religion*, p. 358.
2. Eric Partridge, *Origins: An Etymological Dictionary of Modern English*.
3. Sigmund Freud, *The Interpretation of Dreams*, Penguin Freud Library, Vol. 4.
4. Dodds, E. R., *The Greeks and the Irrational*, p. 104.
5. David Leeming, *Mythology: The Voyage of the Hero*, p. 4.
6. James Hillman, *Dreams and the Underworld*, p. 23.
7. Sigmund Freud, 'Civilization and its Discontents', Penguin Freud Library, Vol. 12, p. 31.
8. Oswald Spengler, *Decline of the West*, Vol. 2, p. 290.
9. C. G. Jung, *Symbols of Transformation*, p. xxv.

CHAPTER 2: WHO WERE THE CELTS?: THE CONTEXT OF THE MYTHOLOGY
1. Proinsias MacCana, *Celtic Mythology*, p. 7.
2. T. W. Rolleston, *Celtic* (Myths and Legends Series), p. 47.
3. Michael Dames, *Mythic Ireland*, p. 10.
4. References to the classical writers have been derived from secondary sources which include MacCana, op. cit.; Miranda Green, *Dictionary of Celtic Myth and Legend*, Frank Delaney, *Legends of the Celts*, Jean Markdale, *Celtic Civilization*, and Nora Chadwick, *The Celts*.
5. For a comprehensive discussion of the theories of Dumézil see C. Scott Littleton, *The New Comparative Mythology*.

CHAPTER 3: THE MYTHOLOGICAL CYCLE: THE ARCHETYPAL STRUGGLE BETWEEN EROS AND THANATOS
1. Alwyn and Brinley Rees, *Celtic Heritage*, p. 104.
2. Marie-Louise Sjoestedt, *Gods and Heroes of the Celts*, p. 3.
3. Jean Markdale, *Celtic Civilization*, p. 15.
4. Rees and Rees, op. cit., p. 210.
5. Sjoestedt, op. cit., p. 11.
6. T. F. O'Rahilly, *Early Irish History and Mythology*, p. 16.

7. MacCana, op. cit., pp. 116–17.

CHAPTER 4: THE GODS: THE MASCULINE ARCHETYPES
1. Nora Chadwick, *The Celts*, p. 170.
2. Luke, 9:12.
3. Daithi O'hOgain, *Myth, Legend and Romance*, p. 273.
4. MacCana, *Celtic Mythology*, p. 69.
5. Sjoestedt, *Gods and Heroes of the Celts*, p. 37.
6. C. G. Jung, *The Archetypes and the Collective Unconscious*, p. 160.
7. Marie-Louise von Franz, *Interpretation of Fairy Tales*, p. 10.
8. C. G. Jung, *The Symbolic Life*, p. 183.

CHAPTER 5: THE SECOND BATTLE OF MAG TUIRED: THE
ARCHETYPAL STRUGGLE BETWEEN LIGHT AND DARK FORCES
1. Sjoestedt, *Gods and Heroes of the Celts*, p. 35.
2. Rees and Rees, *Celtic Heritage*, p. 34.
3. Gerard Murphy, *Saga and Myth in Ancient Ireland*, p. 20.
4. MacCana, *Celtic Mythology*, p. 61.
5. Sjoestedt, op. cit., p. 16.
6. Freud, *Civilization, Society and Religion*, p. 314.

CHAPTER 6: THE GODDESSES: THE FEMININE ARCHETYPES
1. I am indebted to Gearóid Ó Crualaoich of University College, Cork, for introducing me to this figure of Irish mythology.
2. Sjoestedt, *Gods and Heroes of the Celts*, p. 41.
3. MacCana, *Celtic Mythology*, p. 84.
4. Sjoestedt, op. cit., p. 51.
   C. G. Jung, *Psychology and Alchemy*, p. 23.
5. Jeffrey Gantz, *Early Irish Myths and Sagas*, pp. 39–59.
6. Myles Dillon, *Irish Sagas*, pp. 19–26.
7. Marie Heaney, *Over Nine Waves*, pp. 22–36.
8. J. A. MacCulloch, *The Religion of the Ancient Celts*, pp. 348–61.
9. Gantz, op. cit., p. 17.
10. C. G. Jung, *The Practice of Psychotherapy*, p. 218.
11. C. G. Jung, *The Archetypes and the Collective Unconscious*, p. 82.

CHAPTER 7: THE OTHERWORLD I: THE MYTHOLOGY OF THE
UNCONSCIOUS
1. O'Rahilly, *Early Irish History and Mythology*, p. 208.
2. R. A. Macalister, ed. and trans., *Lebor Gabála Eren* (*The Book of Invasions of Ireland*), p. 257.
3. Rees and Rees, *Celtic Heritage*, p. 98.
4. Sjoestedt, *Gods and Heroes of the Celts*, p. 62.

5. MacCana, *Celtic Mythology*, p. 122.

6. Lady Gregory, ed., *Ideals in Ireland*, p. 95.

7. MacCana, op. cit., p. 125.

8. Kenneth Jackson, *Celtic Miscellany*, pp. 143–5.

9. MacCana, op. cit., p. 127.

10. Sjoestedt, op. cit., p. 67.

11. Mircea Eliade, *The Myth of the Eternal Return*, p. 34.

CHAPTER 8: THE OTHERWORLD II

1. Lady Gregory, *Gods and Fighting Men*, p. 93.

2. Jackson, *Celtic Miscellany*, p. 93ff.

3. Peter O'Connor, *Inner Man*, Pan Macmillan Australia, 1991.

4. C. G. Jung, *The Practice of Psychotherapy*, p. 14.

5. John Keats, 'La Belle Dame sans Merci', in *Regency Poets*, Melbourne: Melbourne University Press, 1957, p. 129.

6. I have based this telling on Rees and Rees's version of the original translation by W. Stokes in Whitley Stokes and Ernst Windisch, 'Accalamh na Senarach', *Irische Texte* 4, Leipzig, 1990.

7. Rees and Rees, *Celtic Heritage*, p. 193.

8. Tom Peete Cross, 'Laoghaire Mac Crimthainn's Visit to Fairyland', ed. and trans., *Modern Philology*, 1915–1916, pp. 162ff.

9. Marie Heaney, *Over Nine Waves*, p. 57.

10. C. G. Jung, *Psychology and Religion*, p. 149.

11. C. G. Jung, *The Symbolic Life*, p. 163.

12. Rees and Rees, op. cit., p. 325.

CHAPTER 9: HEROIC EPICS: THE EMERGENCE OF CONSCIOUSNESS

1. Rees and Rees, *Celtic Heritage*, p. 211.

2. Johann Georg von Hahn, *Sagwissenschaftliche Studien*, Jena: Mauke, 1876.

3. Alfred Nutt, 'The Ayran Expulsion and Return Formula in the Folk and Hero Tales of the Celts', *Folk-Lore Record* 4, 1881, pp. 1–44.

4. Otto Rank, In Quest of the Hero, pp. 3–86.

5. Lord Raglan, *The Hero*, London: Methuen, 1936.

6. Joseph Campbell, *The Hero With a Thousand Faces*.

7. Ibid., p. 30.

8. Jan de Vries, *Heroic Song and Heroic Legend*, pp. 211–18.

9. Ibid.

CHAPTER 10: THE ULSTER CYCLE: THE HERO, THE EGO AND THE SHADOW

1. Gantz, *Early Irish Myths and Sagas*, p. 63.

2. Rees and Rees, *Celtic Heritage*, p. 328.
3. W. Stokes, trans., 'Toghail Bruidhne Da Derga', *Revue Celtique* XXII, 1901.
4. Gantz, op. cit., p. 76.
5. O'Rahilly, *Early Irish History and Mythology*, p. 121.
6. Lady Gregory, *Cuchulain of Muirthemne*, Gerrards Cross: Colin Smythe, 1970.
7. Gantz, op cit., pp. 256–67.
8. Thomas Kinsella, *The Táin*, Oxford: Oxford University Press, 1969.
9. Ibid, p. 10.
10. Ibid.
11. Gantz, op. cit., p. 258.
12. Kinsella, op. cit., p. 11.
13. P. W. Joyce, *Old Celtic Romances*, p. 443.
14. Gantz, op. cit., pp. 264–6.

CHAPTER 11: CÚ CHULAINN
1. Kinsella, *The Táin*.
2. Gantz, *Early Irish Myths and Sagas*, p. 136.
3. MacCana, *Celtic Mythology*, p. 102.
4. Sjoestedt, *Gods and Heroes of the Celts*, p. 78.
5. Ibid, p. 83.
6. Kinsella, op. cit., p. 27.
7. *The Hero With a Thousand Faces*, p. 30
8. Tom Peete Cross and Clark H. Slover, *Ancient Irish Tales*, pp. 193 ff.
9. Ibid.
10. Ibid., p. 320 ff.
11. Ibid.
12. Daithi O'hOgain, *Myth, Legend and Romance*, p. 209.

CHAPTER 12: THE FENIAN CYCLE
1. Cross and Slover, *Ancient Irish Tales*, p. 357.
2. Joseph Nagy, *The Wisdom of the Outlaw*, p. 217.
3. Whitley Stokes and Ernst Windisch, eds., 'Accalamh na Senorach', *Irische Texte 4 Part 1*, Leipzig, 1900.
4. Gerard Murphy, *Ossianic Lore and Romantic Tales of Medieval Ireland*, p. 5.
5. O'Rahilly, *Early Irish History and Mythology*, pp. 274–81.
6. Sjoestedt, *Gods and Heroes of the Celts*, pp. 99–110.
7. Kuno Meyer, ed. and trans., 'The Instructions of King Cormac mac Airt', *Todd Lecture Series*, Dublin: Royal Irish Academy, 1909.
8. Proinsias MacCana, *The Learned Tales of Medieval Ireland*, p. 35.
9. O'Rahilly, op. cit., p. 33.

10. Joseph Nagy, 'Liminality and Knowledge in Irish Tradition', *Studia Celtica* 16–17, 1981/82, pp. 135–43.
11. D. W. Winnicott, *Playing and Reality*, pp. 1–30.
12. Robert Gittings, eds., *Letter of John Keats*, p. 43.
13. C. G. Jung, *The Symbolic Life*, p. 399.
14. Joyce, *Old Celtic Romances*, pp. 274–350.
15. Myles Dillon, *Early Irish Literature*, pp. 43–50.
16. Joyce, op. cit., pp. 340–1.
17. Ibid., p. 341.
18. Ibid., p. 342.
19. Ibid.

CONCLUSION
1. Claude Lévi-Strauss, *The Raw and the Cooked*, p. 6.

BIBLIOGRAPHY

Campbell, Joseph, *The Hero With a Thousand Faces*, Princeton: Princeton University Press, 1968

Chadwick, Nora, *The Celts*, Harmondsworth: Penguin, 1991

Cross, Tom Peete, 'Laoghaire Mac Crimthainn's Visit to Fairyland', *Modern Philology XIII*, 1915–16

Cross, Tom Peete and Slover, Clark H., *Ancient Irish Tales*, New York: Barnes & Noble, 1936

Dames, Michael, *Mythic Ireland*, London: Thames & Hudson, 1992

Delaney, Frank, *Legends of the Celts*, London: Grafton, 1991

De Vries, Jan, *Heroic Song and Heroic Legend*, Oxford: Oxford University Press, 1963

Dillon, Myles, *Irish Sagas*, Cork: Mercier Press, 1968
    Early Irish Literature, Dublin: Four Courts Press, 1994

Dodds, E. R., *The Greeks and the Irrational*, Berkeley: University of California Press, 1973

Eliade, Mircea, *The Myth of the Eternal Return*, London: Arkana, 1989

Frazer, J. G., *The Golden Bough: A Study on Magic and Religion*, London: Papermac, 1987

Freud, Sigmund, *The Interpretation of Dreams*, Harmondsworth: Pelican, 1985
    Civilizations, Society and Religion, Harmondsworth: Penguin, 1985

Gantz, Jeffrey, *Early Irish Myths and Sagas*, London: Penguin, 1981

Gittings, Robert, ed., *The Letters of John Keats*, Oxford University Press, 1970.

Green, Miranda, *Dictionary of Celtic Myth and Legend*, London: Thames & Hudson, 1992

Gregory, Lady, ed., *Ideals in Ireland*, London: 1901

Gregory, Lady, *Gods and Fighting Men*, Gerrards Cross: Colin Smythe, 1970
    Cuchulain of Muirthemne, Gerrards Cross: Colin Smythe, 1970

Heaney, Marie, *Over Nine Waves*, London: Faber & Faber, 1995

Hillman, James, *Dream and the Underworld*, New York: Harper & Row, 1979

Jackson, Kenneth, *Celtic Miscellany*, Harmondsworth: Penguin, 1988

Joyce, P. W., *Old Celtic Romances*, Dublin: Roberts Wholesale Books, 1907

Jung, Carl G., *Symbols of Transformation*, London: Routledge & Kegan Paul, 1956
   The Archetypes and the Collective Unconscious, London: Routledge & Kegan Paul, 1959
   The Symbolic Life, London: Routledge & Kegan Paul, 1977
   Psychology and Alchemy, London: Routledge & Kegan Paul, 1953
   The Practice of Psychotherapy, London: Routledge & Kegan Paul, 1954
   Psychology and Religion, London: Routledge & Kegan Paul, 1958
Kinsella, Thomas, *The Táin*, Oxford: Oxford University Press, 1969
Leeming, David, *Mythology: The Voyage of the Hero*, New York: J. B. Lippincott, 1973
Lévi-Strauss, Claude, *The Raw and the Cooked*, Harmondsworth: Penguin, 1992
Littleton, C. Scott, *The New Comparative Mythology*, Berkeley: University of California Press, 1982
Macalister R. A., ed., *Lebor Gabála Eren (The Book of Invasions of Ireland)*, Dublin: Irish Text Society, 5 vols., 1938–56
MacCana, Proinsias, *Celtic Mythology*, New York: Peter Bedrick Books, 1983
   The Learned Tales of Medieval Ireland, Dublin: Institute of Advanced Studies, 1980
MacCulloch, J. A., *The Religion of the Ancient Celts*, London: Constable, 1992
Markdale, Jean, *Celtic Civilization*, London: Gordon & Cremonesi, 1978
Meyer, Kuno, ed. and trans., 'The Instructions of King Cormac mac Airt', *Todd Lecture Series*, Dublin: Royal Irish Academy, 1909
Murphy, Gerard, *Saga and Myth in Ancient Ireland*, Dublin: Three Candles, 1955
   Ossianic Lore and Romantic Tales of Medieval Ireland, Dublin: Three Candles, 1955
Nagy, Joseph, *The Wisdom of the Outlaw*, Berkeley: University of California Press, 1985
   'Liminality and Knowledge in Irish Tradition', *Studia Celtica 16–17*, 1981/82
Nutt, Alfred, 'The Aryan Expulsion and Return Formula in the Folk and Hero Tales of the Celts', *Folk-Lore Record 4*, 1881
O'Connor, Peter A., *The Inner Man*, Pan Macmillan Australia, 1991
O'Grady, Standish H., *Toruigheacht Dhiarmuda agus Grainne/The Pursuit of Duarmuid O'Duibhne and Grainne*, Dublin: Transactions of the Ossianic Society 3, 1857
O'hOgain, Daithi, *Myth, Legend and Romance*, New York: Prentice Hall, 1991
O'Rahilly, T. F., *Early Irish History and Mythology*, Dublin: Dublin Institute for Advanced Studies, 1946

Partridge, Eric, *Origins: An Etymological Dictionary of Modern English*, London, Routledge & Kegan Paul, 1958

Raglan, Lord, *The Hero*, London: Methuen, 1936

Rank, Otto, *In Quest of the Hero*, Princeton: Princeton University Press, 1990

Rees, Alwyn and Brinley, *Celtic Heritage*, London: Thames & Hudson, 1961

Rolleston, T. W., *Celtic* (Myths and Legends series), New York: Avenel Books, 1983

Sjoestedt, Marie-Louise, *Gods and Heroes of the Celts*, Berkeley: Turtle Island Foundation, 1982

Spengler, Oswald, *Decline of the West*, London: Allen & Unwin, 2 vols., 1959

Stokes, Whitley and Windisch, Ernst, eds., ,'Accalamh na Senorach', *Irische Texte 4, Part 1*, Leipzig, 1900

Von Franz, Marie-Louise, *Interpretation of Fairy Tales*, Dallas: Spring, 1978

Von Hahn, Johann Georg, *Sagwissenschaftliche Studien*, Jena: Mauke, 1876

Winnicott, D. W., *Playing and Reality*, Harmondsworth: Penguin, 1986

INDEX